Microsoft® Excel For Windows™

Version 4

SECOND EDITION

Step by Step

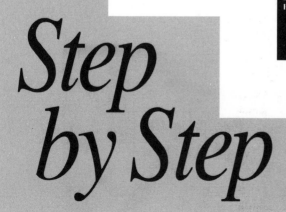

D1318596

PUBLISHED BY
Microsoft Press
A Division of Microsoft Corporation
One Microsoft Way
Redmond, Washington 98052-6399

Copyright © 1992 by Microsoft Corporation

Library of Congress Cataloging-in-Publication Data
Microsoft Excel 4 for Windows step by step / Microsoft Corporation. --
  2nd ed.
      p.   cm.
    Includes index.
    ISBN 1-55615-476-3
     1. Microsoft Excel 4 for Windows. 2. Business--Computer programs.
  3. Electronic spreadsheets. 4. Windows (Computer programs)
  I. Microsoft Corporation.
  HF5548.4.M523M516 1992
  005.369--dc20   92-16106
                                               CIP

Printed and bound in the United States of America.

     5 6 7 8 9 MLML 7 6 5 4 3

Distributed to the book trade in Canada by Macmillan of Canada,
a division of Canada Publishing Corporation.

Distributed to the book trade outside the United States and
Canada by Penguin Books Ltd.

Penguin Books Ltd., Harmondsworth, Middlesex, England
Penguin Books Australia Ltd., Ringwood, Victoria, Australia
Penguin Books N.Z. Ltd., 182-190 Wairau Road, Auckland 10, New Zealand

British Cataloging-in-Publication Data available.

Companies, names, and data used in examples herein are fictitious
unless otherwise noted.

This book was produced using Microsoft Word.

Contents

Part 5 Using Worksheet Databases

Part 6 Creating Charts and Presentations

Appendixes

About This Book

Microsoft® Excel is a powerful spreadsheet application that you can use for analyzing and charting your data and creating effective presentations. *Microsoft Excel Step by Step* is a comprehensive tutorial that shows you how to use Microsoft Excel to simplify your work and increase your productivity. You can use *Microsoft Excel Step by Step* in a classroom setting, or you can use it as a tutorial to learn Microsoft Excel at your own pace and at your own convenience.

This book covers both Microsoft Excel for Windows™ and Microsoft Excel for the Macintosh. The edition you bought, based on the information on the cover, contains the correct type of bound-in disk for your system, whether you're using Microsoft Excel for Windows or Microsoft Excel for the Macintosh. When a procedure differs depending on the software and hardware you're using, you'll see separate instructions, such as "In Microsoft Excel for Windows…" or "In Microsoft Excel for the Macintosh…." Follow the instructions that apply to you.

Because of the similarity of the two products, most of the illustrations in this book apply to both Microsoft Excel for Windows and Microsoft Excel for the Macintosh. When there are substantial differences between the two, you'll see illustrations for both. When the differences do not affect the material being presented, you'll see an illustration from Microsoft Excel for Windows.

You'll get hands-on practice using the practice files on the accompanying disk. Instructions for copying the practice files to your computer's hard disk are given in "Getting Ready" later in this book.

Finding the Best Starting Point for You

This book is designed both for new users learning Microsoft Excel for the first time and for experienced users who want to learn to use the new features in Microsoft Excel version 4.0. Whether you're a novice or an experienced user, *Microsoft Excel Step by Step* will help you to get the most out of Microsoft Excel.

The modular design of this book offers you considerable flexibility in customizing your learning. Lessons 1 and 2 teach basic skills. To decide whether you need to work through these lessons, scan the table on the first page of each one. You can go through the lessons in any order, skip lessons, and repeat lessons later to brush up on certain skills. Each lesson builds on concepts presented in previous lessons, so you may want to back up if you find that you don't understand the concepts or terminology used in a particular lesson.

You start most lessons by opening a practice file from the PRACTICE directory or folder on your hard disk. You then rename the practice file so that the original file remains unchanged while you work on your own version.

The following table recommends starting points based on your experience.

If you are	Follow these steps
New to a computer or graphical environment, such as Microsoft® Windows or the Apple Macintosh	Read "Getting Ready" later in this book. Next, work through Lessons 1 and 2. Work through the other lessons in any order.
Familiar with a graphical computer environment but new to Microsoft Excel	Complete Lesson 1, "Creating a Worksheet." Work through the other lessons in any order.
Familiar with Lotus 1-2-3 but new to Microsoft Excel	Read "Getting Ready" later in this book. Next, work through Lessons 1 and 2. Work through the other lessons in any order.
New to the mouse	Read "If You Are New to Using the Mouse" in "Getting Ready" later in this book.
	Next, work through Lessons 1 and 2. Work through the other lessons in any order.
Experienced with Microsoft Excel	Read Appendix B, "New Features in Microsoft Excel Version 4.0." Complete the lessons that best meet your needs.

Using This Book as a Classroom Aid

If you're an instructor, you can use *Microsoft Excel Step by Step* for teaching Microsoft Excel to novice users and for teaching the new features of Microsoft Excel version 4.0 to experienced users. You may want to select certain lessons that meet your students' needs and incorporate your own demonstrations into the lessons.

If you plan to teach the entire contents of this book, you should probably set aside three full days of classroom time to allow for discussion, questions, and any customized practice you may create.

You can also obtain additional training material to use in conjunction with this book.

- The Microsoft Excel Step by Step Courseware Developer's Kit includes an annotated instructor's version of *Microsoft Excel Step by Step*, overhead files on disk, a reproduction master of *Microsoft Excel Step by Step*, the full text of *Microsoft Excel Step by Step* in Microsoft Word format, and a site license.

- *Microsoft Excel Macros Step by Step* includes detailed macro programming lessons and sample files.

For more information, call (800) MS PRESS.

Conventions Used in This Book

Before you start any of the lessons, it's important that you understand the terms and notational conventions used in this book.

Notational Conventions

- Characters you are to type appear in **bold.**

- Important terms and titles of books appear in *italic*.

Procedural Conventions

- Procedures you are to follow are given in numbered lists (1, 2, and so on). A triangular bullet (▶) indicates a procedure with only one step.

- The word *choose* is used for carrying out a command.

- The word *select* is used for highlighting cells, text, and menu or command names, and for selecting options in a dialog box.

Mouse Conventions

- If you have a multiple-button mouse, Microsoft Excel assumes that you have configured the left mouse button as the primary mouse button. Any procedure that requires you to click the secondary button will refer to it as the right mouse button.

- *Point* means to move the mouse pointer over an object on the screen. For example, "Point to cell A1."

- *Click* means to point to an object and then press and release the mouse button. For example, "Click cell A1."

- *Drag* means to press and hold the mouse button while you move the mouse. For example, "Drag from cell A1 to cell B5."

- *Double-click* means to rapidly press and release the mouse button twice. For example, "Double-click the Microsoft Excel icon to start Microsoft Excel."

You can adjust the mouse tracking speed and double-click speed in Control Panel. For more information, see your system documentation.

Keyboard Conventions

- Names of keys are in small capital letters; for example, TAB and SHIFT.

- You can choose commands with the keyboard. In Microsoft Excel for Windows, press the ALT key to activate the menu bar; then press the keys for the underlined letters in the menu name and the command name. In Microsoft Excel for the Macintosh, press the SLASH (/) key or the PERIOD key on the numeric keypad to activate the menu bar; then press the keys for the underlined letters in the menu name and the command name. For some commands, you can press the key combination listed in the menu.

- The letters you press to choose a command from a menu are underlined in procedures the same way they are underlined on the screen. For example, "From the File menu, choose Open" means that in Microsoft Excel for Windows you can press the ALT key, then the F and O keys. In Microsoft Excel for the Macintosh, you can press the SLASH (/) key, then the F and O keys. If you do not see underlined characters in Microsoft Excel for the Macintosh when you press the SLASH key, choose the Workspace command from the Options menu. Under Command Underline, select the Automatic option button.

- A plus sign (+) between two key names means that you must press those keys at the same time. For example, "Press SHIFT+SPACEBAR" means that you hold down the SHIFT key while you press the SPACEBAR.

- A comma (,) between two key names means that you must press those keys sequentially. In Microsoft Excel for Windows, for example, "press ALT, F, O" means that you first press and release the ALT key, then the F key, and then the O key. In Microsoft Excel for the Macintosh, "press SLASH, F, O" means that you first press and release the SLASH key, then the F key, and then the O key.

- The ENTER key and the RETURN key usually perform the same action in Microsoft Excel. In this book, "Press ENTER" means that you can press either ENTER or RETURN, unless specifically stated otherwise.

- In Microsoft Excel for Windows, if you use the ENTER key on the main keyboard to enter text and choose commands, the wrong cell may be active after certain procedures. You should choose the Workspace command from the Options menu and clear the Move Selection After Enter check box. The ENTER key on the numeric keypad is unaffected by this option.

- In Microsoft Excel for the Macintosh, if you use the RETURN key to enter text and choose commands, the wrong cell may be active after certain procedures. You should choose the Workspace command from the Options menu and clear the Move Selection After Return check box.

- The CTRL key and the CONTROL key perform the same action in Microsoft Excel. The CTRL key appears on keyboards used with Microsoft Excel for Windows, and the CONTROL key appears on keyboards used with Microsoft Excel for the Macintosh.

- In Microsoft Excel for the Macintosh, the COMMAND key is the key marked with a ⌘ symbol.

Other Features of This Book

- You can perform many commands by clicking a tool on a toolbar. When a procedure instructs you to click a tool, a picture of the tool appears in the left margin, as the AutoSum™ tool does here.

If you are familiar with Lotus 1-2-3, read these notes to get useful tips about Microsoft Excel.

- Text in the left margin gives tips or additional useful information for new users of Microsoft Excel who are familiar with Lotus 1-2-3.

- You'll find optional "One Step Further" exercises at the end of most lessons. These exercises, which are less structured than the lessons, help you practice what you learned in the lesson.

Cross-references to Microsoft Excel Documentation

Using *Microsoft Excel Step by Step* will help you learn about your Microsoft Excel documentation. You'll find references to the *Microsoft Excel User's Guide*, online tutorial lessons, and the *Microsoft Excel Function Reference* throughout this book. Using the references to these sources will help you to make greater use of the features in Microsoft Excel.

Microsoft Excel User's Guide, Books 1 and 2   The *User's Guide* is the primary reference for Microsoft Excel features and procedures. Book 1 contains information about creating, editing, printing, and formatting worksheets, charts, and databases. Book 2 contains information about analyzing data, exchanging data with other applications, customizing Microsoft Excel to suit the way you work, and automating your work with macros.

Microsoft Excel Function Reference   This is an alphabetic listing of all worksheet and macro sheet functions. The function topics include notes, examples, descriptions of arguments, and lists of related functions.

Switching to Microsoft Excel from Lotus 1-2-3   (Microsoft Excel for Windows only) This book contains the information you need to make a smooth transition from Lotus 1-2-3.

Help   Microsoft Excel Help provides online information about Microsoft Excel features and gives instructions for performing specific tasks. You'll learn more about Help in "Getting Ready" later in this book.

Online tutorials   Microsoft Excel has two online tutorials: Introducing Microsoft Excel and Learning Microsoft Excel. Introducing Microsoft Excel contains information about the new features in Microsoft Excel and teaches the basic skills you need to become productive in Microsoft Excel. Learning Microsoft Excel provides overviews and hands-on practice for each of the main parts of Microsoft Excel. In Microsoft Excel for Windows, you can go through the tutorials with either the mouse or the keyboard.

You'll learn how to run the tutorials in "Getting Ready" later in this book.

Other references   You'll find a handy bibliography in Appendix C, "For More Information." This will direct you to more information about Microsoft Excel, spreadsheet design, and data presentation.

Getting Ready

This book shows you how to use Microsoft Excel to streamline your everyday work. The lessons begin with the most basic tasks and proceed to more advanced tasks. Each lesson takes approximately 15 to 40 minutes, with optional practices available at the end of each lesson.

Before you begin the lessons, you need to install the practice files on your computer's hard disk and start Microsoft Excel. This section of the book tells you how.

If you have not yet installed Microsoft Excel, you'll need to do so before you begin the lessons. If you need instructions for installing Microsoft Excel version 4.0, see the card *Installing Microsoft Excel*, included with your Microsoft Excel documentation.

Installing the Step by Step Practice Files

Included with this book is a disk named "Microsoft Excel Step by Step Practice Files." Copy the PRACTICE directory or folder with all of its files to the directory or folder on your hard disk in which you installed Microsoft Excel.

Copy the practice files in Microsoft Excel for Windows

The following procedure assumes that Microsoft Windows is already running. To start Windows, see "Starting Microsoft Excel" later in this section.

1 Insert the Microsoft Excel Step by Step Practice Files disk into drive A.

2 In the Program Manager window, open the Main group by double-clicking its icon.

3 In the Main window, start File Manager by double-clicking its icon.

4 In the File Manager window, click the drive A icon.

5 If you have Windows version 3.0, double-click the A directory icon. This step is not necessary in Windows version 3.1.

6 Click the PRACTICE directory to select it.

7 From the File menu, choose the Copy command.

The Copy dialog box appears with PRACTICE in the From box.

8 In the To box, type the name of the directory on your hard disk in which you installed Microsoft Excel; for example, **c:\excel**

9 In Windows version 3.1, click the OK button or press ENTER. In Windows version 3.0, click the Copy button or press ENTER.

For more information about copying the PRACTICE directory using the File Manager, see your Microsoft Windows documentation.

Copy the practice files in Microsoft Excel for the Macintosh

1 Insert the Practice Files disk into the disk drive on your Macintosh.

2 Double-click the Practice Files disk icon to display the contents of the disk.

3 Drag the PRACTICE folder to the folder on your hard disk in which you installed Microsoft Excel; for example, the MICROSOFT EXCEL folder.

4 Eject the Practice Files disk by dragging it to the Trash.

If you need help with this procedure, see your Macintosh documentation.

Using the Practice Files

With the practice files, you can start the tutorial at any lesson, and you can go through the lessons in any order you want. As you go through each lesson, make sure to follow the instructions for renaming the practice files so that you can review the lesson later with a fresh practice file.

The following files are in the PRACTICE directory or folder.

Lesson	Uses this lesson file	Uses this "One Step Further" file
1, "Creating a Worksheet"	01LESSN	None
2, "Entering Numbers and Formulas"	02LESSN	None
3, "Formatting a Worksheet"	03LESSN	03STEP
4, "Working with Formatting and Display Features"	04LESSN	04STEP
5, "Copying and Moving Cell Data and Formats"	05LESSN	05STEP
6, "Putting Formulas to Work"	06LESSN	None
7, "Linking Worksheets"	07LESSN	07STEP
8, "Using Names on a Worksheet"	08LESSN	08STEP
9, "Worksheet Outlining and Data Consolidation"	09LESSN	09STEP
10, "Analyzing Data"	10LESSN	None
11, "Setting Up the Page and Printing"	11LESSN	None
12, "Setting Up a Database"	12LESSN	12STEP
13, "Database Reporting"	13LESSN	None

Lesson	Uses this lesson file	Uses this "One Step Further" file
14, "Creating and Formatting a Chart"	14LESSN	14STEP
15, "Editing Chart Data Series"	15LESSN	None
16, "Creating a Presentation Using Charts and Graphics"	16LESSN	None
17, "Recording Macros"	17LESSN	17STEP

In Microsoft Excel for Windows, the practice files have filename extensions such as .XLS, .XLW, and so on. For example, the Lesson 1 practice file is named 01LESSN.XLS. In this book we refer to the practice files without extensions; for example, 01LESSN.

Because Microsoft Excel works with both Windows and Macintosh files, you can open either format in either version of Microsoft Excel. The practice files for the two versions are identical.

Starting Microsoft Excel

After you have installed Microsoft Excel and copied the practice files, you can start the application.

Starting Microsoft Excel for Windows

Do the following procedures to start Microsoft Windows and Microsoft Excel, and to familiarize yourself with the Windows Program Manager. The appearance of your screen may be different from the illustrations that follow, depending on your particular setup. For more information about Windows, see your Windows documentation.

Start Windows

1 At the system prompt (such as C:\), type **win**

2 Press ENTER.

When you start Windows, the Program Manager window is displayed, as shown in the following illustration. You start all of your applications, including Microsoft Excel, from Program Manager.

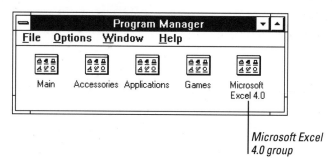

Microsoft Excel 4.0 group

While Windows is active, everything on your screen is displayed in a *window*. You can make each window any size you want and move it anywhere you want on your screen. You can have many windows open at the same time to compare or exchange information easily.

The Program Manager window   Within the Program Manager window are several *icons*. These are symbols representing applications and documents. The icons in the Program Manager window organize the applications in your computer into groups so that you can easily find each application.

The Microsoft Excel 4.0 group   Choosing the Microsoft Excel 4.0 group icon opens another window. The Microsoft Excel 4.0 window contains icons for Microsoft Excel and its companion utility applications.

Start Microsoft Excel for Windows

1   Double-click the Microsoft Excel 4.0 group icon.

This opens the Microsoft Excel 4.0 group.

2   Double-click the Microsoft Excel program icon.

Documents also have icons. Microsoft Excel has five types of documents: worksheets, charts, macro sheets, templates, and workbooks. You can also start Microsoft Excel and open a document by double-clicking a document icon in the Windows File Manager. The following illustration shows a Microsoft Excel document icon.

🖹 **SALES.XLS**

Starting Microsoft Excel for the Macintosh

Use the following procedure to start Microsoft Excel. For more information about the Macintosh, see your Macintosh system documentation.

Start Microsoft Excel for the Macintosh

1   Double-click the MICROSOFT EXCEL folder.

2   Double-click the Microsoft Excel program icon.

You can also start Microsoft Excel by choosing one of its document icons. Microsoft Excel has five types of documents: worksheets, charts, macro sheets, templates, and workbooks. The Microsoft Excel document icons are shown in the following illustration.

Worksheet   Chart   Macro sheet   Workbook   Sheet template

Using the Online Tutorials

Microsoft Excel includes two online tutorials. The tutorials include demonstrations of Microsoft Excel features and activities, and hands-on practices.

Several of the lessons in this book refer to specific tutorial lessons. Follow the procedures below to start a tutorial and begin a lesson.

Run a tutorial in Microsoft Excel for Windows

1 From the Help menu, choose Introducing Microsoft Excel or Learning Microsoft Excel.

2 From the Main Menu, select a lesson.

3 Follow the instructions on the screen.

4 To quit the Introducing Microsoft Excel tutorial, choose the Exit button. To quit the Learning Microsoft Excel tutorial, choose the Controls: Ctrl+F1 button, and then choose the Exit button.

Run a tutorial in Microsoft Excel for the Macintosh

Each tutorial is a HyperCard stack. To run the tutorials, you must have HyperCard version 1.2 or later installed on your computer.

1 Go back to the Finder. If you are running MultiFinder, click the Microsoft Excel icon in the upper-right corner of your screen. Otherwise, you will have to quit Microsoft Excel.

2 Double-click the Introducing Microsoft Excel icon or the Learning Microsoft Excel icon.

3 From the Main Menu, select a lesson.

4 Follow the instructions on the screen.

5 To quit the tutorial, click the question mark icon in the lower-right corner, and click Quit.

If You Are Converting from Lotus 1-2-3

Microsoft Excel has options in the Open and Save As dialog boxes to translate file formats.

This section describes how to convert your worksheets and charts (graphs) between Lotus 1-2-3 and Microsoft Excel.

When you open a 1-2-3 worksheet in Microsoft Excel, your defined graphs are automatically converted into separate chart documents. You can't convert Microsoft Excel charts into 1-2-3 graphs.

When you open a 3-D Lotus 1-2-3 worksheet in Microsoft Excel, it is automatically converted into a Microsoft Excel workbook. Each sheet of the 3-D worksheet becomes a bound worksheet in the workbook. You can't convert Microsoft Excel workbooks into 3-D worksheets.

Opening a 1-2-3 Worksheet in Microsoft Excel

To import data from a file created in another program into a Microsoft Excel worksheet, just open the file.

If you want, you can use Microsoft Excel to open a 1-2-3 worksheet, modify it, and save it in a 1-2-3 file format.

The Open command   With the Open command on the File menu, you can open a file from a disk. Microsoft Excel automatically reads any of the file formats you can select in the Save As dialog box.

Worksheet characteristics such as column width, label alignment, formulas, and most number formats can be converted between Microsoft Excel and 1-2-3. Borders, font formats, custom number formats, and worksheet objects are not converted into Lotus 1-2-3, because they don't exist in 1-2-3.

Open a Lotus 1-2-3 worksheet in Microsoft Excel for Windows

1   From the File menu, choose Open.

2   In the File Name box, type the name of the Lotus 1-2-3 file you want to open.

You can also select Lotus 1-2-3 Files in the List Files Of Type box, and then select the filename you want in the File Name list.

3   Choose the OK button.

Open a Lotus 1-2-3 worksheet in Microsoft Excel for the Macintosh

1   From the File menu, choose Open.

2   In the file list, select the filename you want.

3   Choose the Open button.

Converting 1-2-3 Graphs to Microsoft Excel Charts

When you open a 1-2-3 worksheet that has graphs in Microsoft Excel, Microsoft Excel prompts you to convert the 1-2-3 graphs to Microsoft Excel charts.

Because you can store many graphs on a single worksheet in 1-2-3, you should make sure you don't have so many graphs that you run out of memory when Microsoft Excel tries to create a separate window for each converted chart. Preparing your worksheets in 1-2-3 before you open them in Microsoft Excel can make the conversion easier.

Saving a 1-2-3 Worksheet as a Microsoft Excel Worksheet

You can open a 1-2-3 worksheet with the Open command on the File menu in Microsoft Excel, but it will retain its original file format until you save it in another file format.

The Save As command   You use the Save As command on the File menu to save a document in a different file format. You can save a document from another application in Microsoft Excel format, or you can save a Microsoft Excel document in the format of another application.

Save a Lotus 1-2-3 worksheet in Microsoft Excel for Windows format

1   From the File menu, choose Save As.

2   In the File Name box, type the name with which you want to save the file.

3   In the Save File As Type box, select the Normal file format.

4   Choose the OK button.

Save a Lotus 1-2-3 worksheet in Microsoft Excel for the Macintosh format

1   From the File menu, choose Save As.

2   In the Save Worksheet As box, type the name with which you want to save the file.

3   Choose the Options button.

4   In the File Format box, select the Normal file format.

5   Choose the OK button.

6   Choose the Save button.

Saving a Microsoft Excel Worksheet as a 1-2-3 Worksheet

To export a Microsoft Excel worksheet to another spreadsheet application, you save it in a different file format. Depending on the file format, you may lose some Microsoft Excel formatting.

To save a worksheet in this Lotus 1-2-3 format	Select this option
Release 1A format	WKS
Release 2 format	WK1
Release 3 format	WK3

Save a Microsoft Excel for Windows worksheet in Lotus 1-2-3 format

1   From the File menu, choose Save As.

2   In the File Name box, type the name with which you want to save the file.

3   In the Save File As Type box, select the 1-2-3 file format in which you want to save the file.

4   Choose the OK button.

Save a Microsoft Excel for the Macintosh worksheet in Lotus 1-2-3 format

1   From the File menu, choose Save As.

2   In the Save Worksheet As box, type the name with which you want to save the file.

3   Choose the Options button.

4   In the File Format box, select the 1-2-3 file format in which you want to save the file.

5   Choose the OK button.

6   Choose the Save button.

For Quick Transition from Lotus 1-2-3 to Microsoft Excel for Windows

Microsoft Excel has utilities to help you translate and run 1-2-3 macros.

For an online overview of Microsoft Excel for Windows features that are designed to help you switch from Lotus 1-2-3, see the tutorial Introducing Microsoft Excel.

Run the tutorial in Microsoft Excel for Windows

1   From the Help menu, choose Introducing Microsoft Excel.

2   Select For Lotus 1-2-3 Users.

3   Follow the instructions on the screen.

4   To quit the tutorial, choose the Exit button.

For online help in learning Microsoft Excel commands and procedures, use Help for Lotus 1-2-3 Users. You will practice using this feature in Lesson 1.

Turn on Lotus 1-2-3 Help

1   From the Options menu, choose Workspace.

2   Under Alternate Menu Or Help Key, select the Lotus 1-2-3 Help option button.

3   Choose the OK button.

Now, whenever you press the 1-2-3 command key sequence, you will get help on the equivalent Microsoft Excel command.

For information about	See
Using Help for Lotus 1-2-3 Users Running 1-2-3 macros in Microsoft Excel	*Switching to Microsoft Excel from Lotus 1-2-3* (Microsoft Excel for Windows only)
Microsoft Excel workbooks	"Managing Documents with Workbooks" in Chapter 4 (Book 1) of the *Microsoft Excel User's Guide*

Working in Microsoft Excel

A document in Microsoft Excel is the same as a file in 1-2-3.

When you start Microsoft Excel, it opens a new worksheet called Sheet1 in Microsoft Excel for Windows or Worksheet1 in Microsoft Excel for the Macintosh. The next worksheet you create is called Sheet2 or Worksheet2, and so on. You can rename a document when you save it. Each worksheet is displayed in a window.

The worksheet window in Microsoft Excel for Windows looks like the following illustration.

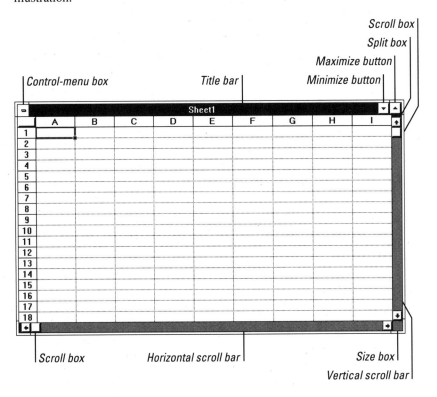

The worksheet window in Microsoft Excel for the Macintosh looks like the following illustration.

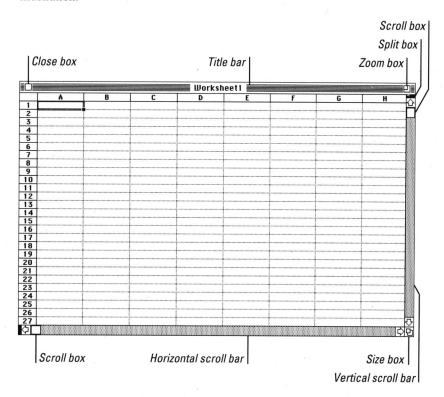

Controlling a window with the mouse You can scroll, move, split, and close a window by using the mouse.

To	Do this
Scroll through a window (to see another part of the document)	Click the scroll bars or drag the scroll box.
Change the size of a window	Drag the size box.
	In Microsoft Excel for Windows, you can also drag any of the window edges or corners.
Enlarge a window to fill the screen	Double-click the title bar.
	In Microsoft Excel for Windows, you can also click the Maximize button.
	In Microsoft Excel for the Macintosh, you can also click the zoom box.

To	Do this
Shrink a document window to an icon in the Microsoft Excel workspace	Click the Minimize button (Microsoft Excel for Windows only).
Restore a window to its previous size	In Microsoft Excel for Windows, click the Restore button.
	In Microsoft Excel for the Macintosh, click the zoom box.
Move a window	Drag the title bar.
Split a window	Drag the split box on the scroll bar to where you want the split.
Close a window	In Microsoft Excel for Windows, double-click the Control-menu box.
	In Microsoft Excel for the Macintosh, click the close box.

Understanding Menus

Microsoft Excel has drop-down menus instead of hierarchical menus.

The menu bar contains menus, and the menus contain commands. In this section you will use commands to create and work with new document windows.

Microsoft Excel menu bars In Microsoft Excel, the menu bars change slightly depending on what type of document you're working on. For example, when a chart is the active document, the menu bar contains a Chart menu and a Gallery menu.

The following illustration shows the Microsoft Excel for Windows menu bar with the Edit menu displayed.

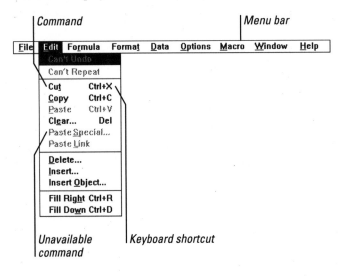

The following illustration shows the Microsoft Excel for the Macintosh menu bar with the Edit menu displayed.

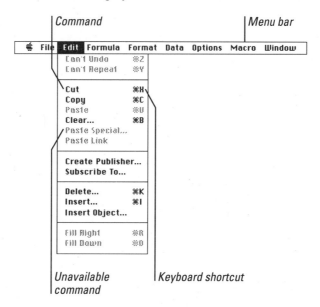

Characteristics of commands   When you open a menu, it displays a list of commands. Some commands have a shortcut key combination listed to the right of the command name. Once you've become familiar with the menus and commands, these shortcut keys can save you time.

When a command name appears dimmed, it doesn't apply to your current situation or is unavailable. For example, the Paste command on the Edit menu appears dimmed if the Copy or Cut command has not been used first.

When a command name has a check mark, the command is already in effect. For example, when you open the Window menu, a check mark appears next to the name of the active window.

Choosing menu commands with the mouse   In Microsoft Excel for Windows, click the menu name and then click the command name. You can also point to the menu name and drag to the command you want. To cancel a menu without choosing a command, click the menu name again.

In Microsoft Excel for the Macintosh, point to the menu name and drag to the command you want. To cancel a menu without choosing a command, move the pointer away from the menu, and then release the mouse button.

You can use the SLASH (/) key as the menu key by defining it with the Workspace command on the Options menu.

Choosing commands with the keyboard in Microsoft Excel for Windows   Press ALT to activate the menu bar, and then press the keys for the underlined letters in the menu and command you want. For example, to choose the Open command from the File menu, press ALT, F, O.

Note   If you are accustomed to using another key to activate the menu bar, such as the SLASH key, you can change the menu key by choosing Workspace from the Options menu and typing the key symbol in the Alternate Menu Or Help Key box.

You can also use the arrow keys to move between menus and commands, and then press ENTER to choose the menu or command you want. To cancel a menu without choosing a command, press ESC. You can also carry out some commands with the keyboard shortcuts listed in the menu.

Choosing commands with the keyboard in Microsoft Excel for the Macintosh   Press the SLASH (/) key or the PERIOD key on the numeric keypad to activate the menu bar, and then press the keys for the underlined letters in the menu and command you want. For example, to choose the Open command from the File menu, press SLASH, F, O. You can also use the arrow keys to move between menus and commands, and press ENTER to choose the menu or command you want. To cancel a menu without choosing a command, press ESC or COMMAND+PERIOD. You can also carry out some commands with the keyboard shortcuts listed in the menu.

If the underlines don't appear in the menu names when you press the SLASH key, choose the Workspace command from the Options menu, and then select the Automatic option button under Command Underline.

Note   If you want to use the PERIOD key on the numeric keypad to choose commands, make sure Num Lock is turned off.

Understanding Dialog Boxes

Microsoft Excel presents options in dialog boxes instead of as menu items.

When you choose a command name that is followed by an ellipsis (. . .), Microsoft Excel displays a dialog box so that you can provide more information. Depending on the dialog box, you type the information or select from a group of options.

For example, the Font dialog box is displayed when you choose the Font command from the Format menu. In the dialog box, you tell Microsoft Excel which font you want.

In Microsoft Excel for Windows, the Font dialog box looks like the following illustration.

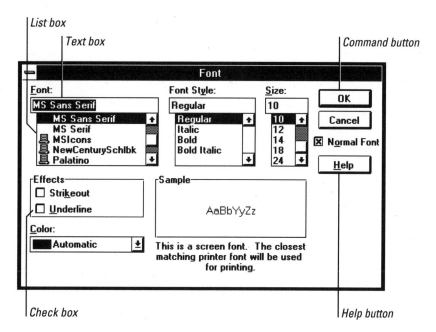

List box

Text box

Command button

Check box

Help button

In Microsoft Excel for the Macintosh, the Font dialog box looks like the following illustration.

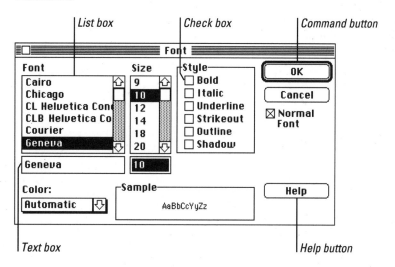

List box

Check box

Command button

Text box

Help button

Every dialog box has one or more of the following areas to help you supply the information necessary to carry out the command.

Help button   You choose the Help button in any dialog box for more detailed information about the options available. If an error message appears on your screen, choose the Help button for an explanation of the error and for help in resolving it.

Command button   You choose a command button to carry out a command or to display more options. Choose the OK button to carry out a command, or choose the Cancel button to cancel a command.

Command buttons use the same conventions as commands on menus. If a button is dimmed, it is unavailable. An ellipsis following the name of a command button means that more options are available. Choosing that command button expands the dialog box or displays another dialog box.

Text box   You type information in a text box. For example, in the Font box you can type the name of the font you want.

List box   Available choices are listed in a list box. In the Size box, you can select a font size from the list. If the list is longer than the box, you can use the scroll bar to see the rest of the list.

Option buttons   You can select only one option at a time from a group of option buttons. In the Clear dialog box, you can select the All, Formats, Formulas, or Notes option button. A selected option button has a black dot in its center.

Check boxes   You select check boxes to choose options that are independent of one another, so you can select more than one at a time. In Microsoft Excel for Windows, you can select the Strikeout check box, the Underline check box, or both under Effects. In Microsoft Excel for the Macintosh, you can select any combination of Bold, Italic, and several other styles. When a check box is selected, an X appears inside the box.

Selecting Dialog Box Options

To move around in a dialog box, click the item you want. You can also press ALT in Microsoft Excel for Windows or COMMAND in Microsoft Excel for the Macintosh while pressing the key for the underlined letter at the same time. In Microsoft Excel for Windows, you can also press TAB to move between items.

Selecting options with the mouse   Use the procedures in this table to select options in a dialog box with the mouse.

To	Do this
Select or clear an option button	Click the option button.
Select or clear a check box	Click the check box.
Select an item in a list box	Click the item.
Move to a text box	Click the text box.
Select text in a text box	Double-click a word or drag through the characters.
Scroll through a list box	Use the scroll bars.

After you've selected the options you want, click the OK button to carry out the command. To cancel the command, click the Cancel button.

Selecting options with the keyboard   You can also select options in a dialog box with the keyboard.

In Microsoft Excel for Windows, press ALT and the underlined letter for the option you want at the same time. Use the arrow keys to scroll through lists.

In Microsoft Excel for the Macintosh, press COMMAND and the underlined letter for the option you want at the same time. Use the arrow keys to scroll through lists. If you don't see underlined letters, choose the Workspace command from the Options menu, and then select the On option button under Command Underlines.

Choosing command buttons with the keyboard   Press ENTER to choose the default button (the button with a dark border). Usually this is the OK button, which carries out the command. Press ESC to choose the Cancel button and cancel the command. In Microsoft Excel for the Macintosh, you can also press COMMAND+PERIOD to choose the Cancel button and cancel the command.

If You Are New to Using the Mouse

Some tasks that require a menu command in 1-2-3 are simple mouse actions in Microsoft Excel.

Toolbars, shortcut menus, and many other features of Microsoft Excel were designed for working with the mouse. Though you can use the keyboard for most actions in Microsoft Excel, many of these actions are easier to do with the mouse.

Mouse Pointers

The mouse controls a pointer on the screen. You move the pointer by sliding the mouse over a flat surface in the direction you want the pointer to move. Usually you don't press the mouse button while you're moving the mouse. If you run out of room to move the mouse, lift it up and put it down again. The pointer moves only when the mouse is touching the flat surface.

Moving the mouse pointer across the screen does not affect the document; the pointer simply indicates a location on the screen. When you press the mouse button, something happens at the location of the pointer.

When the mouse pointer passes over different parts of the Microsoft Excel window, it changes shape, indicating what it will do at that point. Most of your work in this book will use the following mouse pointers.

This pointer	Appears when you point to
⬚ or ➤	The menu bar and toolbars to choose a command or a tool, the title bar to move a window, and the scroll bars to scroll through a document
I	Text in the formula bar you want to edit
⬩	A cell on the worksheet
+	The fill handle on a selected cell or range

This pointer	Appears when you point to
↕ ↔	A column heading boundary or row heading boundary to change column width or row height
◀▶ ↕	A split box on the scroll bar to split a window vertically or horizontally
👆	A button on a worksheet or a term in a Help topic that you can click to go to another topic

Using the Mouse

Moving the mouse and pressing the mouse button are the only skills you need to master *pointing, clicking, double-clicking,* and *dragging.* These are the four basic mouse actions that you will use throughout the lessons in this book.

Pointing   Moving the mouse to place the pointer on an item is called pointing.

Clicking   Pointing to an item on your screen and then quickly pressing and releasing the mouse button is called clicking. You select items on the screen and move around in a document by clicking.

Double-clicking   Pointing to an item and then quickly pressing and releasing the mouse button twice is called double-clicking. This is a convenient shortcut for many tasks in Microsoft Excel.

Dragging   Holding down the mouse button as you move the pointer is called dragging. You can use this technique to select cells in worksheets.

Try the mouse

Take a moment to test drive the mouse. Just slide the mouse so that the pointer moves around the Microsoft Excel screen.

1   Slide the mouse until the pointer is over the menus and tools at the top of the screen. The pointer is a left-pointing arrow.

2   Slide the mouse around the document window, the large open area in the center of the screen.

The document window is the area in which you work with the text on a worksheet. The pointer looks like a large plus sign.

3   With the mouse pointer over any cell in the worksheet, click the mouse button; then slide the mouse pointer over the formula bar, above the worksheet.

The pointer looks like an I-beam.

1 Learning Microsoft Excel Basics

Creating a Worksheet

In this lesson, you'll learn to find your way around a worksheet document. You'll open and close a worksheet, enter text and numbers, and get online Help. If you are a Lotus 1-2-3 user, you can also use Help for Lotus 1-2-3 Users to make your transition to Microsoft Excel easy.

You will learn how to:

- Open and rename a document.
- Scroll through a worksheet document.
- Change the active cell.
- Enter text on a worksheet.
- Work in the formula bar.
- Close a worksheet.
- Use online Help.
- Quit Microsoft Excel.

Estimated lesson time: 15 minutes

Start the lesson

If you quit Microsoft Excel at the end of "Getting Ready," or if you are beginning with this lesson, start Microsoft Excel now.

▶ Start Microsoft Excel.

For information about starting Microsoft Excel, see "Starting Microsoft Excel" in "Getting Ready" earlier in this book.

Opening a Worksheet

You'll open a worksheet to use in this lesson.

The Open command is like /File Retrieve, /File List, /File Directory, and /File Import in 1-2-3.

The Open command   With the Open command, you open a document from a disk and display it in a window. You can open a Microsoft Excel worksheet, chart, macro sheet, or workbook. You can also open a Lotus 1-2-3 worksheet with the Open command.

Changing the current directory or folder   You can use the Open command on the File menu to change the current directory or folder. In Microsoft Excel for Windows, just select a directory from the Directories box, and then choose the OK button. To move to a different directory, select it in the Directories box and choose the OK button. To change disk drives, select a drive from the Drives box and choose the OK button.

In Microsoft Excel for the Macintosh, just select a folder name in the Open Document dialog box, and then choose the Open button. To move to a different folder, point to the folder name at the top of the list box, and then drag to select a folder. To change disk drives, choose the Drive button, or choose the Desktop button if you're using Macintosh system software version 7.0 or later.

Open a worksheet in Microsoft Excel for Windows

1   From the File menu, choose Open.

2   In the Directories box, double-click PRACTICE to switch to the PRACTICE directory.

   If you have no PRACTICE directory, make sure that you followed the instructions in "Getting Ready" for copying it to your hard disk.

3   In the File Name box, select 01LESSN.XLS.

4   Choose the OK button.

   You can click the OK button or press ENTER to choose OK.

Open a worksheet in Microsoft Excel for the Macintosh

1   From the File menu, choose Open.

2   In the Open Document box, double-click PRACTICE to switch to the PRACTICE folder.

   If you have no PRACTICE folder, make sure that you followed the instructions in "Getting Ready" for copying it to your hard disk.

3   Select 01LESSN.

4   Choose the Open button.

The first row of the 01LESSN worksheet is shown in the following illustration.

	A	B	C	D	E
1	Title	WCS Cash Budget: 1993 Fiscal Year			

Enlarging a window   You can quickly enlarge a window to fill the entire workspace. In Microsoft Excel for Windows, click the Maximize button or choose the Maximize command from the Control menu. In Microsoft Excel for the Macintosh, click the zoom box or drag the size box until the window fills the workspace.

Restoring a window   You can quickly restore a maximized window to its previous size. In Microsoft Excel for Windows, click the Restore button or choose the Restore command from the Control menu. In Microsoft Excel for the Macintosh, click the zoom out box.

Enlarge the worksheet window

To see as much of the worksheet as will fit on your display, enlarge the window in the Microsoft Excel workspace.

▶ In Microsoft Excel for Windows, click the Maximize button in the upper-right corner of the 01LESSN.XLS window.

In Microsoft Excel for the Macintosh, click the zoom box in the upper-right corner of the 01LESSN window.

The worksheet window resizes to fill your screen.

Saving a Worksheet

In this lesson, you'll create a budget worksheet for a fictitious company, West Coast Sales. You'll start by renaming 01LESSN as BUDGET.

The Save As command asks for a filename, the same as /File Save in 1-2-3.

The Save As command   Use the Save As command when you need to name a document that you're saving for the first time, or when you want to rename an existing document. You just type the name in the dialog box that appears. You also use Save As to save a document in a different file format.

After you have named a worksheet, the Save File tool is like /File Save Replace in 1-2-3.

The Save File tool   After you've named your document with the Save As command, you can click the Save File tool on the toolbar whenever you want to save your changes. The current version of your document replaces the previous version on the disk. If you click the Save File tool before you've named a document, Microsoft Excel displays the Save As dialog box and prompts you for a name.

Save a worksheet in Microsoft Excel for Windows

1   From the File menu, choose Save As.

2   In the File Name box, type **BUDGET**

Microsoft Excel for Windows automatically saves all worksheets with the .XLS filename extension. You can type a different extension if you prefer.

3   Choose the OK button.

"BUDGET.XLS" now appears in the title bar of the Microsoft Excel window.

Save a worksheet in Microsoft Excel for the Macintosh

1   From the File menu, choose Save As.

2   In the Save Worksheet As box, type **BUDGET**

3   Choose the Save button.

"BUDGET" now appears in the title bar of the active window.

The following illustration shows some important parts of the Microsoft Excel worksheet window. The worksheet window for Microsoft Excel for Windows is shown in the illustration.

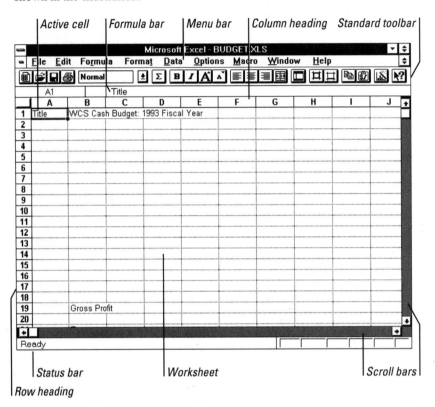

Active cell *Formula bar* *Menu bar* *Column heading* *Standard toolbar*

Status bar *Worksheet* *Scroll bars*

Row heading

The menu bar, formula bar, and status bar are like the control panel in 1-2-3.

The Microsoft Excel window consists of several parts. The *menu bar* displays menus, which contain commands. The *Standard toolbar* includes a Style box and tools for formatting, alignment, creating charts, and other common spreadsheet tasks. You will learn how to use these tools and other toolbars later in this book. You enter and edit cell data in the *formula bar*. The *worksheet* has 256 columns, labeled A through IV, and 16,384 rows. The *row heading* and *column heading* specify the position of cells on the worksheet. The *scroll bars* move the window to a new area of the worksheet. The *status bar* displays messages from Microsoft Excel. The status bar now displays the message "Ready," meaning that Microsoft Excel is ready for you to either choose a command or type data in a cell.

Scrolling Through a Document Window

When a document is too large to fit within a window, you can *scroll* through the document window to see other parts of the document. Scrolling means moving cells across the screen to bring the cells that are currently above, below, or to the side of the window into view. You use the scroll arrows and scroll box located on the scroll bars to move the document cells through the window.

Scroll through the document

To scroll through a worksheet as you do in 1-2-3, choose Workspace from the Options menu and select Alternate Navigation Keys.

You can scroll through the window with the mouse in three ways: click the scroll arrow, drag the scroll box, or click the scroll bar above or below the scroll box. As you scroll, the scroll box moves to indicate your position in the document.

1   Click the down scroll arrow.

The window moves down one row.

2   Drag the scroll box down to the bottom of the scroll bar.

The window moves down to display the end of the worksheet.

3   Click the scroll bar above the scroll box until the scroll box is at the top of the scroll bar.

The window moves up to display the beginning of the worksheet.

Changing the Active Cell

The active cell in Microsoft Excel is like the current cell in 1-2-3.

Cell A1 is the *active cell* when you first open the worksheet. Data you enter is stored in the active cell. You can identify the active cell by its dark border. When you select another cell, it becomes the active cell. You can select cells with the mouse or the keyboard.

Using the mouse to make another cell active   Click the cell you want to move to. If you can't see the cell you want in the window, use the scroll bars to scroll through the window, and then click the cell.

Using the keyboard to make another cell active   The keys you can use to select cells in Microsoft Excel are listed in the following table. In Microsoft Excel for the Macintosh, some of these keys are available only on extended keyboards.

To move	Press
Left one cell	LEFT ARROW
Right one cell	RIGHT ARROW
Up one cell	UP ARROW
Down one cell	DOWN ARROW
Up one screen	PAGE UP
Down one screen	PAGE DOWN

To move	Press
To start of row	CTRL+LEFT ARROW
	In Microsoft Excel for the Macintosh, you can also press COMMAND+LEFT ARROW.
To end of row	CTRL+RIGHT ARROW
	In Microsoft Excel for the Macintosh, you can also press COMMAND+RIGHT ARROW.
To start of worksheet	CTRL+HOME
	In Microsoft Excel for the Macintosh, you can also press COMMAND+HOME.
To end of worksheet	CTRL+END
	In Microsoft Excel for the Macintosh, you can also press COMMAND+END.

In Microsoft Excel for Windows, if you enabled Lotus 1-2-3 navigation keys when you set up Microsoft Excel, you should disable them while you work through this book, or your navigation keys will not work as described. From the Options menu, choose the Workspace command, clear the Alternate Navigation Keys check box, and choose the OK button.

Select cell A3

1   Move the mouse pointer over the cell in column A and row 3.

2   Click the mouse button.

A3 becomes the active cell. You see a border appear around cell A3, and "A3" appears in the reference area to the left of the formula bar.

Entering Text on a Worksheet

You'll start your projected budget worksheet for West Coast Sales (WCS) by entering text in column B to label the rows. You will label other worksheet areas with descriptions such as Introduction, Purpose, and so on. When you document your worksheets, you and others will be able to understand their purpose, logic, and assumptions, and they'll be easier to use.

Text in Microsoft Excel is like labels in 1-2-3.

As soon as you start typing, whatever you type appears in both the active cell and the formula bar. The *cancel box* and the *enter box* appear in the formula bar, and the message in the status bar changes from "Ready" to "Enter."

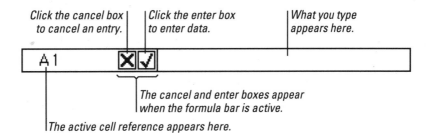

Click the cancel box | Click the enter box | What you type
to cancel an entry. | to enter data. | appears here.

The cancel and enter boxes appear
when the formula bar is active.

The active cell reference appears here.

You can store your data in the active cell by clicking the enter box in the formula bar or by pressing ENTER. You can cancel the entry by clicking the cancel box in the formula bar or by pressing ESC. In Microsoft Excel for the Macintosh, you can also press COMMAND+PERIOD to cancel the entry.

If you make a mistake while you're typing in Microsoft Excel for Windows, you can use the BACKSPACE key or the arrow keys to move the *insertion point*, the blinking vertical line that shows where text is entered in the formula bar. In Microsoft Excel for the Macintosh, you use the DELETE key or OPTION+ARROW keys to move the insertion point.

Enter the heading information

As you type the row titles, long entries will appear to spill into other columns, even though they are stored in column B. You'll learn to change column width in Lesson 3, "Formatting a Worksheet."

1 Type **Created by**

2 Press ENTER.

3 Select cell B3.

4 Type your name.

5 Press ENTER.

If the active cell changes when you press ENTER (or RETURN in Microsoft Excel for the Macintosh), choose the Workspace command from the Options menu. Then clear the Move Selection After Enter or Move Selection After Return check box.

Entering and moving in one step   You don't need to press ENTER after entering text in each cell. You can enter data and move to the next cell in a single step with either the mouse or the keyboard. With the mouse, type your entry and then click the next cell where you want to enter data. With the keyboard, type your entry and then press an arrow key.

Enter row titles for the gross revenue items

1   Select cell A5.

2   Type **Fiscal Model Area**

3   Select cell B7.

4   Type **Gross Revenue**

5   Press ENTER.

Your worksheet should look like the following illustration.

	A	B	C	D	E
1	Title	WCS Cash Budget: 1993 Fiscal Year			
2					
3	Created by	Sam Bryan			
4					
5	Fiscal Model Area				
6					
7		Gross Revenue			
8					

You can save time entering data in a range of cells if you select all of the cells in the range first. As you enter data in each cell, the next selected cell becomes the active cell in a top-to-bottom, left-to-right order. To select a cell range, drag the mouse pointer from the first cell to the last cell in the range.

Select a cell range and enter the row titles

Start by selecting cells B8 through B17, where you will enter the titles for Gross Revenue and Cost of Goods Sold. The first cell you select remains the active cell. After you select the cells, enter the data shown in the following illustration. If you make a typing mistake and want to move backward through the selection, hold down the SHIFT key and press ENTER.

1   Drag from cell B8 to cell B17.

2   Type the remaining entries, as shown in the following illustration.

	A	B	C	D	E
1	Title	WCS Cash Budget: 1993 Fiscal Year			
2					
3	Created by	Sam Bryan			
4					
5	Fiscal Model Area				
6					
7		Gross Revenue			
8		Sales			
9		Shipping			
10		Total			
11					
12		Cost of Goods Sold			
13		Goods			
14		Freight			
15		Markdowns			
16		Miscellaneous			
17		Total			
18					

3 After each entry, press ENTER.

When you reach the last selected cell and press ENTER, the first selected cell becomes the active cell again.

Working in the Formula Bar

You can change a cell entry by typing a new entry over the old one. If you want to edit the existing entry without typing the new one from scratch, you can edit the entry in the formula bar. The formula bar displays the contents of the active cell.

Press F2 to edit a cell, just as you do in 1-2-3.

You can activate the formula bar with either the mouse or the keyboard. With the mouse, click anywhere in the formula bar. You can click the part of the entry you want to edit. To activate the formula bar with the keyboard, press the F2 key in Microsoft Excel for Windows, or press COMMAND+U in Microsoft Excel for the Macintosh. Press ESC to return to the worksheet. In Microsoft Excel for the Macintosh, you can also press COMMAND+PERIOD to return to the worksheet.

The insertion point in Microsoft Excel is like the text cursor in 1-2-3.

The movement and selection keys work differently in the formula bar than they do in the worksheet. In the formula bar, the arrow keys move one character at a time, the HOME key moves the insertion point to the start of the entry, and the END key moves the insertion point to the end of the entry.

With Microsoft Excel, you always select the data you want to act on before you choose the command. You can select the text you want to change with the mouse or the keyboard.

To use the mouse to select	Do this
A word	Double-click the word.
Any character or sequence of characters	Drag across the character or sequence of characters.

After typing a cell entry, press ENTER or ESC, just as you do in 1-2-3.

If you want to cancel your editing changes and restore the previous cell entry, click the cancel box or press ESC before entering the change. In Microsoft Excel for the Macintosh, you can also press COMMAND+PERIOD to cancel your editing changes.

Edit a cell entry

1 Select cell A5.

2 In the formula bar, select "Fiscal" by double-clicking it.

3 Type **Budget**

4 Press ENTER.

Next, save your work.

Save your work

 ▶ Click the Save File tool on the toolbar.

Using Online Help

Microsoft Excel includes Help, a complete online reference. You can get Help information in several ways.

To get Help information	Do this
By topic or activity	In Microsoft Excel for Windows, choose Contents from the Help menu.
	In Microsoft Excel for the Macintosh, choose Help from the appropriate menu (see note below).
While working in a dialog box or message box	Choose the Help button in the dialog box or the message box.
About a specific command, tool, or other element on the screen	Click the Help tool, and then click the command, tool, or other screen element.
By keyword	Double-click the Help tool. In the Search dialog box, type a keyword and then select a Help topic.

Note   In Microsoft Excel for the Macintosh, the command you choose to display the Help Contents window can appear on one of two menus. If you are running Macintosh system software version 7.0 or later and have a 13-inch or larger monitor, the Microsoft Excel Help command appears on the Balloon Help menu. Otherwise, the Help command appears on the Window menu. Choose the Help command from the menu that corresponds to your system.

Display the list of Help topics

▶   In Microsoft Excel for Windows, choose Contents from the Help menu.

In Microsoft Excel for the Macintosh, choose the Help command from the appropriate menu (see note above).

The Help Contents window appears. You can click any underlined word to see that topic. The Help Contents window in Microsoft Excel for Windows is shown in the following illustration. In Microsoft Excel for the Macintosh, the Help Contents window is identical except that the Help menu bar appears at the top of the screen, not at the top of the Help window.

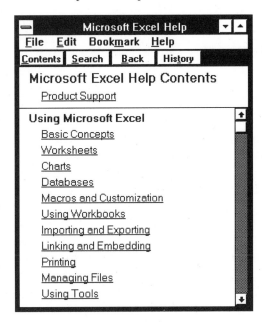

The Help window is like any other window in Microsoft Excel. You can move, size, and scroll through the Help window. You can switch between the Help window and your document, or you can arrange the windows side by side so that you can refer to Help while you work.

View other Help topics

You can select any underlined term from the list of related topics to display that topic in the window.

▶ Scroll down the list until the Commands topic is visible, and then click it.

A list of Microsoft Excel command menus appears in the window.

The Back button   With the Back button in the Help window, you can move from your current topic to the last topic you viewed.

Return to Help Contents

▶ Choose the Contents button.

Close the Help window

▶ In Microsoft Excel for Windows, choose E̲xit from the F̲ile menu in the Help window.

In Microsoft Excel for the Macintosh, choose Close from the File menu.

Getting Help switching to Microsoft Excel   If you have worked with Lotus 1-2-3, you can use Help to look up the command equivalents for Microsoft Excel. If you are familiar with Lotus 1-2-3, go through the next Help exercise to use your knowledge of 1-2-3 to learn about Microsoft Excel. In Microsoft Excel for Windows, you can also look up command equivalents for Microsoft® Multiplan®.

Help for Lotus 1-2-3 Users is useful for looking up or carrying out Microsoft Excel equivalents of 1-2-3 commands.

The Lotus 1-2-3 command in Microsoft Excel for Windows   When you choose the Lotus 1-2-3 command from the Help menu, the Help for Lotus 1-2-3 Users dialog box is displayed. You can select a 1-2-3 command from the Menu box to see the equivalent Microsoft Excel procedure. You can either see a demonstration of the procedure or have the instructions posted on your worksheet while you carry out the command. If you want more information, you can choose the More Help button to start Microsoft Excel Help.

The Lotus 1-2-3 command in Microsoft Excel for the Macintosh   When you choose the Lotus 1-2-3 command from the Window menu or the Balloon Help menu, a dialog box is displayed. In the Command box, you can type the keystrokes of a specific 1-2-3 command for which you want to learn the Microsoft Excel equivalent.

Find the equivalent of File Retrieve in Microsoft Excel for Windows (optional)

Use the Lotus 1-2-3 command on the Help menu to display Help for Lotus 1-2-3 Users.

1   From the H̲elp menu, choose L̲otus 1-2-3.

The following dialog box appears.

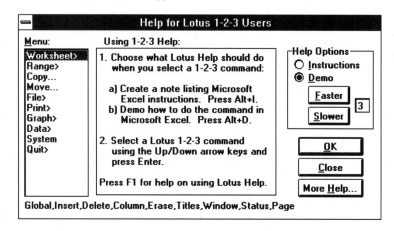

2 Under Help Options, select the Demo option button.

3 In the Menu box, double-click File and then double-click Retrieve.

You can also type **fr** for File Retrieve.

4 Follow the instructions on the screen.

You can select any file within the PRACTICE directory.

5 Choose the OK button.

Microsoft Excel closes the BUDGET file and demonstrates the Open command on the File menu, which is the equivalent of the File Retrieve command.

6 Repeat steps 1 through 3, but select the Instructions option button under Help Options.

Microsoft Excel posts the procedure for opening a file on your worksheet.

7 Press ESC to remove the message from your screen.

If you are an experienced Lotus 1-2-3 user, you may want to have Help for Lotus 1-2-3 Users displayed whenever you press the SLASH key (/). To do this, choose the Workspace command from the Options menu, and under Alternate Menu Or Help Key, select the Lotus 1-2-3 Help option button.

Find the equivalent of File Retrieve in Microsoft Excel for the Macintosh (optional)

1 From the Window menu or the Balloon Help menu, choose Help for 1-2-3 Users, or Lotus 1-2-3 Help.

2 In the Command box, type /**fr**

3 Choose the OK button.

Help displays the procedure for choosing the Open command from the File menu. To close the Help window, double-click the close box.

Closing a Worksheet Window

Closing a worksheet window is like using /Worksheet Erase Yes in 1-2-3.

You can choose the Close command from the File menu to close the active document window. In Microsoft Excel for Windows, you can also use the Close command on the Control menu or double-click the Control-menu box. In Microsoft Excel for the Macintosh, you can also click the close box. If you have made any changes to the worksheet that you haven't saved, Microsoft Excel displays a dialog box asking whether you want to save changes.

Close the worksheet

Now you will close the open worksheet window.

1 From the File menu, choose Close.

2 Choose the No button to cancel changes to the worksheet.

Close the blank worksheet

▶ From the File menu, choose Close.

All document windows are closed. Microsoft Excel is still running, with the *null menu bar* displayed.

You see the null menu bar when all document windows are closed. The null menu bar contains only the File and Help menus in Microsoft Excel for Windows, and only the File, Edit, and Window menus in Microsoft Excel for the Macintosh. Some of the commands that are usually on other menus move to the File menu when all document windows are closed.

Quitting Microsoft Excel

When you quit Microsoft Excel, it is no longer running. You're given the opportunity to save any previously unsaved work before you quit.

The Exit or Quit command on the File menu is like /Quit in 1-2-3.

Commands used to quit Microsoft Excel   In Microsoft Excel for Windows, choose the Exit command from the File menu to end a Microsoft Excel session. In Microsoft Excel for the Macintosh, choose the Quit command from the File menu. If you have any open document windows with unsaved changes, Microsoft Excel displays a dialog box for each of them, asking whether you want to save changes.

Quit Microsoft Excel

▶ In Microsoft Excel for Windows, choose Exit from the File menu.

In Microsoft Excel for the Macintosh, choose Quit from the File menu.

Lesson Summary

To	Do this
Open a document	From the File menu, choose Open. Then select the file you want to open.
Maximize the document window	In Microsoft Excel for Windows, click the Maximize button in the upper-right corner of the document window. In Microsoft Excel for the Macintosh, click the zoom box in the upper-right corner of the document window.
Rename and save a document	From the File menu, choose Save As. Enter a name for the worksheet, and then choose the OK or Save button.
Scroll down a worksheet one row	Click the down scroll arrow.
Scroll down to the bottom of a worksheet	Drag the scroll box down to the bottom of the scroll bar.
Make a different cell the active cell	Click another cell to select it.

To	Do this
Enter text into a cell	Select the cell, and then begin typing. Your entry appears in the formula bar below the toolbar.
Enter text into a range of cells	Select the range. After each entry, press ENTER. The next cell in the selection becomes the active cell.
Edit a cell entry	Select the cell, and then click in the formula bar. Edit the entry, and then press ENTER.
Display the Help Contents	In Microsoft Excel for Windows, choose Contents from the Help menu. In Microsoft Excel for the Macintosh, choose Help from either the Balloon Help menu or the Window menu.
Close a document	From the File menu, choose Close.
End a Microsoft Excel session	In Microsoft Excel for Windows, choose Exit from the File menu. In Microsoft Excel for the Macintosh, choose Quit from the File menu.

For more information about	See in the *Microsoft Excel User's Guide*
Opening, saving, and closing a document	Chapter 4, "Managing Document Files," in Book 1
Scrolling through a worksheet	Chapter 5, "Creating a Worksheet," in Book 1
Entering text and formulas	Chapter 5, "Creating a Worksheet," in Book 1
Using online Help	Chapter 2, "Learning Microsoft Excel," in Book 1

For an online lesson about	Start the tutorial Learning Microsoft Excel and complete this lesson
Microsoft Excel worksheets	"What Is a Worksheet?"
Online Help	"Using Microsoft Excel Help"

For information about starting an online tutorial lesson, see "Using the Online Tutorials" in "Getting Ready" earlier in this book.

Preview of the Next Lesson

In the next lesson, you'll enter some monthly data for the budget you've started. Once you've entered the budget numbers, you'll create several formulas. These will include cell references and a function.

Entering Numbers and Formulas

In this lesson, you'll continue entering data in the monthly budget you started in the previous lesson. You'll enter row and column titles to label items, and you'll enter some budget figures for July, the first month of the fiscal year. You'll finish by writing formulas using cell references and a Microsoft Excel function.

This lesson assumes that you know how to choose menu commands and select dialog box options. If you need help with menu commands or dialog box options, see "Working in Microsoft Excel" in "Getting Ready" earlier in this book.

You will learn how to:

- Quickly create a series of dates.
- Enter text, numbers, and formulas in cells.
- Use references and functions in formulas.

Estimated lesson time: 20 minutes

Start Microsoft Excel

▶ Double-click the Microsoft Excel icon.

If you need help starting Microsoft Excel, see "Starting Microsoft Excel" in "Getting Ready" earlier in this book.

Start the lesson

Follow these steps to open 02LESSN and rename it BUDGET.

1 Open 02LESSN.

2 Save the worksheet as BUDGET.

3 Choose the Yes button to replace the previous BUDGET worksheet.

Enlarge the worksheet window

1 Close any other open windows.

2 In Microsoft Excel for Windows, click the Maximize button.

In Microsoft Excel for the Macintosh, click the zoom box.

Creating a Series of Dates

Dragging the fill handle to enter a series is like using /Data Fill in 1-2-3.

By dragging the *fill handle*, you can create many kinds of series and copy values to adjacent cells. The fill handle is the small square in the lower-right corner of the active cell or range, as shown in the following illustration.

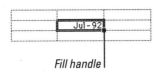

Fill handle

Note   If you do not see a fill handle on the active cell, choose Workspace from the Options menu. Then select the Cell Drag And Drop check box.

Create a series of dates

1   Select cell C6.

You can enter a date or other number the way you want it formatted.

2   Type **Jul-92**

3   Drag the fill handle from C6 to N6.

Look at the reference area of the formula bar as you drag the mouse. The value to be placed in the cell that the mouse pointer is over changes as you drag the fill handle.

Microsoft Excel creates the date series Jul-92 to Jun-93.

4   Scroll back to the left edge of the worksheet.

Your worksheet should look like the following illustration.

	A	B	C	D	E
1	Title	WCS Cash Budget: 1993 Fiscal Year			
2					
3	Created by	Sam Bryan			
4					
5	Budget Model Area				
6			Jul-92	Aug-92	Sep-92
7		Gross Revenue			
8		Sales			
9		Shipping			
10		Total			
11					
12		Cost of Goods Sold			
13		Goods			
14		Freight			
15		Markdown			
16		Miscellaneous			
17		Total			
18					

Entering Data in Worksheet Cells

Enter the budget figures for July

You'll save time by selecting the range of cells where you want to enter data and then pressing ENTER after each entry.

1   Drag from cell C8 to cell C16.

2   Enter the data for July, as shown in the following illustration.

	A	B	C	D	E
1	Title	WCS Cash Budget: 1993	Fiscal Year		
2					
3	Created by	Sam Bryan			
4					
5	Budget Model Area				
6			Jul-92	Aug-92	Sep-92
7		Gross Revenue			
8		Sales	26900		
9		Shipping	5550		
10		Total			
11					
12		Cost of Goods Sold			
13		Goods	17710		
14		Freight	270		
15		Markdown	1240		
16		Miscellaneo	96		
17		Total			
18					

3   Press ENTER after each entry.

Entering Simple Formulas

A number in Microsoft Excel is like a value in 1-2-3.

You can also type @ to begin a formula; Microsoft Excel converts the syntax for you.

A reference is like an address in 1-2-3. Use a colon (:) instead of two periods to indicate a range.

A function is like an @function in 1-2-3.

A formula can consist of numbers, arithmetic operators, cell references, and functions. You can create a formula by typing, by pointing to cells with the keyboard or the mouse, or by pasting names and functions.

To tell Microsoft Excel that you're entering a formula in a cell, begin the entry with an equal sign (=). You can also type +, –, or @ to begin a formula; Microsoft Excel converts these to an equal sign.

References in formulas   A reference in a formula can be the address of a cell or cell range. To indicate a range of cells, you use a colon (:) between the first and last cells; for example, B7:B9 refers to cells B7 through B9. To indicate a list of cells, you use a comma; for example, B7,D3,H9 refers to cells B7, D3, and H9.

Functions in formulas   Microsoft Excel has hundreds of *worksheet functions* to help you perform specialized calculations easily. A worksheet function is a special built-in formula that performs an operation on the values you provide. For example, the formula =SUM(C22:C26) uses a function to add the values in the cell range C22:C26. It returns the same result as the formula =C22+C23+C24+C25+C26, which adds the values individually. Functions can be used alone or nested within other functions. You can enter a function by typing it or by using the Paste Function command on the Formula menu.

Arguments in functions   The arguments in a function tell Microsoft Excel how you want the function carried out. For example, when you use the SUM function, you need to specify which numbers or cells you want summed. The arguments appear in parentheses after the function name. Individual arguments are separated by commas.

You'll create all the formulas for your budget model in a single column. In Lesson 5, "Copying and Moving Cell Data and Formats," you'll copy the formulas to the other columns.

Type a formula

Create a formula in cell C10 to find the sum of the gross revenue items in cells C8 and C9. Remember that you begin a formula by typing an equal sign (=) and that you indicate a cell range by using a colon (:).

1   Select cell C10.

When you enter parentheses in a formula, Microsoft Excel momentarily displays matching parentheses in bold. Notice what happens in the formula bar as you type the first formula. Microsoft Excel adds a matching parenthesis within a formula if you forget to.

2   Type **=sum(c8:c9)**

3   Press ENTER.

The total of Sales and Shipping, 32,450, appears in cell C10.

The Paste Function command   With the Paste Function command on the Formula menu, you can select the function you want from a list of all the available worksheet functions. The Paste Function command is especially useful when you create formulas by pointing with the mouse instead of by typing. If you begin a formula by pasting a function, Microsoft Excel adds the equal sign to the beginning of your formula automatically.

Pointing to add references to formulas   While the formula bar is active, you can use the mouse or the keyboard to point to cells whose references you want to use in the formula. The cells you point to are surrounded by a dotted line called the *moving border*.

Create a formula by pointing

Create a formula in cell C17 to sum the items under Cost of Goods Sold. You'll use the pointing method and the Paste Function command to create the formula.

1   Select cell C17.

2   From the Formula menu, choose Paste Function.

The Paste Function dialog box appears.

3   In the Function Category box, select Math & Trig.

4   In the Paste Function box, select SUM.

In Microsoft Excel for Windows, you can press S to scroll quickly to the first function that begins with S.

5   Clear the Paste Arguments check box.

6   Choose the OK button.

7   Drag from cell C13 to cell C16.

8   Press ENTER.

The total of Cost of Goods Sold, 19,316, appears in cell C17.

Create another formula by pointing

Cell C19 will contain your gross profit. You'll enter a formula to calculate the difference between the Gross Revenue and Cost of Goods Sold results. This formula will contain only arithmetic operators and references.

1   Select cell C19.

2   Type an equal sign (=).

3   Select cell C10.

4   Type a minus sign (–).

5   Select cell C17.

6   Press ENTER.

The difference between Gross Revenues and Cost of Goods Sold, 13,134, appears in cell C19.

 The AutoSum tool   You can click the AutoSum tool on the Standard toolbar to paste the SUM function and a proposed cell range into the active cell. Click the tool again to accept the proposed range and cancel the moving border.

Use the AutoSum tool

1   Select cell C33.

2   Click the AutoSum tool on the toolbar.

Microsoft Excel places the SUM function and a proposed cell range in cell C33. The moving border encloses cells C22:C32.

3   Click the AutoSum tool again or press ENTER to accept the proposed range and enter the formula in the cell.

The total of Expenses, 11,085, appears in cell C33.

Enter the last formula

1   In cell C35, type **=c19–c33**

2   Press ENTER.

The difference between Gross Profit and Total Expenses, 2049, appears in cell C35, as shown in the following illustration.

	A	B	C	D	E
10		Total	32450		
11					
12		Cost of Goods Sold			
13		Goods	17710		
14		Freight	270		
15		Markdown	1240		
16		Miscellaneo	96		
17		Total	19316		
18					
19		Gross Profit	13134		
20					
21		Expenses			
22		Advertising	4000		
23		Salaries	4700		
24		Rent	500		
25		Utilities	75		
26		Insurance	43		
27		Telephone a	280		
28		Office Suppl	147		
29		Training	100		
30		Travel and E	200		
31		Taxes and Li	240		
32		Interest	800		
33		Total	11085		
34					
35		Operating I	2049		
36					

Save and close your worksheet

1   From the File menu, choose Close.

2   Choose the Yes button to save changes to the worksheet.

One Step Further

The West Coast Sales Copier marketing department has been given a budget of $250,000 to promote the license for their newest copier technology. You'll create a worksheet that adds the expenses already incurred and calculates how much is left in the budget.

Use the New command on the File menu to create a new worksheet. Include the creator of the worksheet (type your name), the title of the worksheet (WCS Copier Marketing Budget), and today's date. Save the worksheet as CAMPAIGN.

The marketing department has incurred the following expenses to date.

Category	Amount
Advertising	$100,000
Telemarketing	$25,000
Direct Mail	$50,000

Category	Amount
Clerical Support	$10,000
Consultants	$15,000
General Administration	$5,000

You can open the 02CAMPGN worksheet for comparison with your worksheet. The 02CAMPGN worksheet is in the PRACTICE directory or folder. Close both worksheets when you are finished.

Lesson Summary

To	Do this
Create a series	Enter the starting value, and then drag the fill handle across the range you want to fill.
Type a formula in a cell	In the formula bar, begin the formula with an equal sign (=); then enter the formula and press ENTER.
Use cell references in a formula	After you've started a formula, select the cell or range you want referenced. The formula changes as you select cells.
Use a function in a formula	Click in the formula bar, and place the insertion point at the correct place in the formula. From the Formula menu, choose Paste Function. Select the category and function you want inserted into the formula.
Add a series of numbers	Select the cell in which you want the sum placed. Click the AutoSum tool. Microsoft Excel proposes the sum range. Click the AutoSum tool again to accept this, or select another range and click the AutoSum tool.

For more information about	See in the *Microsoft Excel User's Guide*
Creating a series of dates or numbers	"Creating a Series" in Chapter 5 in Book 1
Entering worksheet data	"Entering Worksheet Data" in Chapter 5 in Book 1
Creating formulas	"Entering a Formula" in Chapter 5 in Book 1

Preview of the Next Lesson

In the next lesson, you'll learn how to format a worksheet. This includes adjusting row and column height, changing fonts and number formats, and quickly formatting a table.

As you complete the next lesson, you'll use new tools such as shortcut menus and different toolbars. You'll also learn how to easily repeat formatting commands and actions.

2 Moving and Formatting Your Data

Formatting a Worksheet

In this lesson, you'll use Microsoft Excel's formatting and display features to dramatically improve your worksheet's appearance.

You will learn how to:

- Change column width and row height.
- Format numbers.
- Create your own number formats.
- Change the alignment of cell entries.

Estimated lesson time: 40 minutes

Start the lesson

1 Open 03LESSN.

2 Save the worksheet as BUDGET.

Selecting Cells and Ranges

Selecting a range of cells is like highlighting a range of cells in 1-2-3. However, in Microsoft Excel you always select cells before you choose a command.

Selecting cells first   As you format the worksheet, you select the cells you want to act on first and then choose the command you want. Whether you want to format a single cell, an entire row or column, or the entire worksheet, you first make the selection and then choose a command.

You may want to change the formatting of entire rows or columns or of the entire worksheet.

If you need to save memory and disk space, format only the cells and cell ranges you need, rather than the entire worksheet.

Selecting entire rows or columns or the entire worksheet   The following table lists the procedures for selecting entire rows, columns, or worksheets.

To select	Do this
One row or column	Click the row or column heading.
Multiple adjacent cells	Hold down SHIFT and double-click the border of the selected cell in the direction you want to extend the selection.
Multiple adjacent rows or columns	Drag across the column headings or row headings.
An entire worksheet	Click the blank box in the upper-left corner of the worksheet grid.

Changing Column Width

The Column Width command is like /Worksheet Global Column-Width and /Worksheet Column Set-Width in 1-2-3.

The Column Width command   With the Column Width command, you can change the width of one or more columns with the Best Fit button, or you can define a width from 0 to 255 characters. You need to select at least one cell in each column you want to change before you choose the command. When you open a new worksheet, the standard column width is 8 characters in Microsoft Excel for Windows or 10 characters in Microsoft Excel for the Macintosh. You can change the standard width for any worksheet.

The Best Fit button   When you choose the Column Width command from the Format menu and choose the Best Fit button, Microsoft Excel widens the selected columns so that the longest string of numbers or text is fully displayed in its own column and does not spill over into other columns.

You can also choose the Best Fit option with the mouse by double-clicking the column boundary to the right of the row heading.

Changing column width with the mouse   You don't need to choose a command to change column width with the mouse. Point to the column boundary to the right of the column heading, and then drag it to the width you want. The mouse pointer changes to ↔ when you point to the boundary. If you want to change the width of more than one column at the same time, select all of the columns and then drag any of the selected column boundaries to increase or decrease the width of the columns.

Change the column width for the entire worksheet

If you want to make a "global" formatting change, start by selecting the entire worksheet.

You can also make changes that affect your entire worksheet. You will change the width of all the columns in the worksheet to 12 characters. First you'll select the entire worksheet.

1   In the upper-left corner of the worksheet grid, click the Select All button.

You can also press CTRL+SHIFT+SPACEBAR in Microsoft Excel for Windows or COMMAND+SHIFT+SPACEBAR in Microsoft Excel for the Macintosh.

The entire worksheet is selected.

2   From the Format menu, choose Column Width.

3   In the Column Width box, type **12**

4   Choose the OK button.

5   Click any cell to cancel the selection of the entire worksheet.

Change the column width for column B

You want all of the row titles in column B to fit within the column. When you want to size an entire column to exactly the right width, double-click the right boundary of the column heading. You can also use the mouse to manually adjust the column width.

1   Select cells B7:B35.

2   From the Format menu, choose Column Width and choose the Best Fit button.

Changing Row Height

You can also change row height by either choosing a command or dragging the mouse.

When you open a new worksheet, the standard row height is set to accommodate the normal font for your worksheet. When you change the size of a font in a cell, Microsoft Excel adjusts row height automatically.

The Row Height command   You can change the height of one or more rows with the Row Height command. Row height is measured in points instead of characters. One inch equals 72 points.

The Standard Height check box   You can select the Standard Height check box to set the correct row height for the largest font in the row. For example, in Microsoft Excel for Windows, with the MS® Sans Serif 10 font, standard row height is 12.75 or 13 points, depending on the graphics display card installed in your computer. In Microsoft Excel for the Macintosh, with the Geneva 10 font, standard row height is 13 points.

The Hide and Unhide buttons   You can choose the Hide or Unhide button to hide or unhide rows on the worksheet. You can also hide rows by setting the row height to zero.

Change the row height for row 11

You want row 11 to act as a border. Make row 11 about half as high as the other rows.

1   Select any cell in row 11.

2   From the Format menu, choose Row Height.

3   In the Row Height box, type **6**

4   Choose the OK button.

Your worksheet should look like the following illustration.

	A	B	C	D
1	Title	WCS Cash Budget: 1993 Fiscal Year		
2				
3	Created by	Sam Bryan		
4				
5	Budget Model Area			
6			Jul-92	Aug-92
7		Gross Revenue		
8		Sales	26900	
9		Shipping	5550	
10		Total	32450	
12		Cost of Goods Sold		
13		Goods	17710	
14		Freight	270	
15		Markdowns	1240	
16		Miscellaneous	96	
17		Total	19316	
18				
19		Gross Profit	13134	

Repeating a Format

The Repeat command   With the Repeat command, you can repeat your most recent action. The name of the Repeat command changes to reflect your last action; for example, Repeat Column Width or Repeat Row Height. To use the Repeat command, you must use a menu command to perform the original action.

Repeat the row height for row 18

You want to set rows 18, 20, and 34 to the same row height as row 11. Since you just changed the row height for row 11, you'll see Repeat Row Height in the Edit menu.

1   Select a cell in row 18.

2   From the Edit menu, choose Repeat Row Height.

Selecting Multiple Cells and Cell Ranges

How to make nonadjacent selections   You can also select and format multiple ranges at the same time. With the mouse, make your first selection, and then hold down the CTRL key in Microsoft Excel for Windows or the COMMAND key in Microsoft Excel for the Macintosh while you make additional selections.

Repeat the row height for rows 20 and 34 in one step

You can save time by selecting a cell in each of these rows and then choosing the Repeat Row Height command from the Edit menu only once.

1   Select a cell in row 20.

2   In Microsoft Excel for Windows, hold down CTRL and click a cell in row 34.

   In Microsoft Excel for the Macintosh, hold down COMMAND and click a cell in row 34.

3   From the Edit menu, choose Repeat Row Height.

Using Shortcut Menus

Microsoft Excel has built-in shortcut menus that contain the most frequently used commands for a selection. The commands on shortcut menus are also located on the menus in the menu bar.

Display a shortcut menu

1   Select cells C7:C35.

2   Move the mouse pointer over the selected range.

3   In Microsoft Excel for Windows, click the right mouse button.

   In Microsoft Excel for the Macintosh, hold down COMMAND+OPTION while you click the mouse button.

Your worksheet should look like the following illustration.

	A	B	C	D	E	F
21		Expenses				
22		Advertising		Cut	Ctrl+X	
23		Salaries		Copy	Ctrl+C	
24		Rent		Paste	Ctrl+V	
25		Utilities		Clear...	Del	
26		Insurance		Delete...		
27		Telephone and Telex		Insert Paste...		
28		Office Supplies				
29		Training		Number...		
30		Travel and Entertainment		Alignment...		
31		Taxes and Licenses		Font...		
32		Interest		Border...		
33		Total		Patterns...		
34						
35		Operating Income	2049			
36						
37						
38						
39						

Formatting Numbers

The Number command is like the /Range Format options in 1-2-3.

The Number command   With the Number command on the Format menu or the shortcut menu, you can format data with a built-in Microsoft Excel number format or your own custom number format. When you choose the Number command, you can select a format from the list or type your own format in the Code box.

The Currency Style tool   You can also format a cell for dollars by clicking the Currency Style tool on the Formatting toolbar.

Format a cell range for dollars

Format the Budget Model Area to display dollar values in whole numbers, with dollar signs, commas separating thousands, and negative numbers in parentheses.

The cell range C7:C35 should still be selected and the shortcut menu displayed. If the shortcut menu is not displayed, select the range and display the shortcut menu.

1   From the shortcut menu, choose Number.

You can also choose <u>N</u>umber from the Forma<u>t</u> menu.

2   In the Category list, select Currency.

3   In the Format Codes list, select the first dollar format: $#,##0_);($#,##0).

4   Choose the OK button.

Creating Custom Number Formats

You use specific symbols to create custom number formats in Microsoft Excel. For example, to format a number this way:

4:06 am, on November 10, 1992

starting with this date entry and General format:

11/10/92 4:06

you would create this number format:

h:mm am/pm", on "mmmm d", "yyyy

Create a custom number format for the month titles

Now create a custom number format for the month titles. Instead of displaying the abbreviated name of the month and the year, display the full name of the month by typing "mmmm" in the Code box.

1   Select cell C6.

2   Hold down the SHIFT key and double-click the right border of cell C6.

Microsoft Excel selects the cell range C6:N6, the month titles.

3   From the Format menu or the shortcut menu, choose Number.

4   In Microsoft Excel for Windows, drag across "mmm-yy" in the Code box at the bottom of the dialog box. This step is not necessary in Microsoft Excel for the Macintosh.

5   In the Code box at the bottom of the dialog box, type **mmmm**

The selected text is replaced by what you type.

6   Choose the OK button.

Your worksheet should look like the following illustration.

	A	B	C	D	E
1	Title	WCS Cash Budget: 1993 Fiscal Year			
2					
3	Created by	Sam Bryan			
4					
5	Budget Model Area				
6			July	August	September
7		Gross Revenue			
8		Sales	$26,900		
9		Shipping	$5,550		
10		Total	$32,450		
12		Cost of Goods Sold			
13		Goods	$17,710		
14		Freight	$270		
15		Markdowns	$1,240		
16		Miscellaneous	$96		
17		Total	$19,316		
19		Gross Profit	$13,134		

Applying Range Formats Automatically

Microsoft Excel has a number of built-in combinations of professionally designed formats that you can apply to any selected range. These formats are combinations of number formats, alignments, fonts, borders, colors, shading, and column widths and row heights. You can adjust any built-in format to retain any formatting you have already applied, such as column widths and number formats.

The AutoFormat command   With the AutoFormat command, you can select from five types of built-in formats: Classic, Colorful, 3-D, Financial, or List. Each of the five types has three different combinations of formats. The format combination you select depends on the way you want your data to appear. When you select a built-in format, a sample of the format is displayed in the AutoFormat dialog box.

Apply a range format

You'll apply a range format designed for financial data. Since you have already applied the column widths, row heights, and number formats you want, you will choose not to apply those formats as part of the range format.

1   Select cells B6:N35.

2   From the Format menu, choose AutoFormat.

3   Select Financial 2.

A sample of the combination of formats used in Financial 2 appears in the Sample box.

4   Choose the Options button.

5   Under Formats to Apply, clear both the Number and Width/Height check boxes.

The sample is updated to show the new combination of formats, as shown in the following illustration.

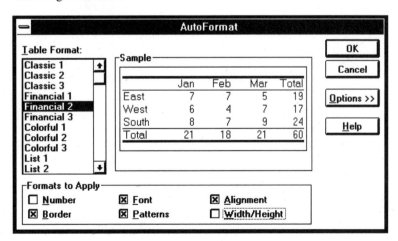

6   Choose the OK button.

Your worksheet should look like the following illustration.

	A	B	C	D	E	F
1	Title	WCS Cash Budget: 1993 Fiscal Year				
2						
3	Created by	Sam Bryan				
4						
5	Budget Model Area					
6			July	August	September	Octob
7		**Gross Revenue**				
8		Sales	$26,900			
9		Shipping	$5,550			
10		Total	$32,450			
12		**Cost of Goods Sold**				
13		Goods	$17,710			
14		Freight	$270			
15		Markdowns	$1,240			
16		Miscellaneous	$96			
17		Total	$19,316			
19		**Gross Profit**	$13,134			

Displaying and Hiding Toolbars

Microsoft Excel has a number of built-in toolbars. Each toolbar contains several tools. Each tool will perform a command or action whenever you click the tool. For example, you can save your worksheet at any time by clicking the Save File tool.

The Standard toolbar   The Standard toolbar, shown in the following illustration, is displayed automatically when you start Microsoft Excel. It contains tools that represent the most commonly performed commands and actions.

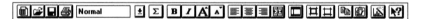

The Formatting toolbar   You can use the Formatting toolbar, shown in the following illustration, when you want to quickly format a worksheet or when you have a lot of formatting tasks to do. The Formatting toolbar contains the formatting tools located on the Standard toolbar as well as additional formatting tools.

Hiding a toolbar   Once you display a toolbar, it remains displayed until you choose to hide it. You can hide a toolbar by choosing Toolbars from the Option menu, selecting the name of the toolbar, and choosing the Hide button.

The toolbar shortcut menu   You can also display or hide a toolbar with the toolbar shortcut menu. Point anywhere in a toolbar, display the shortcut menu, and select the name of the toolbar you want to display or hide.

Display the Formatting toolbar

1 From the Options menu, choose Toolbars.

2 In the Show Toolbars box, double-click Formatting.

Microsoft Excel displays the Formatting toolbar. You can drag a toolbar to any location in the Microsoft Excel window. You can *dock* a toolbar by dragging it to the top or bottom of the Microsoft Excel window.

If you'd like to see a brief description of these tools, move the mouse pointer over any tool and hold down the mouse button. A description of the tool's action appears in the status bar. To continue working without invoking the tool, move the mouse pointer off the tool and release the mouse button.

Aligning Cell Entries

Default text and number alignment is the same as in 1-2-3, but you can change number alignment as well as text alignment in Microsoft Excel.

Microsoft Excel automatically aligns text to the left and numbers to the right. You can change the alignment of text, numbers, and dates with the alignment tools on the Standard toolbar and the Alignment command on the Format menu.

The alignment tools With the alignment tools, you can quickly change the alignment of numbers or text within a cell or cell range. Select the cell or cell range, and then click the Left Align, Center Align, or Right Align tool. You can also center numbers or text across several selected columns with the Center Across Columns tool. The Justify Align tool, located on the Formatting toolbar, fully justifies text and numbers across the width of a cell. The alignment tools are shown in the following illustration.

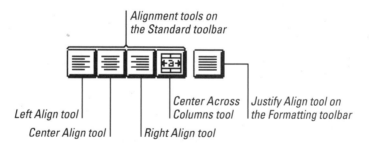

The Alignment command is like /Range Label and /Worksheet Global Label-Prefix in 1-2-3.

The Alignment command You can change the alignment of text or numbers in the selected cells with the Alignment command on the Format menu or the shortcut menu. The Left, Center, Right, Justify, and Center Across Selection option buttons work just like the tools on the Standard or Formatting toolbar. The General option button, which is the default, aligns text to the left and numbers to the right. The Fill option button repeats the characters in a cell to fill the entire cell. If you select the Wrap Text check box, text is wrapped within the cell so that all the text can be displayed in a narrower column width. You can also control the vertical spacing and orientation of text and numbers.

Center the month titles

Your month titles are numbers with a custom date format, so they're right-aligned. Since these serve as headings, you might want to change their alignment.

1 Select cells C6:N6.

2 Click the Center Align tool on the Standard toolbar or the Formatting toolbar.

You can also choose Alignment from the Format menu or the shortcut menu, select the Center option button, and then choose the OK button.

Right-align text in the worksheet area labels

1 Select cells A1:A5.

2 Click the Right Align tool on the Standard toolbar.

You can also choose Alignment from the Format menu or the shortcut menu, select the Right option button, and then choose the OK button.

If you want to use the same alignment prefixes as in 1-2-3, choose Workspace from the Options menu and select Alternate Navigation Keys.

3 Double-click the column A heading boundary for the Best Fit option.

You can also choose Column Width from the Format menu and choose the Best Fit button.

Your worksheet should look like the following illustration.

	A	B	C	D	E
1	Title	WCS Cash Budget: 1993 Fiscal Year			
2					
3	Created by	Sam Bryan			
4					
5	Budget Model Area				
6			July	August	September
7		**Gross Revenue**			
8		Sales	$26,900		
9		Shipping	$5,550		
10		Total	$32,450		
12		**Cost of Goods Sold**			
13		Goods	$17,710		
14		Freight	$270		
15		Markdowns	$1,240		
16		Miscellaneous	$96		
17		Total	$19,316		
19		**Gross Profit**	$13,134		

Changing Fonts

Font refers to the design of the characters in which text and numbers are displayed on the screen and printed by a printer. Each font has a name (such as MS Sans Serif or Courier in Microsoft Excel for Windows, or Geneva or Times in Microsoft Excel for the Macintosh) and comes in various sizes (such as 9-point or 12-point type) and styles (such as normal, bold, or italic).

The screen fonts available in Microsoft Excel depend on your system configuration. The printer fonts available depend on the specific printers you've set up to work with Microsoft Excel. You can use an unlimited number of fonts with Microsoft Excel.

You can change text fonts in Microsoft Excel.

The default screen font for Microsoft Excel for Windows is MS Sans Serif 10-point, and the default screen font for Microsoft Excel for the Macintosh is Geneva 10-point. The row and column headings appear in this font, and standard row height is set to accommodate MS Sans Serif 10 or Geneva 10.

The Font tools on the Formatting toolbar   The Formatting toolbar contains several tools for changing the font, size, and font style of text and numbers.

This tool	Does this
Font Name box	Lists the available fonts
Font Size box	Lists the available sizes for a font
Formatting tools (such as the Bold, Italic, and Underline tools)	Change the style of a chosen font

The font tools on the Formatting toolbar are shown in the following illustration.

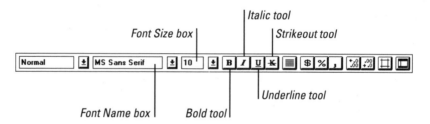

The Font command   In addition to using the tools on the Formatting toolbar, you can use the Font command on the Format menu or the shortcut menu to change the font for a cell or a range of cells. You can use an unlimited number of fonts, styles, and sizes on your worksheet to help organize your data and create striking presentations. If you have a color monitor, you can use up to 16 colors on a worksheet to increase the range of visual effects.

The normal font   Text and numbers appear formatted with the normal font (the default font) until another font is applied. You use the Style command on the Format menu to change the normal font for your worksheet.

Change the worksheet title font

Now you'll change the font of the title from MS Sans Serif 10-point to MS Serif 12-point in Microsoft Excel for Windows, or from Geneva 10-point to Times 12-point in Microsoft Excel for the Macintosh, and you'll add bold formatting.

1 Select cells A1:B1.

2 In the Font Name box on the Formatting toolbar, select MS Serif in Microsoft Excel for Windows or Times in Microsoft Excel for the Macintosh.

3 In the Font Size box on the Formatting toolbar, select 12.

4 Click the Bold tool on the Standard toolbar or the Formatting toolbar.

Your worksheet should look like the following illustration.

	A	B	C	D	E
1	Title	WCS Cash Budget: 1993 Fiscal Year			
2					
3	Created by	Sam Bryan			
4					
5	Budget Model Area				
6			July	August	September
7		Gross Revenue			
8		Sales	$26,900		
9		Shipping	$5,550		
10		Total	$32,450		
12		Cost of Goods Sold			
13		Goods	$17,710		
14		Freight	$270		
15		Markdowns	$1,240		
16		Miscellaneous	$96		
17		Total	$19,316		
19		Gross Profit	$13,134		

Save and close your worksheet

Save your work before taking a break or continuing with the next lesson.

1 Click the Save File tool on the Standard toolbar.

2 From the File menu, choose Close.

One Step Further

In Lesson 2, you created a worksheet that calculated the budget for an ad campaign. In this exercise you will format that worksheet. If you did not go through the "One Step Further" exercise in Lesson 2, you can use the worksheet provided here.

The sample file, suggested procedures, and resulting file provide suggestions for formatting the worksheet.

1 Open 03CAMPGN.

2 Save the worksheet as CAMPAIGN.

3 Change the font and size of the title.

4 Align the row labels to the right.

5 Decrease the row height between titles and listed expenses.

6 Format the numbers as dollars.

7 Open 03CMPGNA and compare it with your work.

You can use the Arrange command on the Window menu to compare the worksheets.

8 Save the CAMPAIGN worksheet, and then close both worksheets when you are finished.

Lesson Summary

To	Do this
Change column width and row height	Change the column width and row height by dragging the column and row boundaries or by using the Column Width and Row Height commands. Use the Best Fit button in the Column Width dialog box to adjust the column to accommodate all cell entries.
Display shortcut menus and toolbars	Display a shortcut menu of frequently used commands by clicking the right mouse button in Microsoft Excel for Windows or by pressing COMMAND+OPTION and clicking the mouse button in Microsoft Excel for the Macintosh. Use the Toolbars command on the Options menu to display a toolbar.
Format numbers	Use the Number command on the Format menu to change the number and date formats.
Create your own number formats	Edit a number format in the Number Format dialog box.
Change the alignment and fonts of cell entries	Click the alignment or font tools on the Standard toolbar or the Formatting toolbar, or choose the Alignment command or the Font command from the Format menu or the shortcut menu.

For more information about	See in the *Microsoft Excel User's Guide*
Formatting techniques	Chapter 7, "Formatting a Worksheet," in Book 1

Preview of the Next Lesson

In the next lesson, you will create, redefine, and apply cell styles, and you will apply and remove cell borders and shading from the BUDGET worksheet. You will also create and name a different view of your worksheet and switch between views.

Working with Formatting and Display Features

In this lesson, you'll use more of Microsoft Excel's formatting and display features to add detail and organization to your worksheet.

You will learn how to:

- Create, apply, and change cell styles with different fonts, number formats, and character alignments.
- Change the worksheet display.
- Add borders and shading to cells.
- Create and name a worksheet view.

Estimated lesson time: 30 minutes

Start the lesson

1   Open 04LESSN.

2   Save the worksheet as BUDGET.

Using Cell Styles

Cell styles are an easy way to quickly and consistently apply cell attributes such as number formats, fonts, alignment, patterns, and protection.

The easiest way to create a style is by example. You format a cell or range with the attributes you want included in the style, and you define that group of attributes as a style. You can then apply that style to other cells with similar types of data.

For example, you may want all summary totals to be bold, centered, and formatted as dollars. You apply this formatting to one cell, and then you define a style called Total for the formatting used in the cell. Instead of applying each format individually to the next cell, you just apply the Total style; the selected cell is instantly formatted. If you decide to change the style from bold to italic, all cells with the Total style change.

You can define a style by using the Style box on the Standard toolbar or the Formatting toolbar, or by using the Style command on the Format menu.

`Normal` **The Style box**   You can use the Style box to define a new style and to apply a style to other cells. First, format a cell using the Number, Alignment, Font, and Cell Protection commands on the Format menu. Click the Style box, type a new style name, and press ENTER.

The Style command   You can also use the Style command to define and apply cell styles. First choose Style from the Format menu, and type a name in the Style Name box. The Description box describes the style of the current selection. To define a new style, choose the Define button. You can choose the Number, Font, Alignment, Pattern, and Protection buttons to open the respective dialog boxes and make any changes to the cell style. Choose the OK button to define the style.

Create a worksheet title cell style

Create a cell style based on the formatted worksheet title. In the preceding lesson, you formatted the worksheet title in MS Serif 12-point bold in Microsoft Excel for Windows or Times 12-point bold in Microsoft Excel for the Macintosh. You will name this style and then use it to format the other worksheet titles in cells A3 and A5.

1   Select cells A1:B1.

 2   Click the Style box on the Standard toolbar or the Formatting toolbar to select Normal.

3   Type **Title**

4   Press ENTER.

The Normal style hasn't been changed; instead, a new style has been created.

The worksheet title and the area labels are aligned differently. Alignment is not part of the Title style.

Apply the Title cell style

1   Select cells A3 and A5.

 2   In the Style box on the Standard toolbar or the Formatting toolbar, click the arrow to display the list.

3   Select the Title cell style.

Cells A1:B1, A3, and A5 are all formatted the same way, as shown in the following illustration.

	A	B	C	D	E	
1	Title	WCS Cash Budget: 1993 Fiscal Year				
2						
3	Created by	Sam Bryan				
4						
5	get Model Area					
6			July	August	September	Oc
7		Gross Revenue				
8		Sales	$26,900			
9		Shipping	$5,550			
10		Total	$32,450			
12		Cost of Goods Sold				
13		Goods	$17,710			
14		Freight	$270			
15		Markdowns	$1,240			
16		Miscellaneous	$96			
17		Total	$19,316			
19		Gross Profit	$13,134			

Wrap the text to fit

The bold text is wider; it is now cut off by the left boundary of column A. You can wrap the text to fit within the column width.

1 With cells A3 and A5 still selected, choose <u>A</u>lignment from the Forma<u>t</u> menu or the shortcut menu.

2 Select the Wrap Text check box.

3 Choose the OK button.

Your worksheet should look like the following illustration.

	A	B	C	D	E	
1	Title	WCS Cash Budget: 1993 Fiscal Year				
2						
3	Created by	Sam Bryan				
4						
5	Budget Model Area					
6			July	August	September	Oc
7		Gross Revenue				
8		Sales	$26,900			
9		Shipping	$5,550			
10		Total	$32,450			
12		Cost of Goods Sold				
13		Goods	$17,710			
14		Freight	$270			
15		Markdowns	$1,240			

Create a heading style for row and column titles

To make the month titles stand out, use the Bold tool on the Standard toolbar or the Formatting toolbar to make them bold.

1 Select cells C6:N6.

2 On the Standard toolbar or the Formatting toolbar, click the Bold tool.

3 From the Forma<u>t</u> menu, choose <u>S</u>tyle.

4 In the Style Name box, type **Heading**

5 Choose the Define button.

6 Under Style Includes, clear the Number, Border, Patterns, Alignment, and Protection check boxes, leaving only the Font check box selected.

7 Choose the OK button to define and apply the style.

Because you left only the Font attribute selected, you can apply the Heading style to cells that are formatted for numbers and dates as well as text. Only the font will be changed.

Create a new style called Total

Now you will define a new cell style with bold and italic formatting. After you define the style in one cell, you will apply the style to other cells.

1 Select cell B10.

2 Click the Bold tool and the Italic tool on the Standard toolbar or the Formatting toolbar.

3 Click the Style box to select Normal.

4 Type **Total**

5 Press ENTER to name the style.

6 Keeping cell B10 selected, select cells B17 and B33.

7 In the Style box, select Total.

Changing a cell style   You can create a new cell style by changing an existing cell style. Remember to clear the check boxes for any attributes you don't want included in the new style.

Format summary figures with bold and color

Format the Summary figures in column C with the Heading style. By changing an existing style, you will create another cell style that includes color.

1 Select cells C10, C17, C19, C33, and C35.

2 From the Format menu, choose Style.

3 Choose the Define button.

4 In the Style Name list, select Heading.

5 Under Change, choose the Font button.

6 In the Color box, click the arrow to display the list.

   If you do not have a color monitor, the names of the colors appear in the Color box instead of the colors themselves. If you later display the worksheet on a color monitor, the color formatting will appear.

7 In the Color list, select Blue.

8 Choose the OK button to close the Font dialog box.

9 In Microsoft Excel for Windows, drag across "Heading" in the Style Name box. This step is not necessary in Microsoft Excel for the Macintosh.

10 In the Style Name box, type **SumData**

11 Choose the OK button to define and apply the style and close the Style dialog box.

12 Click another cell or press an arrow key so that you can see the color.

   If you have a color monitor, the summary data in the selected cells appears in blue.

When you copy the budget figures to columns D through N in Lesson 5, you'll also copy the formats.

Changing the Worksheet Display

You can turn off the display of gridlines to make a Microsoft Excel worksheet look more like a 1-2-3 worksheet.

The Display command   You can change the way your worksheet is displayed with the Display command. You can turn on or off the display of gridlines, row and column headings, zero values, outline symbols, and automatic page breaks. You can display formulas instead of values, and you can change the color of gridlines and row and column headings. These changes apply only to the active worksheet.

Turn off gridlines

1   From the Options menu, choose Display.

2   Under Cells, clear the Gridlines check box.

3   Choose the OK button.

Adding Borders and Shading

You can use borders and shading to create presentation-quality worksheets and more usable templates. By using borders and shading and by adjusting column width and row height, you can create visual effects such as a double-line border.

The Border command   With the Border command on the Format menu, you can add seven types of borders to a cell or range and add a shading pattern to selected cells. You can outline a range of cells or add borders to the top, bottom, left, or right sides of cells. You can also shade a range of cells. You can select from 18 shading patterns with the Patterns command on the Format menu.

Create a border around each month title

Now you will create a border around each of the month titles.

1   Select cells C6:N6.

2   From the Format menu or the shortcut menu, choose Border. The Border dialog box is shown in the following illustration.

3   Under Style, select the third line style from the left.

4   Select the Bottom option.

5   Select the Right option.

6   Select the Left option.

7   Choose the OK button.

8   Select a cell outside your selection to see the outline border clearly.

Outline the income and expense category titles

1   Select cells B7:B35.

2   From the Format menu or the shortcut menu, choose Border.

3   In the Color list, select dark purple.

4   Under Style, select the third line style from the left.

5   Select the Outline option.

6   Choose the OK button.

Remove borders

1   Select cell B6.

2   From the Format menu or the shortcut menu, choose Border.

3   Clear the Top option.

4   Choose the OK button.

Define a shaded border style to divide major budget categories

1   Select cell B11.

2   From the Format menu, choose Style.

3   In the Style Name box, type **Shade**

4   Choose the Define button.

5   Under Change, choose the Patterns button.

6   In the Pattern list, select the third pattern from the top.

7   In the Foreground list, select dark purple.

8   Choose the OK button to close the Patterns dialog box.

9   Under Style Includes, clear the Number, Font, Alignment, and Protection check boxes, leaving only the Border and Patterns check boxes selected.

10   Choose the OK button to define and apply the style.

The Goto command   With the Goto command, you can quickly "go to" (select) another cell or another range. You can choose this command with either the mouse or the keyboard.

Apply the style

1   From the Formula menu, choose Goto.

You can also press F5 in Microsoft Excel for Windows or COMMAND+G in Microsoft Excel for the Macintosh.

2   In the Reference box, type **b18,b20,b34**

3   Choose the OK button.

This selects cells B18, B20, and B34.

4   In the Style box on the Standard toolbar or the Formatting toolbar, select Shade.

Your worksheet should look like the following illustration.

	A	B	C	D	E	F
1		Title	WCS Cash Budget: 1993 Fiscal Year			
2						
3	Created by	Sam Bryan				
4						
5	Budget Model Area					
6			July	August	September	Octobe
7		Gross Revenue				
8		Sales	$26,900			
9		Shipping	$5,550			
10		Total	$32,450			
12		Cost of Goods Sold				
13		Goods	$17,710			
14		Freight	$270			
15		Markdowns	$1,240			
16		Miscellaneous	$96			
17		Total	$19,316			

Naming Views of Your Worksheet

You can create different views of the same worksheet with the View command on the Window menu.

Once you create a view, you can switch to the view rather than save separate versions of the same document.

The settings you can save with a view include print settings, display settings, row heights and column widths, selected cells, window size and position, panes, and frozen titles. You can change any of these settings and save them as a view. The view settings are stored with the worksheet.

Name the current view of your worksheet

You will save the current view of your worksheet so that you can return to this view after you change the display settings.

1 From the Window menu, choose View.

Note   If the View command does not appear on the Window menu, rerun the Setup program to install the View Manager. For more information about adding or removing add-in macros, see "Managing Add-in Commands and Functions" in Chapter 4 in Book 2 of the *Microsoft Excel User's Guide*.

---

2 Choose the Add button.

3 In the Name box, type **Budget**

4 Choose the OK button.

Set up another view of your worksheet

The Freeze Panes command is like /Worksheet Titles in 1-2-3. The Unfreeze Panes command is like /Worksheet Titles Clear in 1-2-3.

Now you will change the display and window settings. With the Freeze Panes command, you will freeze the titles so that they remain on the screen as you scroll through the worksheet to see information.

1 Select cell C7.

2 From the Window menu, choose Freeze Panes.

3 From the Options menu, choose Display.

4 Select the Formulas check box.

5 Clear the Row & Column Headings check box.

6 Choose the OK button.

7 Select cells A1:B5

8 From the Format menu, choose Column Width.

9 Choose the Best Fit button.

Your worksheet should look like the following illustration.

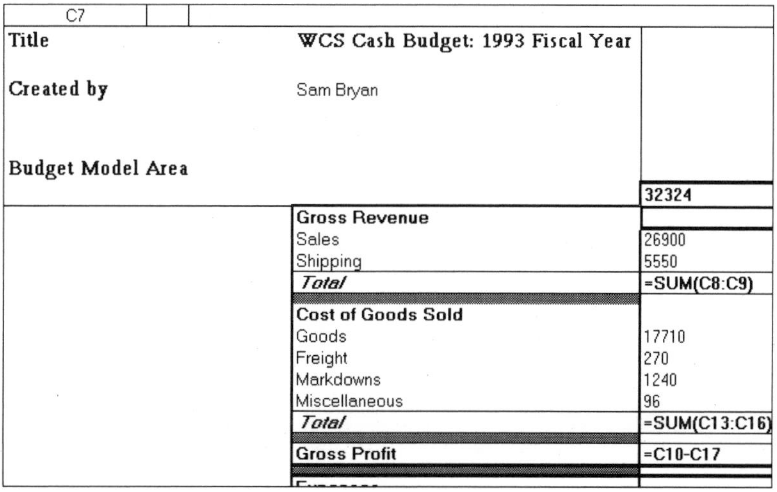

C7		
Title	**WCS Cash Budget: 1993 Fiscal Year**	
Created by	Sam Bryan	
Budget Model Area		
		32324
	Gross Revenue	
	Sales	26900
	Shipping	5550
	Total	=SUM(C8:C9)
	Cost of Goods Sold	
	Goods	17710
	Freight	270
	Markdowns	1240
	Miscellaneous	96
	Total	=SUM(C13:C16)
	Gross Profit	=C10-C17

10 Scroll down to see the rest of the formulas.

Add a different view of your worksheet

Now you will save these display and window settings as a view.

1 From the Window menu, choose View.

2 Choose the Add button.

3 In the Name box, type **Panes**

4 Choose the OK button.

Switch between views of your worksheet

Now you will switch to the Budget view to view the values without the frozen titles.

1 From the Window menu, choose View.

2 In the Views list, select Budget.

3 Choose the Show button.

Your worksheet should look like the following illustration.

	A	B	C	D	E	F
1	Title	WCS Cash Budget: 1993 Fiscal Year				
2						
3	Created by	Sam Bryan				
4						
5	Budget Model Area					
6			July	August	September	Octob
7		Gross Revenue				
8		Sales	$26,900			
9		Shipping	$5,550			
10		*Total*	$32,450			
12		Cost of Goods Sold				
13		Goods	$17,710			
14		Freight	$270			
15		Markdowns	$1,240			
16		Miscellaneous	$96			
17		*Total*	$19,316			

You can use this procedure whenever you want to switch to a different view of your worksheet.

Save and close your worksheet

Save your work before taking a break or continuing with the next lesson.

1   Click the Save File tool on the Standard toolbar.

2   From the File menu, choose Close.

One Step Further

In Lesson 3, you formatted a worksheet that calculated the budget for an ad campaign. In this exercise, you will format that worksheet with styles. If you did not go through the "One Step Further" exercise in Lesson 3, you can use the worksheet provided here.

Use the Microsoft Excel formatting commands to change the appearance of the worksheet. Create a Title style. Create a Heading style for the row and column labels, and add borders and shading.

The sample file, suggested procedures, and resulting file provide suggestions for formatting the worksheet.

1   Open 04CAMPGN.

2   Save it as CAMPAIGN.

3   Create a Title style.

4   Create a Heading style and apply it to the row labels.

5   Turn off the worksheet gridlines.

6 Create an outline border around the row titles.

7 Shade the cells between the titles and the listed expenses.

8 Open 04CMPGNA and compare it with your work.

You can use the Arrange command on the Window menu to compare the worksheets.

9 Save the CAMPAIGN worksheet, and close both worksheets when you are finished.

10 Hide the Formatting toolbar, using the Toolbars command on the Options menu.

Lesson Summary

To	Do this
Create, apply, and change cell styles	Use the Style box on the toolbar to create a style based on an existing cell, or use the Style command on the Format menu to create a style with menu commands.
Change the worksheet display	Use the Display command on the Options menu to turn off the display of gridlines and change other display attributes.
Add borders and shading to cells	Use the Border command on the Format menu to create borders within your worksheet.
Create named views	Use the View command on the Window menu to create different views of your worksheet.

For more information about	See in the *Microsoft Excel User's Guide*
Formatting techniques and naming views	Chapter 7, "Formatting a Worksheet," in Book 1

Preview of the Next Lesson

In the next lesson, you will copy and move cell data and insert and delete rows, columns, and ranges. You'll also learn how to selectively copy cell entries or formats. You will open a new worksheet, work with windows, and copy data from one worksheet to another.

Copying and Moving Cell Data and Formats

In this lesson, you'll insert and delete rows, columns, and cells. You'll also copy and move cell data and formats on a worksheet, and from one worksheet to another.

You will learn how to:

- Copy data to adjacent cells.
- Insert and delete rows, columns, and cells.
- Move cell data.
- Undo a command.
- Copy data to nonadjacent cells.
- Copy cell attributes selectively.
- Switch between multiple worksheets.
- Copy data between worksheets.
- Work with windows.

Estimated lesson time: 40 minutes

Start the lesson

1 Open 05LESSN.

2 Save the worksheet as BUDGET.

Filling Adjacent Cells

Filling adjacent cells is like using /Copy in 1-2-3.

To copy into adjacent cells, you can drag the fill handle in the lower-right corner of the selection, as you did in Lesson 2 to create a series of months, or use the Fill commands on the Edit menu. The fill handle (shown in the following illustration) and the Fill commands copy formulas, formats, or values from a range in a single row or column into an adjacent range with any number of rows or columns. You can copy in any direction.

	A	B	C	D	E	F
1	Title	WCS Cash Budget: 1993 Fiscal Year				
2						
3	Created by	Sam Bryan				
4						
5	Budget Model Area					
6			July	August	September	October
7		Gross Revenue				
8		Sales	$26,900			
9		Shipping	$5,550			
10		*Total*	$32,450			
12		Cost of Goods Sold				
13		Goods	$17,710			
14		Freight	$270			
15		Markdowns	$1,240			
16		Miscellaneous	$96			
17		*Total*	$19,316			
19		Gross Profit	$13,134			

Fill handle

You can copy both cell entries and formats, just as you do in 1-2-3.

The fill handle   With the fill handle, you can copy selected data into adjacent cells. You can drag the fill handle right, left, up, or down to copy data in any direction. If your data is in a series, such as the month titles, you can drag the fill handle to continue the series. If your data is in a series but you want to copy the information into adjacent cells instead of extending the series, press CTRL and drag the fill handle in Microsoft Excel for Windows or press OPTION and drag the fill handle in Microsoft Excel for the Macintosh.

The Fill commands   You can also fill data into adjacent cells with the Fill commands on the Edit menu. The Fill commands do not extend a series but copy the data in the direction you want. Usually, only the Fill Right and Fill Down commands appear on the Edit menu. If you hold down SHIFT when you select the Edit menu, the Fill Up command appears in place of Fill Down and the Fill Left command appears in place of Fill Right.

Many of the budget figures in your worksheet, such as Rent, are the same for each month. You'll copy the formulas for total revenues, cost of goods sold, gross profit, expenses, and operating income from July to the other 11 months. The formulas adjust to calculate each expense correctly.

Copy the figures from July to the other months

You'll drag the fill handle to copy data. First you need to select the range in column C that you want to copy, and then drag the fill handle to include the cells in all the other columns that you want to copy into.

1   Select cells C7:C35.

2   Drag the fill handle to the right to cell N35.

3   Scroll back to the active cell.

You can also select the entire range, including both the cells you want to copy and the cells you want to copy to, and then select the Fill Right command from the Edit menu. With the keyboard, you can also press CTRL+R in Microsoft Excel for Windows or COMMAND+R in Microsoft Excel for the Macintosh.

Your worksheet should look like the following illustration.

	A	B	C	D	E	F
1		Title	WCS Cash Budget: 1993 Fiscal Year			
2						
3	Created by	Sam Bryan				
4						
5	Budget Model Area					
6			July	August	September	October
7		Gross Revenue				
8		Sales	$26,900	$26,900	$26,900	$26,9
9		Shipping	$5,550	$5,550	$5,550	$5,5
10		*Total*	$32,450	$32,450	$32,450	$32,45
12		Cost of Goods Sold				
13		Goods	$17,710	$17,710	$17,710	$17,7
14		Freight	$270	$270	$270	$2
15		Markdowns	$1,240	$1,240	$1,240	$1,2
16		Miscellaneous	$96	$96	$96	$
17		*Total*	$19,316	$19,316	$19,316	$19,31
19		Gross Profit	$13,134	$13,134	$13,134	$13,13

The formatting was also copied.

The formulas you copied from July adjust to the data for every other month. The cell ranges in each of the copied formulas reflect the column that the formula is in. The references in these formulas are *relative references*. When you copy a formula containing relative references, the references are adjusted to reflect the new location. However, *absolute references* always refer to the same cell, regardless of where the formula is copied.

Relative references   A relative reference describes the location of a cell in terms of its distance, in rows and columns, from another cell. Relative references are analogous to giving directions such as "Deliver newspapers to every third house." In the following worksheet, the formula in cell D17 sums the values in cells D13:D16. The formula in cell E17 sums the values in cells E13:E16. Likewise, the formulas in F17 and G17 sum the values in cells F13:F16 and G13:G16, respectively.

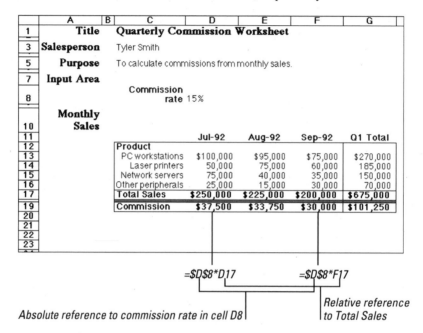

=$D$8*D17   =$D$8*F17

Absolute reference to commission rate in cell D8

Relative reference to Total Sales

Absolute references   An absolute cell reference describes a specific cell address. Absolute references are analogous to giving directions such as "Deliver the newspaper to 403 Oak Street." In the preceding illustration, the formulas in cells D19:F19 calculate commissions based on the total sales for each month. However, each of these formulas refers to cell $D8, the cell that contains the commission rate (15 percent). The dollar signs ($) indicate an absolute reference to cell $D$8. No matter where the commission formula is copied, it always refers to cell $D$8.

Inserting Rows, Columns, and Cells

You can insert an entire row or column by dragging the fill handle. You can also use the Insert command on the Edit menu or the shortcut menu to insert a cell, a row, or a column. The area you select before you choose the command determines what is inserted.

Inserting by dragging   When you select an entire row or column, a fill handle appears next to the row or column heading. To insert a row or column, press SHIFT and drag the fill handle down for rows or toward the right for columns, and select the number of rows or columns you want to insert, as shown in the following illustration.

Press SHIFT and drag the fill handle to insert a selected column.

	A	B	C	D	E	F
1	Title	WCS Cash Budget: 1993 Fiscal Year				
2						
3	Created by	Sam Bryan				
4						
5	Budget Model Area					
6			July	August	September	October
7		Gross Revenue				
8		Sales	$26,900	$26,900	$26,900	$26,9
9		Shipping	$5,550	$5,550	$5,550	$5,5
10		*Total*	$32,450	$32,450	$32,450	$32,45
12		Cost of Goods Sold				
13		Goods	$17,710	$17,710	$17,710	$17,7
14		Freight	$270	$270	$270	$2
15		Markdowns	$1,240	$1,240	$1,240	$1,2
16		Miscellaneous	$96	$96	$96	$
17		*Total*	$19,316	$19,316	$19,316	$19,31
19		Gross Profit	$13,134	$13,134	$13,134	$13,13

The Insert command is like /Worksheet Insert Column and /Worksheet Insert Row in 1-2-3.

Inserting rows, columns, and cells with the Insert command   With the Insert command on the Edit menu or the shortcut menu, you can insert a cell or a range of cells into the worksheet. The Insert command always inserts a cell range equal in size and shape to the selected cell range. To insert a row or column, select the entire row below where you want to insert the new row, or select the entire column to the left of where you want to insert the new column, and then choose the Insert command. If you want to insert a range of cells, select the range where you want to place the insertion, and then choose the Insert command. A dialog box appears, asking whether you want to shift the selected cells down or to the right.

Insert a column at column B

You'll need an extra column for some changes you'll be making to the row titles. Insert a column between columns A and B.

1   Select column A.

Remember, you can select a column by clicking the column heading or by selecting a cell in that column and pressing CTRL+SPACEBAR in Microsoft Excel for Windows or COMMAND+SPACEBAR in Microsoft Excel for the Macintosh.

2   Press SHIFT and drag the fill handle toward the right to include column B.

You can also select column B and then choose Insert from the Edit menu or the shortcut menu.

With the keyboard, you can also press CTRL+SHIFT+PLUS SIGN in Microsoft Excel for Windows. (The PLUS SIGN key is on the main keyboard.) In Microsoft Excel for the Macintosh, you can also press COMMAND+I.

A new column is inserted at column B, shifting the other columns to the right.

Your worksheet should look like the following illustration.

	A	B	C	D	E	F
1	Title		WCS Cash Budget: 1993 Fiscal Year			
2						
3	Created by		Sam Bryan			
4						
5	Budget Model Area					
6				July	August	September
7			Gross Revenue			
8			Sales	$26,900	$26,900	$26,900
9			Shipping	$5,550	$5,550	$5,550
10			*Total*	$32,450	$32,450	$32,450
12			Cost of Goods Sold			
13			Goods	$17,710	$17,710	$17,710
14			Freight	$270	$270	$270
15			Markdowns	$1,240	$1,240	$1,240
16			Miscellaneous	$96	$96	$96
17			*Total*	$19,316	$19,316	$19,316
19			Gross Profit	$13,134	$13,134	$13,134

Deleting Rows, Columns, and Cells

You can delete an entire row or column by dragging the fill handle. You can also use the Delete command on the Edit menu or the shortcut menu to delete a cell, row, or column. As with the Insert command, the area you select before you choose the command determines what is deleted.

Deleting by dragging   When you select an entire row or column, a fill handle appears next to the row or column heading. To delete a row or column, press SHIFT and drag the fill handle up for rows or toward the left for columns to select the number of rows or columns you want to delete.

Deleting cells is different from clearing cells. The Clear command clears the data within a cell but does not delete the cell and move other cells.

The Delete command is like /Worksheet Delete Column and /Worksheet Delete Row in 1-2-3.

Deleting rows, columns, and cells with the Delete command   With the Delete command, you can delete a cell or a range of cells from the worksheet and shift other cells to close the space. The Delete command always deletes a cell range equal in size and shape to the selected cell range. To delete a row or column, select the entire row or column and then choose the Delete command. If you want to delete a range of cells, select the range and then choose the Delete command. A dialog box appears, asking whether you want to shift cells up or to the left to fill the space.

Remember that the Insert and Delete commands physically move cells. If you insert or delete a partial row or column, cells could become separated from their source or dependent data.

Delete row 2

You want to move the figures closer to the worksheet title. Delete row 2 to move the rest of the worksheet up one row.

1   Select row 2.

Remember, you can select a row by clicking the row heading or by selecting a cell in that row and pressing SHIFT+SPACEBAR.

2   Press SHIFT and drag the fill handle up until row 2 appears dimmed.

You can also select row 2 and choose <u>D</u>elete from the <u>E</u>dit menu or the shortcut menu.

With the keyboard, you can also press CTRL+MINUS SIGN in Microsoft Excel for Windows. In Microsoft Excel for the Macintosh, you can also press COMMAND+K .

All cells below row 2 shift up one row. Your worksheet should look like the following illustration.

	A	B	C	D	E	F
1	Title		WCS Cash Budget: 1993 Fiscal Year			
2	Created by		Sam Bryan			
3						
4	Budget Model Area					
5				July	August	September
6			Gross Revenue			
7			Sales	$26,900	$26,900	$26,900
8			Shipping	$5,550	$5,550	$5,550
9			*Total*	$32,450	$32,450	$32,450
11			Cost of Goods Sold			
12			Goods	$17,710	$17,710	$17,710
13			Freight	$270	$270	$270
14			Markdowns	$1,240	$1,240	$1,240
15			Miscellaneous	$96	$96	$96
16			*Total*	$19,316	$19,316	$19,316
18			Gross Profit	$13,134	$13,134	$13,134

Moving Cell Data

Dragging selected cells by their border is like using /Move in 1-2-3.

Moving cell data by dragging You can move cells to another area of a worksheet by dragging the border surrounding the selection. The pointer changes to an arrow when it's positioned over the border. When you drag the border, the border moves to indicate the size and position of the selection, as shown in the following illustration.

	A	B	C	D	E	F
1	Title		WCS Cash Budget	1993 Fiscal Year		
2	Created by		Sam Bryan			
3						
4	Budget Model Area					
5				July	August	September
6			Gross Revenue			
7			Sales	$26,900	$26,900	$26,900
8			Shipping	$5,550	$5,550	$5,550
9			*Total*	**$32,450**	**$32,450**	**$32,450**
11			Cost of Goods Sold			
12			Goods	$17,710	$17,710	$17,710
13			Freight	$270	$270	$270
14			Markdowns	$1,240	$1,240	$1,240
15			Miscellaneous	$96	$96	$96
16			*Total*	**$19,316**	**$19,316**	**$19,316**
18			Gross Profit	**$13,134**	**$13,134**	**$13,134**

You can insert cells between cells by holding SHIFT and dragging the border to a row or column gridline. Along a row gridline, the border collapses horizontally; along a column gridline, the border collapses vertically.

The Cut and Paste commands You can also use two commands together to move data: the Cut command on the Edit menu to cut selected data, and the Paste command on the Edit menu to paste it into a new location. Unlike the Delete command, the Cut command does not physically remove a cell. Rather, it cuts the data within the cell so that you can paste it elsewhere. The moving border indicates the cells that will be cut or copied from the worksheet.

When you choose the Cut command, the data you want to move is stored on the Clipboard. The cell data remains on the Clipboard until it is replaced by another cut or copied selection.You can do other tasks, such as opening another document, and then choose the Paste command when you're ready to paste data into the other document.

The selected data on the worksheet is surrounded by a moving border until you press ESC or cut or copy another selection.

Move the worksheet title and author one cell to the left

Now move the worksheet title and author back to column B by dragging cells C1:C2.

1   Select cells C1:C2.

2   Drag the border of the selection to cells B1:B2.

Your worksheet should look like the following illustration.

	A	B	C	D	E	F
1		Title	WCS Cash Budget: 1993 Fiscal Year			
2		Created by	Sam Bryan			
3						
4		Budget Model Area				
5				July	August	September
6			Gross Revenue			
7			Sales	$26,900	$26,900	$26,900
8			Shipping	$5,550	$5,550	$5,550
9			*Total*	$32,450	$32,450	$32,450
11			Cost of Goods Sold			
12			Goods	$17,710	$17,710	$17,710
13			Freight	$270	$270	$270
14			Markdowns	$1,240	$1,240	$1,240
15			Miscellaneous	$96	$96	$96
16			*Total*	$19,316	$19,316	$19,316
18			Gross Profit	$13,134	$13,134	$13,134

Move a formula

Moving a formula is different from copying a formula. When you move a formula, the cell references still refer to the original cells. When you copy a formula, relative cell references adjust to the new location.

1   Select cell D9.

2   Drag the cell by the border to cell D4.

The value appears in the cell. The formula, as displayed in the formula bar, did not change. It is still =SUM(D7:D8).

The Undo command   If you make a mistake or change your mind, you can reverse most commands and actions by choosing the Undo command from the Edit menu. The name of the Undo command changes to reflect your last action. For example, if you find that you incorrectly dragged data in the worksheet, you can choose the Undo Drag and Drop command, because dragging the data was the last action you performed.

Undo the last action

To reverse your last editing change, you can use the Undo Drag and Drop command on the Edit menu.

▶ From the Edit menu, choose Undo Drag and Drop.

Copying to Nonadjacent Cells

Pressing CTRL or OPTION and dragging selected cells by their border is like using /Copy in 1-2-3.

Copying by dragging   You already used the fill handle to copy cell contents into adjacent cells. When the cells you want to copy to are not next to the cells you want to copy from, you can press CTRL in Microsoft Excel for Windows or OPTION in Microsoft Excel for the Macintosh and drag the border surrounding the selection to copy cell data to other worksheet cells.

You can insert the copied cells between cells by pressing CTRL+SHIFT in Microsoft Excel for Windows or OPTION+SHIFT in Microsoft Excel for the Macintosh and dragging the border to a row or column gridline.

The Copy command   You can also use two commands together: the Copy command on the Edit menu to define the data you want to copy, and the Paste command on the Edit menu to paste it into a new location. You will use the Copy and Paste commands to copy data between worksheets later in this lesson. You can also use the Copy tool on the Standard toolbar instead of the Copy command.

The Paste command   When you use the Copy and Paste commands on the Edit menu to copy cell data, the selection you defined remains both in its original location and on the Clipboard. As long as the moving border is present, you can paste the selection from the Clipboard as many times as you want.

The Insert Paste command   The Insert Paste command on the Edit menu inserts cells to contain the pasted data and pastes the data in one step. As with the Paste command, you can also use the Insert Paste command to paste a selection from the Clipboard as many times as you want. After you choose the Cut or Copy command, the Insert command changes to Insert Paste.

In the following steps, you'll change the way budgeted insurance expenses are allocated over the year. To save on billing costs, the company will pay $236.50 twice a year, in July and January, rather than paying $43 a month.

Enter new insurance figures

First, change the budgeted insurance expenses for the first six months. The expense will be $236.50 for July and $0 for August through December.

1   Select cell D25.

2   Type **236.50**

3   Press the RIGHT ARROW key.

The number is displayed as $237 because of your number format.

4   In cell E25, type **0**

5   Click the enter box or press ENTER.

6   With cell E25 selected, drag the fill handle to the right to cell I25.

Copy the insurance figures to the second six months

The monthly insurance budget is the same for January through June as it is for July through December. Use the Copy and Paste commands on the Edit menu to copy the figures from the first six months of the fiscal year to the second six months.

1   Select cells D25:I25.

2   In Microsoft Excel for Windows, press CTRL and drag the border to cells J25:O25, as shown in the following illustration.

	C	D	E	F	G	H
18	Gross Profit					
20	Expenses					
21	Advertising	$4,000	$4,000	$4,000	$4,000	$4,00
22	Salaries	$4,700	$4,700	$4,700	$4,700	$4,70
23	Rent	$500	$500	$500	$500	$50
24	Utilities	$75	$75	$75	$75	$7
25	Insurance	$237	$0	$0	$0	$
26	Telephone and Telex	$280	$280	$280	$280	$28
27	Office Supplies	$147	$147	$147	$147	$14
28	Training	$100	$100	$100	$100	$10
29	Travel and Entertainme	$200	$200	$200	$200	$20
30	Taxes and Licenses	$240	$240	$240	$240	$24
31	Interest	$800	$800	$800	$800	$80

Use the mouse to copy a selection to another location by dragging its border.

In Microsoft Excel for the Macintosh, press OPTION and drag the border to outline cells J25:O25.

You can also select cells D25:I25, choose Copy from the Edit menu or the shortcut menu, select cells J25:O25, choose Paste from the Edit menu or the shortcut menu, and then press ESC to cancel the moving border. In Microsoft Excel for the Macintosh, you can also press COMMAND+PERIOD to cancel the moving border.

Copying Cell Attributes Selectively

Sometimes you may want to copy only certain cell attributes, such as formulas, values, formats, or cell notes. You use the Paste Special command on the Edit menu to paste cell attributes selectively.

The Paste Special command   With the Paste Special command, you can paste certain attributes of the copy selection into the paste area. A dialog box appears in which you select the attribute you want to paste. You can also paste using an operation, such as addition or subtraction.

You will find many uses for the Paste Special command. If you want to convert formulas into values, you can select Values in the Paste box. If you want to add a block of numbers to a similar block of numbers, you can select Add in the Operation box. Paste Special is also useful for copying formats from one cell or cell range to another.

The Transpose check box in the Paste Special dialog box is like /Range Transpose in 1-2-3.

Select the Skip Blanks check box if you don't want to paste blank cells contained in the copy selection. The Transpose check box pastes rows as columns and columns as rows.

In the next procedure, you'll use the Paste Special command to copy the formats from shaded cells in column C to columns D through O to create identical borders in those columns.

Copy the formats from cell C10 to columns D through O

1   Select cell C10.

2   Click the Copy tool.

You can also choose <u>C</u>opy from the <u>E</u>dit menu.

3   Select cells D10:O10, D17:O17, D19:O19, and D33:O33.

4   From the <u>E</u>dit menu, choose Paste <u>S</u>pecial.

The Paste Special dialog box appears, as shown in the following illustration.

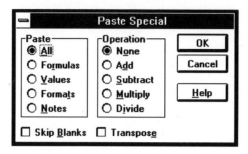

5   Under Paste, select the Formats option button.

6   Choose the OK button.

7   From the Forma<u>t</u> menu or the shortcut menu, choose <u>B</u>order.

8   Clear the Left and Right options.

9   Choose the OK button.

10   Press ESC to cancel the moving border.

Your worksheet should look like the following illustration.

	A	B	C	D	E	F
1		Title	WCS Cash Budget: 1993 Fiscal Year			
2	Created by	Sam Bryan				
3						
4	Budget Model	Area				
5				July	August	September
6			Gross Revenue			
7			Sales	$26,900	$26,900	$26,900
8			Shipping	$5,550	$5,550	$5,550
9			*Total*	**$32,450**	**$32,450**	**$32,450**
11			Cost of Goods Sold			
12			Goods	$17,710	$17,710	$17,710
13			Freight	$270	$270	$270
14			Markdowns	$1,240	$1,240	$1,240
15			Miscellaneous	$96	$96	$96
16			*Total*	**$19,316**	**$19,316**	**$19,316**
18			**Gross Profit**	**$13,134**	**$13,134**	**$13,134**

Copy all cell attributes to column B

You'll create an indented look for your row titles by placing some of the titles in column B and some in column C. Use the fill handle to copy the data in column C to column B.

1   Select cells C6:C34.

2   Drag the fill handle to the left to include cells B6:B34.

You can also select cells B6:C35, press SHIFT, and choose Fill Left from the Edit menu.

Your worksheet should look like the following illustration.

	A	B	C	D	E	F
1		Title	WCS Cash Budget: 1993 Fiscal Year			
2		**Created by**	Sam Bryan			
3						
4		**Budget Model Area**				
5				July	August	September
6		Gross Re	Gross Revenue			
7		Sales	Sales	$26,900	$26,900	$26,900
8		Shipping	Shipping	$5,550	$5,550	$5,550
9		*Total*	*Total*	**$32,450**	**$32,450**	**$32,450**
11		Cost of G	Cost of Goods Sold			
12		Goods	Goods	$17,710	$17,710	$17,710
13		Freight	Freight	$270	$270	$270
14		Markdown	Markdowns	$1,240	$1,240	$1,240
15		Miscellan	Miscellaneous	$96	$96	$96
16		*Total*	*Total*	**$19,316**	**$19,316**	**$19,316**
18		Gross Pr	Gross Profit	**$13,134**	**$13,134**	**$13,134**

You need to clear the individual item titles from column B and the bold category titles from column C.

Clearing Cell Entries

The Clear command is like /Range Erase in 1-2-3, except that you can specify which cell attributes you want to clear.

The Clear command   With the Clear command, you can selectively clear specific cell attributes, such as formatting, or you can clear everything from the cell at once.

Clear the bold titles from column C

Clear the category and total titles from column C, leaving only the individual items. Then the bold titles in column B will spill into column C, hiding the vertical borders.

1   Select cells C6, C9, C11, C16, C18, C20, C32, and C34.

2   From the Edit menu, choose Clear.

You can also press DELETE in Microsoft Excel for Windows or COMMAND+B in Microsoft Excel for the Macintosh.

3   Choose the OK button.

Clear the individual item titles from column B

Clear everything but the bold titles from column B.

1   Select cells B7:B8, B12:B15, and B21:B31.

2   From the Edit menu, choose Clear.

3   Choose the OK button.

Insert a column

Insert a column between column A and column B to separate the worksheet area titles from the data.

1   Select column A.

2   Press SHIFT and drag the fill handle to include column B.

You can also select column B and choose Insert from the Edit menu.

Change column width for columns B and C

Change the width of columns B and C to make them each two characters wide.

1   Select columns B and C.

2   Drag the column C heading boundary to the left until "Width: 2.00" is displayed in the reference area of the formula bar.

You can also choose Column Width from the Format menu, type **2**, and choose the OK button.

Remove the right border in column C

You also copied the outline border format to column C. Remove the border between columns C and D to create one border around columns C and D.

1   Select cells C6:C34.

2   From the Format menu, choose Border.

3   Under Border, clear the Right option.

4   Choose the OK button.

5   Select cells D6:D34.

6   From the Format menu, choose Border.

7   Clear the Left option.

8   Choose the OK button.

Your worksheet should look like the following illustration.

	A	B	C	D	E	F	G	
1	Title			WCS Cash Budget: 1993 Fiscal Year				
2	Created by			Sam Bryan				
3								
4	Budget Model Area							
5					July	August	September	Oc
6			Gross Revenue					
7			Sales		$26,900	$26,900	$26,900	
8			Shipping		$5,550	$5,550	$5,550	
9			*Total*		**$32,450**	**$32,450**	**$32,450**	
11			Cost of Goods Sold					
12			Goods		$17,710	$17,710	$17,710	
13			Freight		$270	$270	$270	
14			Markdowns		$1,240	$1,240	$1,240	
15			Miscellaneous		$96	$96	$96	
16			*Total*		**$19,316**	**$19,316**	**$19,316**	
18			Gross Profit		**$13,134**	**$13,134**	**$13,134**	
20								

Creating a New Document

When you create a new document in Microsoft Excel, it is displayed in its own window. You can have many document windows open at the same time.

The New command   You use the New command to create a new document. You name the document when you save it.

 The New Worksheet tool   You can also create a new worksheet by clicking the New Worksheet tool on the Standard toolbar.

Create a new worksheet

Now you will create a new blank worksheet for a separate expense report.

1   From the File menu, choose New.

Microsoft Excel displays the New dialog box, as shown in the following illustration.

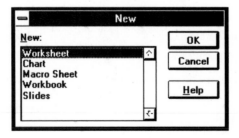

The New dialog box lists the types of documents you can create: worksheet, chart, macro sheet, or workbook. "Worksheet" is already selected by default, so you can just choose the OK button.

2   Choose the OK button.

Microsoft Excel displays a new worksheet named Sheet2 (Worksheet2). BUDGET is still open behind Sheet2 (Worksheet2).

Save the new worksheet

1   From the File menu, choose Save As.

2   Save the worksheet as EXPENSE.

3   In Microsoft Excel for Windows, choose the OK button.

In Microsoft Excel for the Macintosh, choose the Save button.

Switching Between Windows

You can only work on the document in the active window. You can tell which document window is active by the dark title bar and the dark border.

When you have more than one document open, you can switch to another document by choosing the document name from the bottom of the Window menu. All open windows are listed alphabetically and numbered at the bottom of the Window menu. The active window has a check mark next to its name.

You can also switch between windows by using the mouse or the keyboard. With the mouse, move and size windows until the one you want is visible, and then click anywhere in the window. In Microsoft Excel for Windows, with the keyboard, press CTRL+F6 to switch to the next window and CTRL+SHIFT+F6 to switch to the previous window. In Microsoft Excel for the Macintosh, press COMMAND+M.

If you have an extended keyboard for the Macintosh, you can also press COMMAND+F6 to switch to the next window and COMMAND+SHIFT+F6 to switch to the previous window.

Switch to the BUDGET worksheet window

▶   From the Window menu, choose 1 BUDGET.

The BUDGET window is now active. When document windows overlap, the active window is in front.

Moving, Sizing, and Arranging Windows

The Arrange command   With the Arrange command, you can quickly lay out all the open document windows so that none of them overlap. This way, you can see all the open document windows at the same time. You can also use the Arrange command to fit a single document window to the workspace. If you later display your document on a computer with a different size screen, such as a portable computer, your document will still fill the workspace exactly.

Arrange all windows on the workspace

1   From the Window menu, choose Arrange.

Under Arrange, the Tiled option button is already selected.

2   Choose the OK button.

The windows are arranged to fill the workspace. You can tell that BUDGET is the active window by the presence of scroll bars and the dark title bar, as shown in the following illustration. In Microsoft Excel for the Macintosh, the filenames do not include the .XLS extension.

Close the Sheet1 (Worksheet1) window

1   Switch to Sheet1 (Worksheet1).

2   In Microsoft Excel for Windows, double-click the Control-menu box in the upper-left corner of Sheet1.

In Microsoft Excel for the Macintosh, click the close box in the upper-left corner of Worksheet1.

Sizing a window manually   You can make a window the exact size you want. In Microsoft Excel for Windows, with the mouse, drag the size box or any edge or corner of the window until it is the size you want. With the keyboard, choose the Size command from the Control menu, and use the arrow keys to change the size of the window.

In Microsoft Excel for the Macintosh, you can make a window the exact size you want by dragging the size box with the mouse. The size box is in the lower-right corner of the document window.

Size the EXPENSE window

1   Switch to EXPENSE.

2   In the lower-right corner of the window, drag the size box down.

In Microsoft Excel for Windows, you can also choose Size from the Control menu. Use the DOWN ARROW and RIGHT ARROW keys to size the window, and then press ENTER.

BUDGET.XLS				EXPENSE.XLS				
	A	B C	D		A	B	C	D
1	Title		WCS Cash Budget:	1				
2	Created by		Sam Bryan	2				
3				3				
	Budget Model			4				
4		Area		5				
5				6				
6			Gross Revenue	7				
7			Sales	8				
8			Shipping	9				
9			*Total*	10				
				11				
11			Cost of Goods Sold	12				
12			Goods	13				
13			Freight	14				
14			Markdowns	15				
15			Miscellaneous	16				
16			*Total*	17				
				18				
18			Gross Profit	19				

Copying Data Between Windows

Now you'll copy the expense information from the BUDGET worksheet to the EXPENSE worksheet.

Copy the expense data to another worksheet

1   Switch to BUDGET.

2   Select cells C20:P32.

 3   Click the Copy tool.

You can also choose Copy from the Edit menu or the shortcut menu.

4   Switch to the EXPENSE window.

5 Enlarge the EXPENSE window.

6 Select cell B5.

7 From the Edit menu or the shortcut menu, choose Paste.

All of the data and formats are copied to the new worksheet.

Your worksheet should look like the following illustration.

	A	B	C	D	E	F	G	H	I	
1										
2										
3										
4										
5		Expenses								
6			Advertisin	$4,000	$4,000	$4,000	$4,000	$4,000	$4,000	
7			Salaries	$4,700	$4,700	$4,700	$4,700	$4,700	$4,700	
8			Rent	$500	$500	$500	$500	$500	$500	
9			Utilities	$75	$75	$75	$75	$75	$75	
10			Insurance	$43	$43	$43	$43	$43	$43	
11			Telephon	$280	$280	$280	$280	$280	$280	
12			Office Sup	$147	$147	$147	$147	$147	$147	
13			Training	$100	$100	$100	$100	$100	$100	
14			Travel and	$200	$200	$200	$200	$200	$200	
15			Taxes and	$240	$240	$240	$240	$240	$240	
16			Interest	$800	$800	$800	$800	$800	$800	
17		*Total*		$11,085	$11,085	$11,085	$11,085	$11,085	$11,085	$1
18										
19										
20										

Save and close the worksheets

1 Click the Save File tool.

2 From the File menu, choose Close.

Microsoft Excel switches to the BUDGET worksheet.

3 Click the Save File tool.

4 From the File menu, choose Close.

One Step Further

In this lesson, you learned to copy and move cell data and formats. In the following exercise, you will practice the skills you learned.

The WCS Copier advertising campaign will extend from July through September. The July expenses have already been entered in the worksheet. You need to modify the worksheet to reflect the following changes:

- Advertising is now divided into two expenses. Ad Production has a one-time budget of $75,000, and Periodical Advertising Space has a monthly budget of $25,000.

- Expenses for Clerical Support and General Administration will remain the same from July through September.

- Telemarketing expenses will occur in August, but not in September.

- Direct mail expenses will occur in September, but not in August.

- An additional $50,000 will be allocated in August for the advertising campaign.

- Consulting expenses will occur in July only.

Follow these steps to make the changes.

1 Open the 05CAMPGN worksheet.

2 Save it as CAMPAIGN.

3 Use the fill handle to label the columns for July through September in the Input and Budget area of the worksheet.

4 Copy the cell data to the appropriate cells as previously described.

5 Use the Copy and Paste Special commands on the Edit menu to copy the formatting from the July column to the August and September columns.

6 Copy the formatting in column C to columns D through F. You will need to reapply the number format and the SumData style.

7 Copy the formulas for adding Expenses and calculating Funds Remaining to August and September.

8 Change the Funds Remaining formula to reflect any additional budget allocations for August and September.

To see one possible result of this exercise, open 05CMPGNA. For more information, you can double-click any cell with a note indicator.

9 Save the CAMPAIGN worksheet and close both worksheets when you are finished.

Lesson Summary

To	Do this
Copy data to adjacent cells	Use the fill handle to copy cell data and formulas to adjacent cells. Relative references in formulas copied to adjacent cells automatically adjust to calculate their new rows or columns.
Insert and delete rows and columns	Select the row or column, and then press SHIFT and drag the fill handle to insert and delete rows and columns.
Move cell data	Drag the border surrounding the selection to move cell data.
Undo a command or action	Use the Undo command on the Edit menu to reverse an action.
Copy data to non-adjacent cells	Press CTRL in Microsoft Excel for Windows or OPTION in Microsoft Excel for the Macintosh, and drag the border surrounding the selection to copy cell data to nonadjacent cells.

To	Do this
Copy cell attributes selectively	Use the Copy tool and the Paste Special command on the Edit menu to selectively paste attributes such as formatting.
Arrange windows	Use the Arrange command on the Window menu to arrange windows.
Move, size, close, enlarge, and restore windows	Use the mouse or the commands on the Control menu in Microsoft Excel for Windows to control the size and position of windows.
Copy data between worksheets	Use the Copy tool and the Paste command on the Edit menu to copy cell data and formatting from one worksheet to another.

For more information about	See in the *Microsoft Excel User's Guide*
Creating formulas Using absolute and relative references	Chapter 5, "Creating a Worksheet," in Book 1
Moving and copying	Chapter 6, "Editing a Worksheet," in Book 1

Preview of the Next Lesson

In the next lesson, you'll use sample documents to see how formulas can work for you. You'll use several useful worksheet features, such as goal seeking and lookup tables, and you'll get an introduction to custom functions and conditional functions.

Part

3 Analyzing, Linking, and Summarizing Data

Putting Formulas to Work

In this lesson, instead of building a worksheet of your own, you will examine sample documents to learn about advanced worksheet features, including arrays, goal seeking, custom functions, the IF function, and lookup tables. By completing the online examples, you'll learn what features are available in Microsoft Excel and where to look when you want to use them in your work.

You will learn how to:

- Use array formulas.

- Create a decision-making conditional formula with the IF function.

- Create a formula with a nested function.

- Use custom functions to automate frequently used formulas.

- Find an entry in a lookup table.

- Protect cells and documents.

- Hide and unhide documents.

Estimated lesson time: 30 minutes

Start the lesson

The 06LESSN workbook file opens the 06INTRO, 06ARRAYS, 06NESTFN, 06IF_FUN, 06LOOKTB, and 06CUSTFN worksheets, and the 06CUSTFN macro sheet. It also opens a hidden macro sheet, 06HIDDEN. You can test the examples in these documents to learn about complex formulas.

 ▶ Open the 06LESSN workbook.

The 06INTRO worksheet appears. Your screen should look like the following illustration.

You'll use the buttons at the top of the worksheet to display the examples while you read about them.

Using the buttons Clicking a button at the top of each sample worksheet activates a different worksheet. You can also press CTRL in Microsoft Excel for Windows or COMMAND+OPTION in Microsoft Excel for the Macintosh, and the underlined letter in each button.

Array Formulas and Functions

You'll click the Arrays button to make the 06ARRAYS worksheet the active document.

Switch to the 06ARRAYS worksheet

▶ Click the Arrays button.

The 06ARRAYS worksheet becomes the active document.

You can use arrays for writing multiple-value formulas and improving worksheet efficiency.

Array formulas and functions With arrays, you can build formulas that produce multiple results or that operate on a range of cells. An array formula occupies only one cell, but it can calculate values in many cells in which you need to do similar calculations. You can greatly improve the efficiency of your worksheet by using array formulas instead of ordinary single-value formulas.

In this exercise, you will enter an array formula into a single cell. The formula will calculate the cost of purchasing a fleet of trucks, vans, and cars, given the cost of each type of vehicle and the number to be bought. Without an array formula, you would have to calculate the cost of the trucks, vans, and cars separately and then calculate the sum of those separate values. With an array formula, you can calculate the cost with a single mathematical operation.

Enter an array formula

This example demonstrates how to use an array formula to multiply and add a group of cells in one formula, rather than using separate formulas to multiply price by units and then sum the total cost of all units.

You enter a normal formula by clicking the enter box or pressing ENTER. In Microsoft Excel for Windows, you enter an array formula by pressing CTRL+SHIFT+ENTER. In Microsoft Excel for the Macintosh, you enter an array formula by pressing COMMAND+ENTER.

▶ Follow the instructions on the worksheet to edit the formula.

The total cost of the fleet of cars and trucks, $219,000, appears in cell E14.

Entering an array formula in a range of cells Most results that you want to compute on a worksheet can be described by single values. However, some results can be described only by the multiple values of an array formula entered in a range of cells—called an *array range. Microsoft Excel Step by Step* does not include a lesson on array ranges. For more information about array ranges, see "Entering an Array Formula in a Range of Cells" in Chapter 5 in Book 1 of the *Microsoft Excel User's Guide.*

The LINEST and TREND functions are like /Data Regression in 1-2-3.

Some Microsoft Excel functions are array functions. For example, to perform regression analysis in Microsoft Excel, you use the TREND, GROWTH, LINEST, and LOGEST array functions. For more information about these functions, see the *Microsoft Excel Function Reference.*

Making Decisions Using an IF Function

Formulas with IF functions You can use an IF function to build a conditional formula. It will return one value if the conditions are true and another value if the conditions are false. An IF function can be used to apply different formulas, based on its conditions—that is, to make a decision based on the results of a TRUE/FALSE test. For example, a payroll worksheet can use an IF function to determine whether to award sales bonuses based on monthly sales.

Build a formula with an IF function

The example uses an IF function to calculate bonuses based on the salesperson's commissions. If the commissions are less than $5000, the salesperson receives no bonus. If the commissions are $5000 or greater, the salesperson receives an additional 10 percent.

1 Click the IF Function button to switch to the 06IF_FUN worksheet.

2 Follow the instructions on the worksheet to edit and copy the formula.

After the formula evaluates the conditions, C. Tyler receives no bonus and S. Bryan receives a bonus of $750.

Building a Formula with a Nested Function

Functions within another function   In Lesson 2, you learned that a function takes a value or values (its *arguments*) and performs some type of operation on them. A function's arguments can be anything that produces a desired data type. For example, the first argument to the IF function you used in the preceding exercise is a *logical* value—either TRUE or FALSE. When you enter the argument, you could specify the actual logical value TRUE or FALSE, but you will usually use a reference to a cell, a name that refers to a formula or cell, or another function that returns the value you want. When an argument to a function is itself a function, it is said to be *nested*.

Build a formula with a nested function

This example uses an AND function nested within an IF function to calculate bonuses based on the salesperson's sales of copiers and printers. If the sales of copiers are greater than $55,000 and the sales of printers are greater than $50,000, the salesperson receives a bonus.

1   Click the Nested Functions button to switch to the 06NESTFN worksheet.

2   Follow the instructions on the worksheet to edit and copy the formula.

After the formula evaluates the conditions, C. Tyler receives no bonus and S. Bryan receives a bonus of $750.

Creating Custom Functions

You can write your own custom functions to automate specialized calculations that you perform often. You create a custom function on a macro sheet by using the ARGUMENT function to specify the function's arguments, entering the formula that the custom function should calculate, and using the RETURN function to return the result of the calculation. Once you define and name a custom function, you can use it as you would any worksheet function, such as SUM. The custom function appears in the Paste Function dialog box, under the category you specify, whenever the macro sheet is open.

Use a custom function in a formula

First you will look at the 06CUSTFN macro sheet where the FAHRENHEIT and CELSIUS custom functions are defined. Then you will switch to the 06CUSTFN worksheet, where the functions are used.

1 At the top of the worksheet, click the Custom Functions button to switch to the 06CUSTFN macro sheet.

2 Examine the macro statements and comments that make up the custom functions. Every custom function has these three parts: the arguments, the formula, and the value returned. The comments explain how this custom function is written.

3 Select cells C14:C16.

4 From the Formula menu, choose Define Name.

5 In the Name box, type **Celsius**

6 Under Macro, select the Function option button.

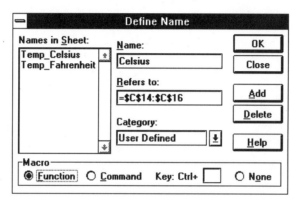

7 Choose the Add button.

8 In the Name box, type **Fahrenheit**

9 Move to the Refers To box and delete any cell references.

10 Select cells C18:C20.

You may have to move the Define Name dialog box so that you can select the cells.

11 Under Macro, select the Function option button.

12 Choose the OK button.

13 At the right side of the macro sheet, click the Custom Function Worksheet button.

14 Follow the instructions on the worksheet to edit and use the formulas.

The initial data is the respective boiling points for Fahrenheit and Celsius. The formulas convert the initial data from Fahrenheit to Celsius, and vice versa. You can change the initial data to test the conversion formulas.

Using a Lookup Table

Lookup tables are like the @VLOOKUP and @HLOOKUP functions in 1-2-3. To make sure they work the same as in 1-2-3, choose Calculation from the Options menu and select Alternate Expression Evaluation.

Lookup values and compare values You can use a *lookup table* to find a piece of information based on another piece of information that you already know. The information you know is called a *lookup value*. For example, when you look up someone's telephone number in a directory, you are using the person's name as the lookup value, and you must compare your lookup value to other names, which are the *compare values*.

In Microsoft Excel, a lookup table consists of a row or column of compare values, in ascending order, and adjacent rows or columns containing data that you want to find.

You will use a known income as a lookup value to find a corresponding tax rate, as shown in the following illustration.

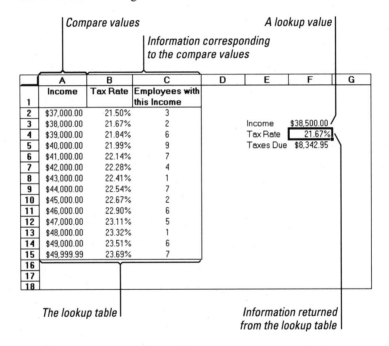

Lookup functions You get data from the lookup table by using the lookup functions HLOOKUP, VLOOKUP, and LOOKUP. With these functions, you specify the lookup value, the table's location, and the row or column from which matching values in the table will be returned.

If your compare values	Use
Are in the first row of the lookup table	HLOOKUP
Are in the first column of the lookup table	VLOOKUP
Aren't adjacent to your data	LOOKUP

For more information about these functions, see the *Microsoft Excel Function Reference*.

Look up a tax rate

This example demonstrates how to find a tax rate for a given income using a lookup table. You will use the VLOOKUP function to search through the lookup table and return data from the second column.

1   Click the Lookup Tables button to switch to the 06LOOKTB worksheet.

2   Follow the instructions on the worksheet to complete the formula.

The VLOOKUP formula searches through the first column to find the largest value that is less than or equal to 38,500. That value is 38,000. The formula returns the corresponding tax rate, 0.2167 or 21.67 percent.

Annotating a Worksheet

Some of the worksheets and macro sheets in this lesson include text boxes to give you tips and instructions, macro buttons to guide you from one worksheet to another, or cell notes to explain a formula in more detail. You can use these tools to provide helpful information about documents containing complex formulas.

 Text boxes   If you want additional information to appear right on your worksheet, create a text box with the Text Box tool on the Utility toolbar, and type the information you want in the box. In the sample documents, text boxes contain information about each worksheet or macro sheet. Text boxes can be moved, sized, attached to cells, or sized with cells. You can format the text within each box with multiple fonts, styles, and sizes. You can also format the text box itself with a variety of colors and patterns. You'll learn more about text boxes in Lesson 16, "Creating a Presentation Using Charts and Graphics."

 Buttons   You can create a button on your worksheet with the Button tool on the Utility toolbar and then use the button to run a command macro. Buttons, like text boxes, can be moved, sized, attached to cells, or sized with cells. You can type a name in the button and change the font, style, and size of the button name. You'll learn more about buttons in Lesson 17, "Recording Macros."

The Note command   Use the Note command to attach a cell note to a cell. Notes do not appear in the cell, but they can be printed with the worksheet. Cells with notes attached are indicated by a note indicator in the upper-right corner. Adding a note to a cell is useful for documenting assumptions, "footnoting" the source of your cell data, or explaining a formula. To read a cell note, double-click the cell.

Read a cell note

Cell F17 on the 06LOOKTB worksheet contains a cell note.

1   On the 06LOOKTB worksheet, double-click cell F17.

2   Read the note, and then choose the Close button.

Protecting a Worksheet

Some of the worksheets and macro sheets in this lesson were either protected to prevent accidental changes or hidden to keep them out of your way.

The Cell Protection command is like /Range Protect and /Range Unprotect in 1-2-3.

The Cell Protection and Object Protection commands With the Cell Protection and Object Protection commands, you can protect data in the selected cells or in objects such as text boxes, buttons, or charts from being edited or displayed in the formula bar. These commands specify which cells and objects will be affected when you choose the Protect Document command.

The Protect Document command is like /Worksheet Global Protection Enable in 1-2-3.

The Protect Document and Unprotect Document commands With the Protect Document command, you can turn on cell protection. You can also protect the worksheet window so that it can't be sized or closed. If you want extra protection, you can type a password. Be sure that you don't lose your password, or you won't be able to reverse protection of the worksheet. To unprotect a worksheet, choose the Unprotect Document command, and then type your password if one is required.

Unprotect a worksheet

Many of the sample worksheets are protected, except for the cells in which you will enter data. No password was used to protect the documents, so you can protect and unprotect them.

1   On the 06LOOKTB worksheet, select any cell other than the ones you edited, and try to enter data.

The message "Locked cells cannot be changed" is displayed.

2   From the Options menu, choose Unprotect Document.

You can now change the data in any cell or object on the worksheet.

The Hide and Unhide commands With the Hide command, you can hide the active window. With the Unhide command, you can unhide a hidden window. Hiding windows is useful when you want a document to be open but not visible. A hidden window is closed when you choose the Close All command from the File menu. To close only the hidden window, you need to unhide the window and then choose the Close command.

Unhide a macro sheet

The hidden 06HIDDEN macro sheet contains the macros you ran when you clicked the buttons on the sample documents. Unhide the macro sheet window.

1   From the Window menu, choose Unhide.

2   Select the 06HIDDEN macro sheet.

3   Choose the OK button.

The 06HIDDEN macro sheet appears on your screen.

Close the sample documents

Close all of the documents, but do not save the changes.

1   From the File menu, choose Close All.

Remember to press SHIFT to choose Close All.

2   For each document, choose the No button when Microsoft Excel asks whether you want to save changes.

Lesson Summary

To	Do this
Enter an array formula	Select the range of cells into which you want to enter the formula, type the formula in the formula bar, and press CTRL+SHIFT+ENTER in Microsoft Excel for Windows or COMMAND+ENTER in Microsoft Excel for the Macintosh.
Make a decision using an IF function	Enter the IF formula in the formula bar. The first argument is a mathematical TRUE/FALSE test, the second argument is a formula you want Microsoft Excel to use if the test is TRUE, and the third argument is a formula to use if the test is FALSE.
Build a formula with a nested function	Enter the formula in the formula bar, specifying one function as an argument to another function.
Create a custom function	Enter the custom function on a macro sheet. Use the ARGUMENT function to define the custom function's arguments. Enter the mathematical formula that the custom function will calculate. Use the RETURN function to return the result of the calculation. Select the range of cells containing the custom function. Choose the Define Name command from the Formula menu to name the function, to define it as a function, and to assign it to a function category.
Look up a value in a lookup table	Create the lookup table. The first row or column contains compare values; any other rows or columns contain information corresponding to the com-pare values. Use one of the lookup functions (HLOOKUP, LOOKUP, or VLOOKUP) to look up a value in the table. The first argument to the function is the lookup value, the second argument is the range of cells containing the lookup table, and the third argument specifies which row or column in the table con-tains the information you want returned.
Annotate your work-sheets with text boxes, buttons, and notes	Use the Text Box and Button tools on the Utility toolbar to add text boxes and buttons. Choose the Note command from the Formula menu to add cell notes. Double-click a cell to read the note assigned to it.

To	Do this
Protect or unprotect cells and objects	Choose the Cell Protection or Object Protection command from the Format menu to specify which cells or objects you want to protect. Then use the Protect or Unprotect Document command on the Options menu to actually implement or remove the protection.
Hide or unhide documents	Choose the Hide or Unhide command from the Window menu.

For more information about	See in the *Microsoft Excel User's Guide*
Array formulas	"Creating and Using an Array Formula" in Chapter 5 in Book 1
Custom functions	Chapter 5, "Creating and Using Custom Worksheet Functions," in Book 2
Lookup tables	"Creating a Lookup Table" in Chapter 1 in Book 2

For more information about	See in the *Microsoft Excel Function Reference*
The IF function	IF (form 1, worksheets)

Preview of the Next Lesson

In the next lesson, you'll write formulas to link information from one worksheet to another. You will use the linking capabilities of Microsoft Excel to work more flexibly. Instead of creating one large worksheet, you will create smaller, simpler worksheets that are linked together.

Linking Worksheets

In this lesson, you'll link one worksheet to another. You'll see how you can work efficiently with multiple documents. You'll also learn to save a group of documents as a workbook file so that you can open them all at once.

You will learn how to:

- Write a formula that links one worksheet to another.

- Save and open a workbook file.

Estimated lesson time: 30 minutes

Start the lesson

In this lesson, you'll work with a version of the BUDGET worksheet that has purpose and summary information added. The SALEHIST worksheet tracks the history of companywide and industrywide sales. You will use these worksheets to learn more about linking.

1 Open 07LESSNA.

2 Save the worksheet as BUDGET.

3 Open 07LESSNB.

4 Save the worksheet as SALEHIST.

Your screen should look like the following illustration. In Microsoft Excel for the Macintosh, the .XLS extensions do not appear.

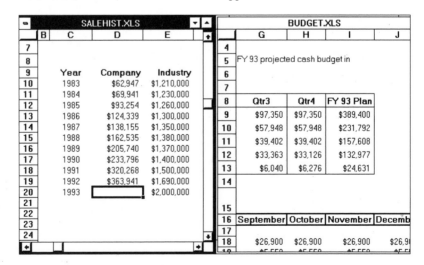

Notes attached to cells A5 and A8 of the BUDGET worksheet contain information about the Purpose cell, the Summary Area cell, and other worksheet changes. You can read cell notes by double-clicking any cell that has a note indicator. A note indicator appears as a dot in the upper-right corner of the cell.

Creating a Formula to Link One Worksheet to Another

Your BUDGET worksheet already contains the projected revenue data that you need in the SALEHIST worksheet. You'll create a formula that will link revenue data in the BUDGET worksheet to the SALEHIST worksheet.

External references   A linking formula contains an *external reference*, which is a reference to another document. An external reference consists of a document name and a cell reference, separated by an exclamation point. For example, you'll create a formula in SALEHIST that uses the following external reference:

=BUDGET.XLS!$I$9

In Microsoft Excel for the Macintosh, the formula will use this external reference:

=BUDGET!$I$9

Create a linking formula

Because you can create a linking formula by pointing, it's as easy to create as any other formula. Create a formula in SALEHIST to total the projected monthly revenues from BUDGET.

1   On the SALEHIST worksheet, select cell D20.

2   Type an equal sign (=).

3   Switch to the BUDGET worksheet by clicking it.

4   On the BUDGET worksheet, select cell I9.

5   Click the enter box or press ENTER.

Your screen should look like the following illustration. In Microsoft Excel for the Macintosh, the .XLS extensions do not appear.

| D20 | | =BUDGET.XLS!$I$9 | | | | | | | |

SALEHIST.XLS						BUDGET.XLS			
---	C	D	E			G	H	I	J
7					4				
8					5	FY 93 projected cash budget in			
9	Year	Company	Industry		6				
10	1983	$62,947	$1,210,000		7				
11	1984	$69,941	$1,230,000						
12	1985	$93,254	$1,260,000		8	Qtr3	Qtr4	FY 93 Plan	
13	1986	$124,339	$1,300,000		9	$97,350	$97,350	$389,400	
14	1987	$138,155	$1,350,000		10	$57,948	$57,948	$231,792	
15	1988	$162,535	$1,380,000		11	$39,402	$39,402	$157,608	
16	1989	$205,740	$1,370,000		12	$33,363	$33,126	$132,977	
17	1990	$233,796	$1,400,000		13	$6,040	$6,276	$24,631	
18	1991	$320,268	$1,500,000		14				
19	1992	$363,941	$1,690,000						
20	1993	$389,400	$2,000,000		15				
21					16	September	October	November	Decemb
22					17				
23					18	$26,900	$26,900	$26,900	$26,9

When you create a linking formula by pointing, Microsoft Excel uses absolute references. With absolute references, the formula will still refer to the same cells on the BUDGET worksheet if you copy the formula to another location on the SALEHIST worksheet.

Dependent and source documents   The formula in SALEHIST depends on cells in BUDGET. The linking formula in SALEHIST returns an error value if you delete the BUDGET worksheet. SALEHIST is the *dependent worksheet,* and BUDGET is the *source worksheet.*

Change the July budgeted sales revenues

Change the July projected sales revenues in BUDGET to see how changing your source worksheet affects your dependent worksheet.

1   Switch to the BUDGET worksheet by clicking it.

2   Select cell E18.

3   Type **27000**

4   Click the enter box or press ENTER.

The value in cell D20 on SALEHIST changes from $389,400 to $389,500.

Managing Links

You need to keep the dependent and source document relationship in mind as you create and use a system of linked worksheets. Here are some guidelines for managing links.

 Saving linked worksheets   It's good practice to save the source worksheet before saving the dependent worksheet. This way the correct names will be saved in the dependent worksheet when you quit Microsoft Excel. For example, if you change the name of the source worksheet, BUDGET, and later save the dependent worksheet, SALEHIST, the linking formulas in the dependent worksheet will contain the new name.

Moving linked worksheets with your operating system   In Microsoft Excel for Windows, if you use File Manager instead of Microsoft Excel to copy your dependent worksheet to a different disk or directory, you also need to copy the source worksheet. In Microsoft Excel for the Macintosh, if you use the Finder instead of Microsoft Excel to copy your dependent worksheet to a different disk or folder, you also need to copy the source worksheet.

The Links command   If your links become disconnected, which happens if the source worksheet is deleted, you can redirect them with the Links command. To redirect links to a source worksheet you've renamed or moved, open the dependent worksheet, choose Links from the File menu, choose the Change button, select the name of the source worksheet to which you want to redirect the links, and choose the Change button again.

Save and close the worksheet

Although the formula includes a reference to an external document (the BUDGET worksheet), the value in cell D20 of the SALEHIST worksheet remains the same.

As you close the BUDGET worksheet, watch the linking formula in the formula bar.

 1   Click the Save File tool.

2   From the File menu, choose Close.

When you close the source document, the linking formula in cell D20 of the SALEHIST worksheet changes to show the source document's full path (location). When you open the BUDGET worksheet again, the formula changes back to show only the worksheet name.

Recently opened file list   In Microsoft Excel for Windows, and in Microsoft Excel for the Macintosh if you have a large screen, the names of the last four files you opened are listed at the bottom of the File menu. You can reopen any of these files by choosing the filename from the list in the File menu.

If you have a 9-inch Macintosh screen, the recently opened file list isn't available. You need to choose the Open command from the File menu to reopen a file.

Reopen the worksheet

▶ From the File menu, choose BUDGET, or choose Open from the File menu and select BUDGET.

Insert rows to move the Summary Area and its formulas

Just as references in formulas on the same worksheet are adjusted when you move the supporting cells, external references are also adjusted. You will move the Summary Area along with its formulas by inserting rows into the worksheet.

1 On the BUDGET worksheet, select rows 8 through 10.

2 From the Edit menu, choose Insert.

3 Switch to the SALEHIST worksheet by clicking it.

The formula in cell D20 of SALEHIST adjusts to display the new reference for the gross revenue formula (BUDGET.XLS!$I$12 in Microsoft Excel for Windows or BUDGET!$I$12 in Microsoft Excel for the Macintosh). Whenever you move an absolute reference, such as $I$12, formulas in dependent cells automatically adjust to reflect the new location on the worksheet.

Saving a Workbook File

With a Microsoft Excel workbook file, you can save and open a group of documents at once rather than opening each document individually.

A workbook file that contains only worksheets is like a 3-D worksheet in Lotus 1-2-3 Release 3.0.

The Save Workbook command You can use the Save Workbook command to save a *workbook*, which includes the open documents themselves, their position and arrangement, and their workbook settings. Think of the individual documents as being "pages" within the workbook file. When you choose Save Workbook from the File menu, a dialog box appears so that you can name the workbook file. In Microsoft Excel for Windows, the .XLW extension is added to all workbook files.

Save the workbook

Now you will save a workbook file to use when you want to work with BUDGET and SALEHIST at the same time.

1 From the File menu, choose Save Workbook.

2 Save the workbook as BUDGETWK.

Microsoft Excel creates a workbook file and displays the Workbook Contents window. From the Workbook Contents window, you can add documents to and remove documents from the workbook, control the workbook options, and switch from one document to another. Think of switching from one document to another as "turning pages" in the workbook. The Workbook Contents window is shown in the following illustration.

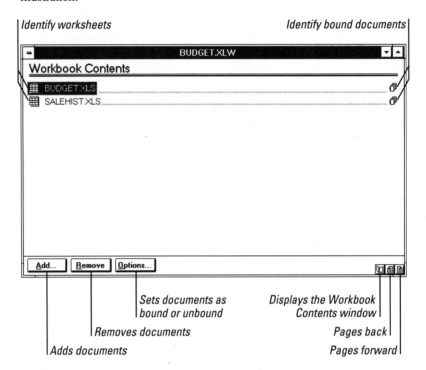

Identify worksheets

Identify bound documents

Sets documents as bound or unbound

Displays the Workbook Contents window

Removes documents

Pages back

Adds documents

Pages forward

Bound and Unbound Workbook Files

A workbook is a type of Microsoft Excel document in which you store either other documents or information about other documents. A document stored in a workbook file is *bound* in the workbook. An *unbound* document appears in a workbook's list of documents, but the document file itself is stored outside the workbook file. While bound documents can be bound in only one workbook at a time, unbound documents can appear in several workbooks at a time.

Note   Bound documents can have names that are up to 31 characters long. To name a bound document, choose the Options button in the Workbook Contents window and type the name in the Document Name box. The maximum length of an unbound document name is determined by your operating system.

Unbind the worksheets into separate documents

The BUDGET and SALEHIST worksheets are bound in the BUDGET workbook. You will choose the Options button in the Workbook Contents window to make the worksheets unbound.

1   In the Workbook Contents window, select the BUDGET worksheet.

2   Choose the Options button.

3   Under Store Document In, select the Separate File (Unbound) option button.

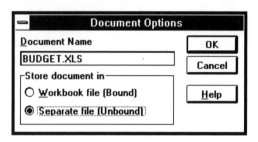

4   Choose the OK button.

5   In the Workbook Contents window, select the SALEHIST worksheet.

6   Choose the Options button.

7   Under Store Document In, select the Separate File (Unbound) option button.

8   Choose the OK button.

You can also click the icon to change the file from bound to unbound.

The icons at the right side of the Workbook Contents window change to "loose-leaf pages" to indicate that the worksheets are unbound, as shown in the following illustration.

Identify unbound documents

Close the worksheets

1   From the File menu, choose Close All (remember to press the SHIFT key).

2   Choose the Yes button to save your changes in each worksheet.

The Save As dialog box appears.

3   In Microsoft Excel for Windows, choose the OK button. Choose the OK button again to replace the worksheet.

In Microsoft Excel for the Macintosh, choose the Save button. Choose the Yes button to replace the worksheet.

One Step Further

In the preceding lessons, you created a worksheet to keep track of a three-month advertising budget. In this exercise, you will link a worksheet detailing quarterly consulting expenses to a worksheet containing your advertising budget. You will link the Total Expenses cells on the 07CONSLT worksheet for July, August, and September to the Consultants cells for those three months on the 07CAMPGN worksheet.

 1   Open the 07STEP workbook file that contains the 07CAMPGN and 07CONSLT worksheets.

2   On 07CAMPGN, enter a formula for the July Consultants' Expense that links to the July Total Consulting Expenses cell on 07CONSLT.

3   Create similar formulas for the August and September Consultants' Expenses cells that link to 07CONSLT.

Your worksheets should look like the following illustration. In Microsoft Excel for the Macintosh, the .XLS extensions do not appear.

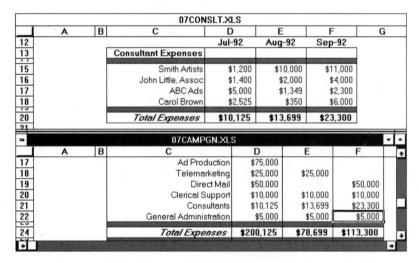

4   Close the worksheets when you are finished. Do not save the changes, because you may want to use these files again.

Lesson Summary

To	Do this
Link one worksheet to another	In a cell on the dependent worksheet, create a linking formula with an external reference to a source worksheet. You can do this by typing an equal sign (=) and clicking a cell on the source worksheet.
Save a workbook file	Choose the Save Workbook command from the File menu. After the workbook is created, you can choose the Options button in the Workbook Contents window to specify whether the documents in the workbook are bound or unbound.

For more information about	See in the *Microsoft Excel User's Guide*
Linking worksheets	"Linking Microsoft Excel Worksheets" in Chapter 11 in Book 1
Creating and using workbooks	"Managing Documents with Workbooks" in Chapter 4 in Book 1

Preview of the Next Lesson

In the next lesson, you will create and use names in a worksheet. Names help you find areas of your worksheet quickly and easily, and they make your formulas easier to understand.

Using Names on a Worksheet

In this lesson, you'll learn how to create and use names. You'll use names to simplify worksheet formulas and to define areas of the worksheet so that you can find them easily. Using names will help you to create clear, easy-to-use, and well-documented worksheets.

You will learn how to:

- Create names for cells and cell ranges.
- Use cell names and cell range names in formulas.
- Apply names to existing formulas to replace cell references.
- Name formulas containing relative references and constants.

Estimated lesson time: 45 minutes

Opening the Workbook File

You will continue to use the BUDGET and SALEHIST worksheets for this lesson. The worksheets are the same as those you were working with at the end of Lesson 7, except for the addition of an initial data area on the BUDGET worksheet. This data area contains variables for sales growth and increases in cost of goods sold (COGS), which you will use in worksheet formulas. You can open both worksheets at the same time by opening a workbook file.

Start the lesson

Open the workbook file that includes 08LESSNA and 08LESSNB.

 ▶ Open the 08LESSN workbook file.

Rename the 08LESSNA worksheet

1 Switch to the 08LESSNA worksheet.

2 Save the worksheet as BUDGET.

Rename the 08LESSNB worksheet

1 Switch to the 08LESSNB worksheet.

2 Save the worksheet as SALEHIST.

Your screen should look like the following illustration. In Microsoft Excel for the Macintosh, the filenames do not include the .XLS extension.

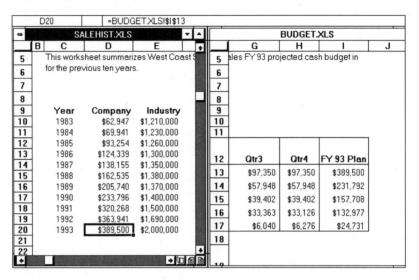

| D20 | =BUDGET.XLS!$I$13 |

	SALEHIST.XLS			BUDGET.XLS			
B	C	D	E	G	H	I	J
5	This worksheet summarizes West Coast S			ales FY 93 projected cash budget in			
6	for the previous ten years.						
7							
8							
9	**Year**	**Company**	**Industry**				
10	1983	$62,947	$1,210,000				
11	1984	$69,941	$1,230,000				
12	1985	$93,254	$1,260,000	**Qtr3**	**Qtr4**	**FY 93 Plan**	
13	1986	$124,339	$1,300,000	$97,350	$97,350	$389,500	
14	1987	$138,155	$1,350,000	$57,948	$57,948	$231,792	
15	1988	$162,535	$1,380,000	$39,402	$39,402	$157,708	
16	1989	$205,740	$1,370,000	$33,363	$33,126	$132,977	
17	1990	$233,796	$1,400,000	$6,040	$6,276	$24,731	
18	1991	$320,268	$1,500,000				
19	1992	$363,941	$1,690,000				
20	1993	$389,500	$2,000,000				
21							
22							

Creating and Using Names

Names make your worksheets and formulas easier to update and understand. The following illustration shows how named worksheet ranges interrelate.

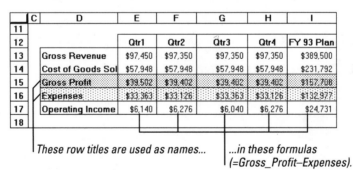

C	D	E	F	G	H	I
11						
12		**Qtr1**	**Qtr2**	**Qtr3**	**Qtr4**	**FY 93 Plan**
13	Gross Revenue	$97,450	$97,350	$97,350	$97,350	$389,500
14	Cost of Goods Sol	$57,948	$57,948	$57,948	$57,948	$231,792
15	Gross Profit	$39,502	$39,402	$39,402	$39,402	$157,708
16	Expenses	$33,363	$33,126	$33,363	$33,126	$132,977
17	Operating Income	$6,140	$6,276	$6,040	$6,276	$24,731
18						

These row titles are used as names...   *...in these formulas (=Gross_Profit–Expenses).*

The Define Name command is like /Range Name Create and /Range Name Delete in 1-2-3.

The Define Name command   You can name a cell range, constant value, or formula with the Define Name command. You can also change or delete an existing name with Define Name.

Name the cell containing annual budgeted sales

Use the Define Name command on the Formula menu to assign the name "Total_Revenues" to the cell that contains your total revenues formula.

1   In the BUDGET worksheet, select cell I13.

2   From the Formula menu, choose <u>D</u>efine Name.

3   In the Name box, type **Total_Revenues**

You must type an underline character between the words, because names cannot contain spaces.

4   Choose the OK button.

Microsoft Excel names cell I13 "Total_Revenues." If a name is assigned to the active cell, the reference area displays the cell's name instead of the cell's reference, as shown in the following illustration.

The reference area displays the name of the active cell if a name has been defined for it.

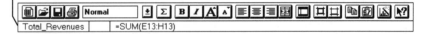

The Paste List button works the same way as /Range Name Table in 1-2-3.

The Paste Name command   You can use the Paste Name command to paste a name into a formula you're creating. With Paste Name on the Formula menu, you can make sure that the name is defined and that it's spelled correctly in your formula. You can also use the Paste Name tool on the Macro toolbar.

Create a new linking formula using a name

If you want to use names as you do in 1-2-3, choose Calculation from the Options menu and select Alternate Formula Entry.

You'll create a new linking formula that uses the name "Total_Revenues" rather than a cell reference. Instead of typing the formula, you will use the Paste Name command on the Formula menu.

1   Switch to the SALEHIST worksheet.

2   Select cell D20.

3   Type an equal sign (=) to begin a new formula.

4   Switch to the BUDGET worksheet.

5   From the Formula menu, choose <u>P</u>aste Name.

6   In the Paste Name box, select Total_Revenues.

7   Choose the OK button.

8   Click the enter box or press ENTER.

Your new formula appears in the formula bar. Your screen should look similar to the following illustration. In Microsoft Excel for the Macintosh, the .XLS extensions do not appear in the formula.

D20		=BUDGET.XLS!Total_Revenues							
SALEHIST.XLS					**BUDGET.XLS**				
B	C	D	E			G	H	I	J
5	This worksheet summarizes West Coast S			**5**	ales FY 93 projected cash budget in				
6	for the previous 10 years.			**6**					
7				**7**					
8				**8**					
9	Year	Company	Industry	**9**					
10	1983	$62,947	$1,210,000	**10**					
11	1984	$69,941	$1,230,000	**11**					
12	1985	$93,254	$1,260,000	**12**		Qtr3	Qtr4	FY 93 Plan	
13	1986	$124,339	$1,300,000	**13**		$97,350	$97,350	$389,500	
14	1987	$138,155	$1,350,000	**14**		$57,948	$57,948	$231,792	
15	1988	$162,535	$1,380,000	**15**		$39,402	$39,402	$157,708	
16	1989	$205,740	$1,370,000	**16**		$33,363	$33,126	$132,977	
17	1990	$233,796	$1,400,000	**17**		$6,040	$6,276	$24,731	
18	1991	$320,268	$1,500,000	**18**					
19	1992	$363,941	$1,690,000						
20	1993	$389,500	$2,000,000						
21									
22									

Enlarge the BUDGET worksheet window

For the rest of this lesson, you'll work only with the BUDGET worksheet. Close the SALEHIST worksheet, and enlarge the BUDGET worksheet to fill the workspace.

1 Close the SALEHIST worksheet.

2 Choose the Yes button to save your changes.

3 In the upper-right corner of the BUDGET window, click the Maximize button in Microsoft Excel for Windows, or click the zoom box in Microsoft Excel for the Macintosh.

The Create Names command is like /Range Name Labels in 1-2-3, except that Create Names acts on multiple cell ranges.

The Create Names command With the Create Names command, you can define many names at once by using row and column titles as the names.

Create names in the Summary Area

You'll use the row titles in the Summary Area to create names for Gross Revenue, Cost of Goods Sold, Gross Profit, Expenses, and Operating Income.

1 Select cells D13:H17.

2 From the Formula menu, choose Create Names.

3   Make sure that the Left Column check box is selected.

4   Choose the OK button.

If you want to see the names you created, choose the Define Name command from the Formula menu. Choose the Close button to close the dialog box.

The Apply Names command   The Apply Names command replaces cell references in your formulas with the names you've created.

Apply names to the formulas in the Summary Area

You've already written formulas to total quarterly figures in the Summary Area of the worksheet. You will use the Apply Names command on the Formula menu to change cell references in these formulas to names. For example, the formula in cell I13 will change from =SUM(E13:H13) to =SUM(Gross_Revenue).

1   Select cells I13:I17.

2   From the Formula menu, choose Apply Names.

3   Choose the OK button.

The formula bar shows the new formula in cell I13. Your screen should look like the following illustration.

	I13		=SUM(Gross_Revenue)						
	C	D	E	F	G	H	I	J	
5		This worksheet presents the West Coast Sales FY 93 projected cash budget in							
6		monthly detail and quarterly summaries.							
7									
8		**Monthly Growth:**							
9		Sales Growth 1.50%							
10		COGS Increase 0.90%							
11									
12			Qtr1	Qtr2	Qtr3	Qtr4	FY 93 Plan		
13		Gross Revenue	$97,450	$97,350	$97,350	$97,350	$389,500		
14		Cost of Goods Sol	$57,948	$57,948	$57,948	$57,948	$231,792		
15		Gross Profit	$39,502	$39,402	$39,402	$39,402	$157,708		
16		Expenses	$33,363	$33,126	$33,363	$33,126	$132,977		
17		Operating Income	$6,140	$6,276	$6,040	$6,276	$24,731		
18									

You can move to each cell in the range I13:I17 to see how names were applied to each formula.

Use names to find cell data

You can use the Goto command on the Formula menu to find intersecting cells in named rows and columns. In this procedure, you will name the columns of quarterly data in the Summary Area and then use the Goto command to find projected expenses for Qtr2.

1   Select cells E12:I17.

2   From the Formula menu, choose Create Names.

3   Make sure that the Top Row check box is selected.

4   Choose the OK button.

5   From the Formula menu, choose Goto.

6   In the Reference box, type **Qtr2 Expenses**

7   Choose the OK button.

Microsoft Excel selects cell F16, the cell containing the second-quarter expenses.

Naming Values

The Define Name and Create Names commands on the Formula menu can also be used to name a value. Using names is an easy way to refer to values.

Create names for the monthly growth variables

The variables for sales growth and COGS increase appear in the Initial Data area of the worksheet. Sales Growth refers to a monthly growth rate of 1.50 percent, and COGS Increase refers to an increase rate of 0.90 percent. You will name these variables and use them in worksheet formulas to project your budget.

Use the Create Names command on the Formula menu to name these new variables.

1   Select cells D9:E10.

2   From the Formula menu, choose Create Names.

3   Make sure that the Left Column check box is selected.

4   Choose the OK button.

Use the Sales Growth variable in a formula

Use the Sales Growth variable in a formula to forecast sales revenues. You'll enter the formula in the cell for August sales. Use July sales as the starting point for the rest of your calculations.

1   Select cell F22.

2   Type an equal sign (=).

3   Select cell E22.

4   Type *(1+

5 From the Formula menu, choose Paste Name.

6 Select Sales_Growth.

7 Choose the OK button.

8 Type)

9 Click the enter box or press ENTER.

The formula =E22*(1+Sales_Growth) appears in the formula bar.

You multiply 1+Sales_Growth by the previous month's sales, rather than multiplying by the Sales_Growth variable and then adding the product to the previous month's total in a second formula.

Naming Formulas

In Microsoft Excel, you can name formulas and constants, not just the cells containing formulas or values.

You can also name a formula with the Define Name command on the Formula menu. When the Define Name dialog box appears, type the name in the Name box, type the formula in the Refers To box, and then choose the Add or OK button. The Add button adds the name to the list and leaves the dialog box open. The OK button adds the name to the list and closes the dialog box.

Name a formula for sales growth

You created a formula to calculate revenue growth based on a previous month's revenue projections. The formula 1+Sales_Growth automatically increases the previous month's sales projection. Use "Frm" to identify the name as a formula in the Paste Name dialog box. You will give the name FrmSales_Growth to the formula 1+Sales_Growth.

1 From the Formula menu, choose Define Name.

2 In the Name box, type **FrmSales_Growth**

3 In the Refers To box, type **=1+Sales_Growth**

4 Choose the OK button.

Use the named formula to calculate shipping revenues

Replace the August shipping revenue value with a formula. You will use the name FrmSales_Growth as part of this new formula.

1 Select cell F23.

2 Type **=e23***

3 From the Formula menu, choose Paste Name.

4 Select FrmSales_Growth.

5 Choose the OK button.

6 Click the enter box or press ENTER.

Cell F23 displays a new value, $5633, reflecting a 1.50-percent increase over the previous month.

Copy the August revenue formulas to the rest of the months

Use the fill handle to copy the August sales and shipping revenue projection formulas to September through June.

1 Select cells F22:F23.

2 Drag the fill handle to cell P23.

3 Scroll your worksheet back to the Summary Area.

The Summary Area data depends on the Budget Model Area data. A 1.50-percent growth rate in monthly shipping revenues results in a new projected gross revenue figure of $424,491 in cell I13. Your worksheet should look like the following illustration.

C	D	E	F	G	H	I
8	Monthly Growth:					
9	Sales Growth 1.50%					
10	COGS Increase 0.90%					
11						
12		Qtr1	Qtr2	Qtr3	Qtr4	FY 93 Plan
13	Gross Revenue	$99,122	$103,650	$108,384	$113,335	$424,491
14	Cost of Goods Sold	$57,948	$57,948	$57,948	$57,948	$231,792
15	Gross Profit	$41,174	$45,702	$50,436	$55,387	$192,699
16	Expenses	$33,363	$33,126	$33,363	$33,126	$132,977
17	Operating Income	$7,812	$12,576	$17,074	$22,261	$59,722
18						
19						
20		July	August	September	October	November
21	Gross Revenue					
22	Sales	$27,000	$27,405	$27,816	$28,233	$28,657
23	Shipping	$5,550	$5,633	$5,718	$5,804	$5,891
24	*Total*	$32,550	$33,038	$33,534	$34,037	$34,547
26	Cost of Goods Sold					
27	Goods	$17,710	$17,710	$17,710	$17,710	$17,710
28	Freight	$270	$270	$270	$270	$270

Next, you will project the increases in cost of goods sold and variable expenses that go along with increasing revenues.

Name a formula for COGS growth

You will name a formula to use for projecting cost of goods sold and variable expenses for the 1993 fiscal year. This formula will add 1 to the COGS Increase rate and multiply the result by the previous month's value. The result of the formula includes the previous month's value plus the projected increase. You will create this formula the same way you created the formula to calculate sales growth.

1 Select cell F27.

2 From the Formula menu, choose <u>D</u>efine Name.

3 In the Name box, type **FrmCOGS_Increase**

4 In the Refers To box, type **=1+COGS_Increase**

5 Choose the OK button.

The August sales and shipping formulas used cell references for the July sales and shipping formulas. Rather than using a cell reference, you can name a formula that acts as a reference.

Naming a Formula to Act as a Relative Reference

With the Define Name command on the Formula menu, you can name a formula to act as a relative reference. This can help you clarify your formulas. Choose Define Name, type the name in the Name box, and then type a relative cell reference in the Refers To box. For example, if the active cell is B1 and you want the name to refer to one cell to the left, type **A1** in the Refers To box.

You can also point to cell A1 rather than typing the reference. If you enter a cell reference by pointing to it rather than typing it, be sure to remove the dollar signs ($), either by editing the reference in the Refers To box or by using the Reference command on the Formula menu.

Name a relative reference

You will define a formula named PreviousMonth to refer to the data in the cell to the left of the formula. You will use PreviousMonth in formulas for projecting expenses.

1   With cell F27 still selected, choose Define Name from the Formula menu.

2   In the Name box, type **PreviousMonth**

3   In the Refers To box, type **=e27**

4   Choose the OK button.

Calculate August goods costs

You will replace the August goods value with a formula.

1   With cell F27 still selected, type an equal sign (=).

2   From the Formula menu, choose Paste Name.

3   In the Paste Name box, select PreviousMonth.

4   Choose the OK button to paste the name in the formula.

5   Type an asterisk (*).

6   From the Formula menu, choose Paste Name.

7   Select FrmCOGS_Increase.

8   Choose the OK button to paste the name in the formula.

9   Click the enter box or press ENTER to enter the formula in the worksheet.

The formula bar displays the formula =PreviousMonth*FrmCOGS_Increase.

Copy the formula to Freight, Markdowns, and Miscellaneous

You will use the Copy tool on the Standard toolbar to replace the other Cost of Goods Sold and variable expense values with the August goods formula.

1   With cell F27 still selected, click the Copy tool.

2   Select cells F28:F30, F41, F44, and F46 (the remaining August variable expenses).

Remember to use the CTRL key in Microsoft Excel for Windows or the COMMAND key in Microsoft Excel for the Macintosh to make nonadjacent selections.

3   From the Edit menu, choose Paste.

4   Press ESC to cancel the moving border.

In Microsoft Excel for the Macintosh, you can also press COMMAND+PERIOD to cancel the moving border.

The formula is copied to each of the selected cells. The formula replaces values and recalculates data based on the previous month's costs.

Your screen should look like the following illustration.

	C	D	E	F	G	H	I	J
26		Cost of Goods Sold						
27		Goods	$17,710	$17,869	$17,710	$17,710	$17,710	$17,71(
28		Freight	$270	$272	$270	$270	$270	$27(
29		Markdowns	$1,240	$1,251	$1,240	$1,240	$1,240	$1,24(
30		Miscellaneous	$96	$97	$96	$96	$96	$9(
31		*Total*						
33		**Gross Profit**						
35		**Expenses**						
36		Advertising	$4,000	$4,000	$4,000	$4,000	$4,000	$4,00(
37		Salaries	$4,700	$4,700	$4,700	$4,700	$4,700	$4,70(
38		Rent	$500	$500	$500	$500	$500	$50(
39		Utilities	$75	$75	$75	$75	$75	$7(
40		Insurance	$237	$0	$0	$0	$0	$(
41		Telephone and Telex	$280	$283	$280	$280	$280	$28(
42		Office Supplies	$147	$147	$147	$147	$147	$14(
43		Training	$100	$100	$100	$100	$100	$10(
44		Travel and Entertainment	$200	$202	$200	$200	$200	$20(
45		Taxes and Licenses	$240	$240	$240	$240	$240	$24(
46		Interest	$800	$807	$800	$800	$800	$80(

The remaining expenses are fixed expenses. You will replace each August fixed expense value with a formula that refers to the July fixed expense. By creating a formula that refers to a single cell, you can enter data once and have it automatically entered in any other dependent cells.

Create formulas for August fixed expenses

July fixed expenses will be allocated the same way for the remainder of the year. You will use the formula named PreviousMonth, which sets a cell's value to that of the previous month.

1   Select cell F36, the cell containing the August advertising expense.

2   Type an equal sign (=).

3   From the Formula menu, choose Paste Name.

4   Select PreviousMonth.

5   Choose the OK button to paste the name in the formula.

6   Click the enter box or press ENTER to enter the formula in the worksheet.

 7   Click the Copy tool.

8   Select cells F37:F39, F42:F43, and F45.

9   From the Edit menu, choose Paste.

The copied formula is pasted in all the selected cells.

10 Press ESC to cancel the moving border.

In Microsoft Excel for the Macintosh, you can also press COMMAND+PERIOD to cancel the moving border.

Your screen should look like the following illustration.

	C	D	E	F	G	H	I	J
26		Cost of Goods Sold						
27		Goods	$17,710	$17,869	$17,710	$17,710	$17,710	$17,71(
28		Freight	$270	$272	$270	$270	$270	$27(
29		Markdowns	$1,240	$1,251	$1,240	$1,240	$1,240	$1,24(
30		Miscellaneous	$96	$97	$96	$96	$96	$9(
31		*Total*						
33		**Gross Profit**						
35		**Expenses**						
36		Advertising	$4,000	$4,000	$4,000	$4,000	$4,000	$4,00(
37		Salaries	$4,700	$4,700	$4,700	$4,700	$4,700	$4,70(
38		Rent	$500	$500	$500	$500	$500	$50(
39		Utilities	$75	$75	$75	$75	$75	$7!
40		Insurance	$237	$0	$0	$0	$0	$(
41		Telephone and Telex	$280	$283	$280	$280	$280	$28(
42		Office Supplies	$147	$147	$147	$147	$147	$14
43		Training	$100	$100	$100	$100	$100	$10(
44		Travel and Entertainment	$200	$202	$200	$200	$200	$20(
45		Taxes and Licenses	$240	$240	$240	$240	$240	$24(
46		Interest	$800	$807	$800	$800	$800	$80(

Use a formula for January insurance

Change the January insurance expense to a formula.

1 Select cell K40.

2 Type an equal sign (=).

3 Select cell E40.

4 Click the enter box or press ENTER.

Copy the expense formulas through the rest of the fiscal year

You will copy the August cost and expense formulas to September through June.

1 Select cells F27:F30.

2 Drag the fill handle to cell P30.

3 Select cells F36:F39.

4 Drag the fill handle to cell P39.

5 Select cells F41:F46.

6 Drag the fill handle to cell P46.

The Gross Revenue, Cost of Goods Sold, and Expense values are replaced with formulas. Your worksheet should look like the following illustration.

	C	D	E	F	G	H	I
20			July	August	September	October	November
21	Gross Revenue						
22		Sales	$27,000	$27,405	$27,816	$28,233	$28,657
23		Shipping	$5,550	$5,633	$5,718	$5,804	$5,891
24	Total		$32,550	$33,038	$33,534	$34,037	$34,547
26	Cost of Goods Sold						
27		Goods	$17,710	$17,869	$18,030	$18,192	$18,356
28		Freight	$270	$272	$275	$277	$280
29		Markdowns	$1,240	$1,251	$1,262	$1,274	$1,285
30		Miscellaneous	$96	$97	$98	$99	$100
31	Total		$19,316	$19,490	$19,665	$19,842	$20,021
33	Gross Profit		$13,234	$13,548	$13,869	$14,195	$14,527
35	Expenses						
36		Advertising	$4,000	$4,000	$4,000	$4,000	$4,000
37		Salaries	$4,700	$4,700	$4,700	$4,700	$4,700
38		Rent	$500	$500	$500	$500	$500
39		Utilities	$75	$75	$75	$75	$75
40		Insurance	$237	$0	$0	$0	$0
41		Telephone and Telex	$280	$283	$285	$288	$290
42		Office Supplies	$147	$147	$147	$147	$147
43		Training	$100	$100	$100	$100	$100
44		Travel and Entertainment	$200	$202	$204	$205	$207
45		Taxes and Licenses	$240	$240	$240	$240	$240
46		Interest	$800	$807	$814	$822	$829
47	Total		$11,279	$11,054	$11,065	$11,077	$11,089
49	Operating Income		$1,956	$2,495	$2,803	$3,118	$3,438

Save and close the worksheet

Save and close the worksheet. If you want to continue with the "One Step Further" exercise, you will use another version of the BUDGET worksheet.

1   Click the Save File tool.

2   From the File menu, choose Close to close the worksheet.

3   From the File menu, choose Close Workbook. Choose the No button when Microsoft Excel asks whether you want to save changes to the workbook.

One Step Further

Now you will complete the BUDGET worksheet, using what you have learned. Open the 08STEP worksheet and rename it BUDGET. The worksheet now includes additions to the Initial Data area for entry of initial revenue, COGS, and expense data. The Initial Data area also includes variables for monthly sales growth and COGS increase.

To complete the worksheet, you need to copy the data from July Revenue, COGS, and Expenses to their respective categories in the Initial Data area; create names for each of the initial data categories; and replace the July budget values with formulas that refer to each budget category in the Initial Data area. You will use the names for the categories in the Initial Data area in the July formulas.

1   Open the 08STEP worksheet.

2   Save the worksheet as BUDGET.

3   Copy the July revenue, COGS, and expense values to their corresponding budget categories in the Initial Data area.

4   Use Create Names on the Formula menu to create a name for each budget category in the Initial Data area.

5   Use any method to replace the July revenue, COGS, and expense values with formulas that refer to the same categories in the Initial Data area.

6   You can change any of the Initial Data area values, including monthly sales growth and COGS increase, to project different budget scenarios.

To see a possible solution to this exercise, open 08LESSNC.

7   Save the BUDGET worksheet.

8   Close both worksheets but do not save any changes.

Lesson Summary

To	Do this
Create names for cells and cell ranges	Choose the Define Name command from the Formula menu. In the Refers To box, enter the cell range using absolute references. If the selected range contains row or column headings, you can assign those names to adjacent cells using the Create Names command on the Formula menu.
Use cell and cell range names in formulas	In the formula bar, type the name, or choose the Paste Name command from the Formula menu, or click the Paste Name tool on the Macro toolbar.
Apply names to existing formulas to replace cell references	Choose the Apply Names command from the Formula menu.
Name formulas containing relative references and constants	Choose the Define Name command from the Formula menu. In the Refers To box, type the complete formula, including the equal sign (=).

For more information about	See in the *Microsoft Excel User's Guide*
Defining and using names	"Naming a Cell, Range, or Formula" in Chapter 8 in Book 1

Preview of the Next Lesson

In the next lesson, you will learn about worksheet outlining and data consolidation. With these powerful Microsoft Excel features, you can easily analyze and summarize your data.

Worksheet Outlining and Data Consolidation

In this lesson, you'll use three powerful Microsoft Excel features: worksheet outlining, group editing, and data consolidation. With outlining, you can switch between summary and detail views of your data. Group editing is used for sharing data and formatting between documents. It is useful for setting up and formatting a group of worksheets in preparation for consolidating data. Data consolidation summarizes the data from several worksheets into one worksheet.

The worksheets in this lesson examine the number of employees and payroll costs for the three divisions of West Coast Sales. Each division includes marketing, engineering, research and development, and administrative departments.

In the first part of this lesson, you'll use a worksheet that breaks down personnel statistics within each division by department. Then you'll format a group of worksheets containing personnel statistics for each division. You'll consolidate the data in these worksheets by department so that you can compare the total costs of administration, marketing, engineering, and research and development throughout the company.

You will learn how to:

- Create an outline on a worksheet.
- Expand and collapse an outline.
- Format a group of worksheets at the same time.
- Consolidate data from different worksheets.

Estimated lesson time: 45 minutes

Start the lesson

You'll create an outline on this worksheet and examine the data in different ways by switching between summary and detail views. You must have a mouse to do some of these procedures.

1 Open 09LESSNA.

2 Save the worksheet as WCSDIV.

Creating a Worksheet Outline

Outlining a worksheet differs from outlining a text document such as a report or a proposal. In a text document, the subordinate information appears below a heading. When you outline a worksheet, subordinate information typically appears above or to the left of the summary information.

A worksheet can be outlined horizontally by rows or vertically by columns, or both, depending on how the summary formulas are calculated. To create an outline, you must write your formulas so that references consistently point in one direction, such as summary rows always referring to the rows above and summary columns always referring to the columns to the left.

The Outline command   You can use the Outline command to create a worksheet outline. You can create an outline on a new or existing worksheet, but you can have only one outline on a worksheet at a time. Outlines can contain up to seven levels of information. You can create both horizontal and vertical outlines of the data. You can also apply styles consistently to your worksheets by selecting the Automatic Styles check box.

Create a worksheet outline

Use the Outline command on the Formula menu to outline the Personnel Cost Data area on the WCSDIV worksheet. Create both horizontal and vertical outlines of the data.

1   Select cells D9:H24.

2   From the Formula menu, choose Outline.

The check boxes are already selected for Automatic Styles, Summary Rows Below Detail, and Summary Columns To Right Of Detail.

3   Choose the Create button.

Outline symbols appear to the left of the row and column headings.

Your worksheet should look like the following illustration.

Row level buttons

Column level bar

Column level buttons

Collapse button

	C	D	E	F	G	H
			Number of			Personnel
9		Department	Employees	Payroll	Benefits	Costs
	Copier					
10	Division	Marketing	4	$177,000	$53,100	**$230,100**
11		Engineering	7	$303,500	$91,050	**$394,550**
12		R and D	2	$98,000	$29,400	**$127,400**
13		Administrative	4	$160,000	$48,000	**$208,000**
14		**Copier Total**	**17**	**$738,500**	**$221,550**	**$960,050**
	Fax					
15	Division	Marketing	2	$105,000	$31,500	**$136,500**
16		Engineering	6	$250,500	$75,150	**$325,650**
17		R and D	2	$97,000	$29,100	**$126,100**
18		Administrative	3	$132,000	$39,600	**$171,600**
19		**Fax Total**	**13**	**$584,500**	**$175,350**	**$759,850**
	Printer					
20	Division	Marketing	7	$320,500	$96,150	**$416,650**
21		Engineering	14	$655,000	$196,500	**$851,500**
22		R and D	5	$214,000	$64,200	**$278,200**
23		Administrative	4	$179,000	$53,700	**$232,700**
24		**Printer Total**	**30**	**$1,368,500**	**$410,550**	**$1,779,050**
25						
26						

Row level bar

Expand button   Expands (displays) the hidden subordinate data.

Collapse button   Collapses (hides) the rows or columns enclosed by the row or column level bar.

Row and column level buttons   Display specified levels of data. For example, in an outline with three levels of data, clicking the 2 button displays information for the first two levels.

Row and column level bars   Show the hierarchy of the levels of data. To hide the detail rows and columns, click the collapse button on the level bar.

Collapse the outline to level 1

Now that you've outlined the worksheet, view the division summaries.

1 Click the row level 1 button.

Your worksheet should look like the following illustration.

Expand button

2 Click the column level 1 button.

Your worksheet should look like the following illustration.

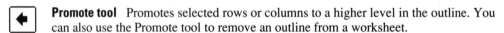

Some of the outlining controls are on the Utility toolbar. The following illustration shows the outlining tools on the Utility toolbar.

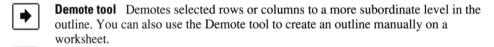

Outlining tools

Promote tool Promotes selected rows or columns to a higher level in the outline. You can also use the Promote tool to remove an outline from a worksheet.

Demote tool Demotes selected rows or columns to a more subordinate level in the outline. You can also use the Demote tool to create an outline manually on a worksheet.

Show Outline Symbols tool Displays or hides the outline symbols on your worksheet.

Select Visible Cells tool Selects only the visible cells when the outline is collapsed. You can work with the visible cells to plot a chart or to copy only a specific level of information.

Display the Utility toolbar

▶ From the toolbar shortcut menu, choose Utility.

Demote the columns

The Number of Employees column is not part of your outline because the summary formulas in column H don't refer to the data in column E. If you select column E and click the Demote tool, the column will become level 2 data in your worksheet. Once you have demoted the Number of Employees column, demote the Payroll and Benefits columns to level 3.

1   Select column E.

2   On the Utility toolbar, click the Demote tool.

3   Click the expand button above column H to expand the outline.

4   Select columns F and G.

5   On the Utility toolbar, click the Demote tool.

The outline symbols for the columns reflect your changes. Your worksheet should look like the following illustration.

	C	D	E	F	G	H
9		Department	Number of Employees	Payroll	Benefits	Personnel Costs
14		Copier Total	17	$738,500	$221,550	$960,050
19		Fax Total	13	$584,500	$175,350	$759,850
24		Printer Total	30	$1,368,500	$410,550	$1,779,050
25						

Collapse and expand the outline

Now that you've changed the column levels, view the level 1 and level 2 columns with the level 1 rows.

1   Click the column level 1 button.

Your worksheet should look like the following illustration.

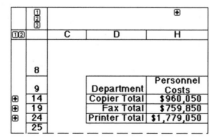

2   Click the expand buttons to see the detail.

Save the outline view

Now that you've created an outline, save the outline view of your worksheet so that you can switch to this view without recreating the outline each time.

1   From the <u>W</u>indow menu, choose <u>V</u>iew.

> **Note**   If the View command does not appear on the File menu, rerun the Setup program to install the View Manager. For more information about adding or removing add-in macros, see "Managing Add-in Commands and Functions" in Chapter 4 in Book 2 of the *Microsoft Excel User's Guide*.

2   Choose the Add button.

3   In the Name box, type **Outline**

4   Choose the OK button.

Remove the outline

To remove the outline, select the rows or columns and promote them until the outline symbols disappear.

1   Select rows 9 through 24.

2   On the Utility toolbar, click the Promote tool until the outline symbols disappear.

3   Select columns D through H.

4   On the Utility toolbar, click the Promote tool until the outline symbols disappear.

If you just want to turn off the display of outline symbols without removing the outline, click the Show Outline Symbols tool on the Utility toolbar.

Save and close the worksheet

In the remainder of the lesson, you will work with a different group of worksheets that contain the same data. Save and close the WCSDIV worksheet.

1   Click the Save File tool on the Standard toolbar.

2   From the <u>F</u>ile menu, choose <u>C</u>lose.

Formatting a Group

With Microsoft Excel, you can save time by entering data and editing, formatting, and changing display options in several worksheets at the same time. You do this by defining similar worksheets as a *group*. Any changes you make in the active worksheet are duplicated in all the sheets in the group.

Open the workbook

The 09LESSNB workbook file contains the 09WCSDPT, 09FAX, 09COPIER, and 09PRINTER worksheets. You will format these worksheets as a group and then consolidate their data into one worksheet.

1   Open the 09LESSNB workbook file.

2   Switch to the 09WCSDPT worksheet.

Rename the worksheets

Change the names of the worksheets to WCSDEPT, FAX, COPIER, and PRINTER.

1   With the 09WCSDPT worksheet active, choose Save <u>A</u>s from the <u>F</u>ile menu.

2   Save the worksheet as WCSDEPT.

3   In Microsoft Excel for Windows, choose the OK button.

In Microsoft Excel for the Macintosh, choose the Save button.

4   Repeat steps 1 through 3 for each of the worksheets, renaming them FAX, COPIER, and PRINTER.

5   Switch to WCSDEPT.

Your screen should look like the following illustration. In Microsoft Excel for the Macintosh, the filename does not have the .XLS extension.

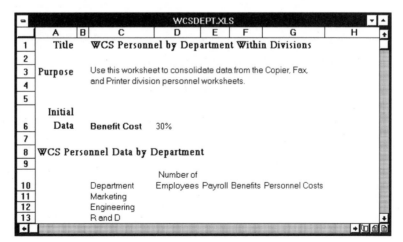

The Group Edit command   You can use the Group Edit command to group several worksheets for formatting, editing, or data entry. Working with a group is useful for preparing your worksheets for operations such as data consolidation.

Start the group editing session

You'll start a group editing session to format all of the open worksheets at once.

1   Switch to the WCSDEPT worksheet, if it is not already the active sheet.

2   From the Options menu, choose Group Edit.

3   The names of the four worksheets should be selected. If not, hold down SHIFT in Microsoft Excel for Windows or COMMAND in Microsoft Excel for the Macintosh, and click the name of each worksheet.

4   Choose the OK button.

The word "Group" appears within brackets after the worksheet name in each title bar.

Format the group

You will format all of the worksheets at the same time by formatting the active worksheet. Format the row and column labels.

1   Select cells C10:C15 and D10:G10.

2   In the Style box on the Standard toolbar, select the Heading style.

3   Select columns D through F.

4   From the Format menu, choose Column Width.

5   Choose the Best Fit button.

6   Select cells C10:C15.

7   Click the Right Align tool on the Standard toolbar.

Your worksheet should look like the following illustration. In Microsoft Excel for the Macintosh, the filename in the worksheet title bar does not have the .XLS extension.

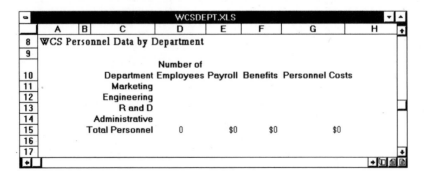

	A	B	C	D	E	F	G	H
8	WCS Personnel Data by Department							
9								
10			Department	Number of Employees	Payroll	Benefits	Personnel Costs	
11			Marketing					
12			Engineering					
13			R and D					
14			Administrative					
15			Total Personnel	0	$0	$0	$0	
16								
17								

The Fill Group command Once you create a group, you can also use the Fill Group command to copy the contents of a cell in the active sheet to the other worksheets.

End the group editing session

You are finished working with the group. To end the group editing session, switch to another worksheet. Use the paging buttons to switch to the PRINTER worksheet.

▶ Click the left paging button.

The worksheets are no longer part of a group. You can now work with each worksheet individually.

Consolidating Data from Multiple Worksheets

You can use consolidation to summarize data from several worksheets into one worksheet. For example, you can take the sales figures for several products from separate worksheets, add them together, and display the totals in another worksheet. When you choose the Consolidate command from the Data menu, Microsoft Excel consolidates the source ranges you specify.

The Consolidate command You can use the Consolidate command to summarize data from several *source* areas into a *destination* area. You can use 11 different functions, including AVERAGE, COUNT, MAX, and SUM, to consolidate data into the destination area.

In Microsoft Excel, you can consolidate data by category as well as by position.

Consolidating by category of data You consolidate data by category when the source areas are in different locations but contain similar data. To consolidate by category, you select the Top Row check box or the Left Column check box if there are category labels in the top row or the left column of the source areas. You can select both check boxes for a single consolidation.

If the worksheets you want to consolidate are in a workbook and you want to consolidate by position, you can use 3-D formulas to consolidate your data.

Consolidating by position of data You consolidate data by position when the source worksheets are created from identical templates and the data to be consolidated is located in the same cells in each worksheet. For example, individual expense reports created from the same template can be consolidated by position into a destination worksheet.

Creating links to source data You can create links to source data by choosing the Consolidate command from the Data menu and selecting the Create Links To Source Data check box. When you create links to source data, Microsoft Excel also creates a linking formula for each cell, inserting rows and columns in your destination area to hold the linking formulas. Microsoft Excel creates an outline and subordinates the source data references in the destination area. Make sure that the inserted rows and columns for the linked source data do not disrupt or shift data in other parts of your worksheet.

Consolidate the data by department

With the WCSDEPT worksheet active, you'll choose the Consolidate command from the Data menu and define source areas for consolidation on the COPIER, FAX, and PRINTER worksheets.

1 Click the right paging button to switch to the WCSDEPT worksheet.

2 Select cells C10:G14.

3 From the Data menu, choose Consolidate.

4 Move to the Reference box.

5 With the Data Consolidate dialog box still open, click the paging button twice to switch to the COPIER worksheet.

6 Select cells C10:G14. You can scroll to see the cells, and you can drag the dialog box by its title bar if it is in your way.

In Microsoft Excel for Windows, COPIER.XLS!$C$10:$G$14 appears in the Reference box. In Microsoft Excel for the Macintosh, COPIER!$C$10:$G$14 appears in the Reference box.

7 Choose the Add button.

8 Repeat steps 5 through 7 for the FAX and PRINTER worksheets.

9 Select the Top Row and Left Column check boxes.

10 Select the Create Links To Source Data check box.

11 Choose the OK button.

You can select cells E10:G27 and set the column width to best fit so that you can see all of your data. Your worksheet should look like the following illustration.

		A	B	C	D	E	F	G	H	
	8	WCS Personnel Data by Department								
	9									
	10	Department				Number of Employees	Payroll	Benefits	Personnel Costs	
⊞	14	Marketing				13	$602,500	$180,750	$783,250	
⊞	18	Engineering				27	$1,209,000	$362,700	$1,571,700	
⊞	22	R and D				9	$409,000	$122,700	$531,700	
⊞	26	Administrative				11	$471,000	$141,300	$612,300	
	27	Total Personnel				60	$2,691,500	$807,450	$3,498,950	
	28									

You created links to the source worksheets. Microsoft Excel consolidated the data in the source areas, inserted references to the source data, and created an outline.

Expand the outline

Expand the outline to examine the detail.

▶ Click the row level 2 button.

Notice that rows 11, 12, and 13 took on the formatting of row 10. Format these rows to look like the following illustration.

1 2		A	B C D	E	F	G	H	
	10	Department		Number of Employees	Payroll	Benefits	Personnel Costs	
	11		Copier	4	$177,000	$53,100	$230,100	
	12		Fax	2	$105,000	$31,500	$136,500	
	13		Printer	7	$320,500	$96,150	$416,650	
	14	Marketing		13	$602,500	$180,750	$783,250	
	15		Copier	7	$303,500	$91,050	$394,550	
	16		Fax	6	$250,500	$75,150	$325,650	
	17		Printer	14	$655,000	$196,500	$851,500	
	18	Engineering		27	$1,209,000	$362,700	$1,571,700	
	19		Copier	2	$98,000	$29,400	$127,400	
	20		Fax	2	$97,000	$29,100	$126,100	
	21		Printer	5	$214,000	$64,200	$278,200	
	22	R and D		9	$409,000	$122,700	$531,700	
	23		Copier	4	$160,000	$48,000	$208,000	
	24		Fax	3	$132,000	$39,600	$171,600	
	25		Printer	4	$179,000	$53,700	$232,700	
	26	Administrative		11	$471,000	$141,300	$612,300	

Save and close the workbook

1 From the File menu, choose Close All.

2 Choose the Yes button to save your changes in each worksheet.

One Step Further

West Coast Sales issues a consolidated sales report for all products from its two sales regions. Open the 09STEP workbook file to open the 09SALRPT, 09NORTH, and 09SOUTH worksheets.

Rename each worksheet with the Save As command on the File menu, removing the "09" from each name. Use the Group Edit command on the Options menu to create a group; then format the source worksheets. Consolidate the products sold onto the SALRPT worksheet.

1 Open the 09STEP workbook file.

2 Rename each worksheet. The worksheet names should be SALRPT, NORTH, and SOUTH.

3 Create a group containing the SALRPT, NORTH, and SOUTH worksheets.

4 Format cells C13:E13 with the Heading style.

5 Change the column width, if necessary, so that you can see all of the data.

6 End the group editing session.

7 Switch to SALERPT.

8 Select cells C13:E24.

9 From the Data menu, choose Consolidate.

10 Select cells C13:E20 on the NORTH and SOUTH worksheets.

11 Select the Top Row and Left Column check boxes.

12 Choose the OK button.

Your worksheet should look like the following illustration.

	A	B	C	D	E	F
11	Sales Data		Company-Wide Sales Fiscal Year 1993 Qtr 2			
12						
13			Product	Units Sold	Revenues (in thousands)	
14			Compact Printer	39,000	$9,750	
15			Impact Printer	52,500	$7,875	
16			Laser Printer	17,000	$25,500	
17			XL 150 Copier	12,500	$11,875	
18			XL 225 Copier	11,000	$16,500	
19			XL 500 Copier	9,000	$19,800	
20			XL 700 Printer	5,000	$25,000	
21			Letter Printer	23,000	$5,750	
22			XL 100 Copier	13,000	$11,310	
23			XL 250 Copier	15,000	$26,250	
24			XL 300 Copier	11,000	$19,250	
25						

Save and close the worksheets when you are finished.

Lesson Summary

To	Do this
Create an outline on a worksheet	Select an area of a worksheet and choose Outline from the Format menu.
Expand and collapse an outline	Click the expand and collapse buttons to expand and collapse parts of the outline.
Format a group of worksheets at the same time	Create a group with the Group Edit command on the Options menu and then format the active sheet.
Consolidate data from different worksheets	Choose Consolidate from the Data menu to consolidate data from source worksheets into a destination worksheet.

For more information about	See in the *Microsoft Excel User's Guide*
Worksheet outlining	Chapter 8, "Organizing and Documenting a Worksheet," in Book 1
Consolidating data Group editing and formatting	Chapter 11, "Working with Multiple Microsoft Excel Documents," in Book 1

Preview of the Next Lesson

In the next lesson, you'll learn some techniques for analyzing data. You'll use a data table to compare different solutions to an equation, use goal seeking to find a value, and use the What-If macro and Scenario Manager to perform "what-if" analysis.

Analyzing Data

In this lesson, you'll learn how to analyze your worksheet data. Microsoft Excel provides a number of techniques to help you analyze data, including data tables, goal seeking, the What-If macro, Microsoft Excel Solver, and Scenario Manager. You can use these tools to conduct "what-if" analysis. With what-if analysis, you can substitute different input data in your worksheet formulas and compare the results.

You will learn how to:

- Compare different solutions to an equation using a data table.
- Find a value using goal seeking.
- Test different values using the What-If add-in macro.
- Save different groups of values using Scenario Manager.

Estimated lesson time: 45 minutes

Start the lesson

The 10LESSN workbook contains two worksheets. The 10LESSNA worksheet contains the information you need to complete a one-input data table, and the 10LESSNB worksheet contains the information you need to create a two-input data table.

1 Open the 10LESSN workbook file.

2 If the 10LESSNA worksheet is not in the active window, switch to it.

3 Save the 10LESSNA worksheet as ONEINPUT.

Using Data Tables

The Table command is like /Data Table 1 or /Data Table 2 in 1-2-3, except that data tables in Microsoft Excel are recalculated when you change the source data.

Once you have entered formulas on your worksheet, you may want to perform "what-if" analysis to see how changing certain values in your formulas affects the results of the formulas. *Data tables* can provide a shortcut for calculating all of the variations in one operation.

A data table is a range of cells that shows the results of substituting different values in one or more formulas. There are two types of data tables: one-input tables and two-input tables. With a one-input table, you enter different values for one variable and see the effect on one or more formulas. With a two-input table, you enter different values for two variables and see the effect on one formula.

Using a One-Input Data Table

You will use a one-input data table to calculate mortgage loan payments based on different interest rates.

Enter the formula for the data table

1   In cell C8, type **=PMT(Interest_Rate/12,Number_of_Months,–Loan_Amount)**

2   Click the enter box or press ENTER.

Your worksheet should look like the following illustration.

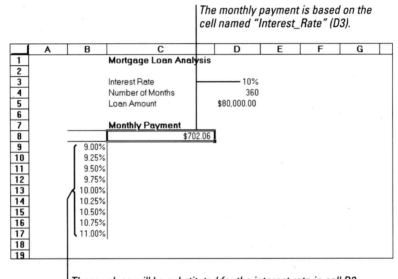

The monthly payment is based on the cell named "Interest_Rate" (D3).

These values will be substituted for the interest rate in cell D3.

The PMT function returns the monthly payment of $702.06, based on a 10-percent interest rate.

You will set up a data table so that the interest rates in column B (the *input values*) will be substituted in cell D3 (the *input cell*) and the resulting monthly payments will be entered in the cells below the formula in cell C8. When the input values are in a column, as in this case, you enter the formula that refers to the input cell in the row above the first input value and one cell to the right of the column of input values. This is why you entered your formula in cell C8. If the input values are in a row, you enter the formula one cell below and to the left of them.

Fill in the one-input data table

1   Select cells B8:C17.

2   From the Data menu, choose Table.

3   In the Column Input Cell box, type **Interest_Rate**

The input values are in a column. "Interest_Rate" refers to cell D3.

4   Choose the OK button.

Your worksheet should look like the following illustration.

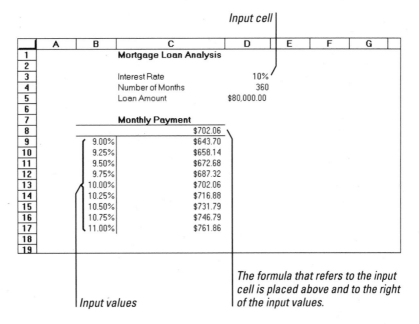

Input cell

	A	B	C	D	E	F	G
1			Mortgage Loan Analysis				
2							
3			Interest Rate	10%			
4			Number of Months	360			
5			Loan Amount	$80,000.00			
6							
7			Monthly Payment				
8			$702.06				
9		9.00%	$643.70				
10		9.25%	$658.14				
11		9.50%	$672.68				
12		9.75%	$687.32				
13		10.00%	$702.06				
14		10.25%	$716.88				
15		10.50%	$731.79				
16		10.75%	$746.79				
17		11.00%	$761.86				
18							
19							

Input values

The formula that refers to the input cell is placed above and to the right of the input values.

Microsoft Excel substitutes the values in cells B9:B17 in the input cell and fills in the table with the results of the formulas.

Add a formula to an existing data table

The preceding example shows how to use a one-input data table to see the effect of changing interest rates on a single formula. To see the effect of changing interest rates on more than one formula, you will add a formula to the existing one-input data table. This formula totals the interest paid over the life of the loan.

1 In cell D8, type =(**C8*Number_of_Months**)–**Loan_Amount**

2 Click the enter box or press ENTER.

Microsoft Excel calculates the total interest paid based on a 10-percent interest rate.

3 Select cells B8:D17.

4 From the Data menu, choose Table.

5 In the Column Input Cell box, type **Interest_Rate**

6 Choose the OK button.

Microsoft Excel substitutes each value in the input cell and fills in the table with the results of the formulas.

7 Format your worksheet as shown in the following illustration.

This cell calculates the total interest. It refers to cell C8, which refers to cell D3 (the input cell).

	A	B	C	D	E	F	G
1			Mortgage Loan Analysis				
2							
3			Interest Rate	10%			
4			Number of Months	360			
5			Loan Amount	$80,000.00			
6							
7			Monthly Payment	Interest Paid			
8			$702.06	$172,740.61			
9		9.00%	$643.70	$151,731.31			
10		9.25%	$658.14	$156,930.52			
11		9.50%	$672.68	$162,166.01			
12		9.75%	$687.32	$167,436.47			
13		10.00%	$702.06	$172,740.61			
14		10.25%	$716.88	$178,077.17			
15		10.50%	$731.79	$183,444.92			
16		10.75%	$746.79	$188,842.63			
17		11.00%	$761.86	$194,269.14			
18							
19							

8 Save the ONEINPUT worksheet.

Using a Two-Input Data Table

If you want to see how changes in two variables affect one formula, use a two-input data table. You will see how your monthly payment changes depending on both the interest rate and the term of the loan. The 10LESSNB worksheet contains the information you need to complete the two-input data table.

Set up a two-input data table

1 Switch to the 10LESSNB worksheet.

2 Save the worksheet as TWOINPUT.

3 In cell A8, type =PMT(Interest_Rate/12,Number_of_Months,–Loan_Amount)

4 Click the enter box or press ENTER.

You will set up a data table so that interest rates entered in column A will be substituted in one input cell (E3) and loan terms entered in row 8 will be substituted in a second input cell (E4), as in the following illustration. The resulting monthly payments will be entered in the cells below row 8 and to the right of column A when you calculate the table using the Table command on the Data menu.

Column input cell   _Row input cell_

	A	B	C	D	E		F	G	H	
1			Mortgage Loan Analysis							
2										
3			Interest Rate		10%					
4			Number of Months		360					
5			Loan Amount		$80,000.00					
6										
7										
8	$702.06	180	240	300	360		420	480		
9	9.00%									
10	9.25%									
11	9.50%									
12	9.75%									
13	10.00%									
14	10.25%									
15	10.50%									
16	10.75%									
17	11.00%									
18										
19										

These values will be substituted in cell E3.   _These values will be substituted in cell E4._

Fill in a two-input data table

1 Select cells A8:G17.

2 From the Data menu, choose Table.

3 In the Row Input Cell box, type **Number_of_Months**

The values for the number of months are in a row. "Number_of_Months" refers to cell E4.

4 In the Column Input Cell box, type **Interest_Rate**

The values for the interest rate are in a column. "Interest_Rate" refers to cell E3.

5 Choose the OK button.

Microsoft Excel substitutes each value in the input cells and fills in the table with the results of the formulas.

Your two-input data table should look like the following illustration.

	A	B	C	D	E	F	G	H
1			Mortgage Loan Analysis					
2								
3			Interest Rate		10%			
4			Number of Months		360			
5			Loan Amount		$80,000.00			
6								
7								
8	$702.06	180	240	300	360	420	480	
9	9.00%	$811.41	$719.78	$671.36	$643.70	$627.19	$617.09	
10	9.25%	$823.35	$732.69	$685.11	$658.14	$642.20	$632.53	
11	9.50%	$835.38	$745.70	$698.96	$672.68	$657.29	$648.05	
12	9.75%	$847.49	$758.81	$712.91	$687.32	$672.47	$663.65	
13	10.00%	$859.68	$772.02	$726.96	$702.06	$687.74	$679.32	
14	10.25%	$871.96	$785.31	$741.11	$716.88	$703.08	$695.05	
15	10.50%	$884.32	$798.70	$755.35	$731.79	$718.51	$710.86	
16	10.75%	$896.76	$812.18	$769.67	$746.79	$734.00	$726.72	
17	11.00%	$909.28	$825.75	$784.09	$761.86	$749.57	$742.64	
18								
19								

6 Save the TWOINPUT worksheet.

7 From the File menu, choose Close All.

Remember to hold down SHIFT to choose Close All.

8 Choose the No button so that you don't save changes to the workbook.

Editing a Data Table

You can edit the input values or formulas in the top row or the left column of a data table. Microsoft Excel recalculates the table after you edit any cells that affect the table results.

Because the resulting values in a data table are an *array*, you cannot edit them individually. If you try to edit the data table values, Microsoft Excel displays a message telling you that you cannot change part of a table. If you want to edit data table results, you can convert the results into a range of constant values. Use the Values option in the Paste Special dialog box.

You can also copy values from a data table. When you do this, only the values are copied, not the formulas for those values. To recalculate, move, or delete a table, you must first select the entire table, including the formulas and the input values.

You cannot clear individual values in a data table; you must clear all of the values. Make sure not to select the formulas and the input values. If these are selected, Microsoft Excel clears the entire table, including the formulas and the input values.

Goal Seeking

In this exercise, you will use the West Coast Sales budget worksheet you have used in previous lessons.

Open the worksheet

1   Open the 10LESSNC worksheet.

2   Save the worksheet as ANALYZE.

The Goal Seek command   You can use the Goal Seek command to find the values that a formula needs to reach a specific value. When you use goal seeking, Microsoft Excel varies the value in a cell you specify until a formula dependent on that cell returns the value you want.

The ANALYZE worksheet contains a summary of revenue, cost of goods sold (COGS), gross profit, expenses, and operating income. You can use goal seeking to find out how much the rate of sales must increase in order to increase operating income to a specific value. The connection between rate of sales growth and operating income involves several formulas. The growth formulas determine future sales and COGS. Sales and shipping determine gross revenue. Gross revenue and COGS determine gross profit. Gross profit and expenses determine operating income. Microsoft Excel will recalculate all of the interconnecting formulas each time it varies the rate of sales growth until the operating income reaches the value you specify.

Seek a specific solution to a formula

You will use the Goal Seek command on the Formula menu to find the rate of sales growth that will increase operating income from $47,114 to $60,000.

1   Select cell I32, the cell containing total projected operating income.

2   From the Formula menu, choose Goal Seek.

Microsoft Excel assumes that you want to change the value of cell I32.

3   In the To Value box, type **60000**

4   Move to the By Changing Cell box.

5   Click cell E24.

6   Choose the OK button to seek a solution.

7   Choose the OK button to change the value in cell E24.

Your worksheet should look like the following illustration.

Microsoft Excel changes the value of this cell...

	C	D	E	F	G	H	I	J
22				Travel and Entertainment	$200			
23		**Monthly Growth**		Taxes and Licenses	$240			
24		Sales Growth	2.03%	Interest	$800			
25		COGS Increase	0.90%					
26								
27			Qtr1	Qtr2	Qtr3	Qtr4	FY 93 Plan	
28		**Gross Revenue**	$99,649	$105,851	$112,440	$119,438	$437,378	
29		**Cost of Goods Sold**	$58,471	$60,064	$61,700	$63,381	$243,617	
30		**Gross Profit**	$41,178	$45,787	$50,739	$56,057	$193,761	
31		**Expenses**	$33,397	$33,266	$33,611	$33,486	$133,761	
32		**Operating Income**	$7,781	$12,521	$17,128	$22,571	$60,000	
33								

...until this cell reaches $60,000.

8   Save the ANALYZE worksheet.

In order for operating income to reach $60,000, sales must increase by 2.03 percent each month. Now you will learn how to answer "what-if" questions by changing several variables at once.

Using the What-If Add-In Macro

In order for West Coast Sales to achieve its desired increase in sales, it must increase advertising or hire another salesperson, or both. The What-If macro can show how different combinations of these expenses affect operating income.

The What If command   You use the What If command on the Formula menu to start the What-If add-in macro. With the What-If macro, you can perform what-if analysis by creating or specifying a *data sheet* for your worksheet model. A data sheet is a worksheet on which you save a collection of input values that you want to substitute in your worksheet cells. You can then have Microsoft Excel calculate your worksheet for every possible combination of values stored on the data sheet.

Create a data sheet

You will use the What If command on the Formula menu to create a data sheet that contains advertising costs of $4000, $5000, and $6000 and salary costs of $4700 and $7700. Advertising will be "variable #1," and salaries will be "variable #2."

1   In Microsoft Excel for Windows, switch to the LIBRARY directory, located in the same directory as Microsoft Excel, and open the file WHATIF.XLA.

In Microsoft Excel for the Macintosh, switch to the LIBRARY folder, located in the same folder as Microsoft Excel, and open the file WHAT IF.

If the Macro library is not installed, rerun the Setup program to install it.

2   From the Formula menu, choose What If.

3   Choose the New button to create a new data sheet.

4   In the Reference Of Variable #1 box, type **Advertising**.

"Advertising" refers to cell G14.

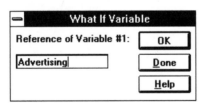

5   Choose the OK button.

6   In the Value #1 For Advertising box, type **4000**

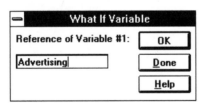

7 Choose the OK button.

8 In the Value #2 For Advertising box, type **5000** and then choose the OK button.

9 In the Value #3 For Advertising box, type **6000** and then choose the OK button.

10 Choose the Done button.

11 In the Reference Of Variable #2 box, type **Salaries** and then choose the OK button. "Salaries" refers to cell G15.

12 In the Value #1 For Salaries box, type **4700** and then choose the OK button.

13 In the Value #2 For Salaries box, type **7700** and then choose the OK button.

14 Choose the Done button.

15 Choose the Done button again to create the data sheet.

Microsoft Excel creates a new worksheet that the What-If macro will use as its data sheet. The data sheet is not in the active window, so your screen does not change.

View the data sheet

▶ Switch to the data sheet.

The name that Microsoft Excel gives to the data sheet varies, but it should be the only other open document. Your data sheet should look like the following illustration.

	A	B	C	D	E
1		2	Advertising	Salaries		
2			1	1	
3			4000	4700	
4			5000	7700	
5			6000		
6					
7					
8					
9					
10					

The What-If macro will substitute these values for Advertising and Salaries.

Editing a data sheet Once you have created a data sheet, you can change or add input values. To add an input value, insert the new input value in the column of values for that variable.

Specify the data sheet

The What-If macro needs to know where to get the data that it will substitute in your worksheet. You will specify the data sheet you just created.

1 Switch to the ANALYZE worksheet.

2 From the Formula menu, choose What If.

3 In the Data Sheet box, select the name of the data sheet you just created.

4 Choose the OK button.

Now you will see how to substitute these values in the ANALYZE worksheet. You can cycle through the variables all at once or one variable at a time.

Cycle through all of the variables at once

You will substitute new values for Advertising and Salaries at the same time. You will split the worksheet window into two panes so that you can see how different values for advertising and salaries affect operating income.

1 Drag the split box to split the worksheet window into panes, and scroll the panes so that your worksheet looks like the following illustration.

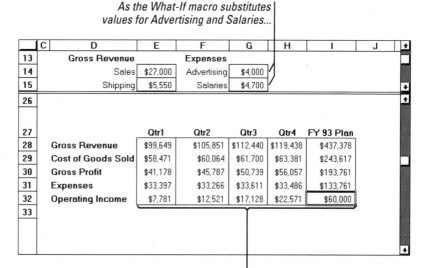

As the What-If macro substitutes values for Advertising and Salaries...

	C	D	E	F	G	H	I	J	
13		Gross Revenue		Expenses					
14		Sales	$27,000	Advertising	$4,000				
15		Shipping	$5,550	Salaries	$4,700				
26									
27			Qtr1	Qtr2	Qtr3	Qtr4	FY 93 Plan		
28		Gross Revenue	$99,649	$105,851	$112,440	$119,438	$437,378		
29		Cost of Goods Sold	$58,471	$60,064	$61,700	$63,381	$243,617		
30		Gross Profit	$41,178	$45,787	$50,739	$56,057	$193,761		
31		Expenses	$33,397	$33,266	$33,611	$33,486	$133,761		
32		Operating Income	$7,781	$12,521	$17,128	$22,571	$60,000		
33									

...Microsoft Excel recalculates the rest of the worksheet.

2 In Microsoft Excel for Windows, press CTRL+SHIFT+T.

In Microsoft Excel for the Macintosh, press COMMAND+OPTION+SHIFT+T.

Microsoft Excel substitutes the first Advertising value, 4000, which is the same as the value that was already there, so you will not see a change on the worksheet.

3 Press CTRL+SHIFT+T (or COMMAND+OPTION+SHIFT+T) again.

Microsoft Excel substitutes the next Advertising value and recalculates the summary table.

4 Press CTRL+SHIFT+T (or COMMAND+OPTION+SHIFT+T) until the value in cell I32 reaches zero.

Microsoft Excel cycles through all of the combinations of Advertising and Sales values.

Cycle through one variable at a time

Now you will substitute new values for Advertising while Salaries remains constant, and you will substitute new values for Salaries while Advertising remains constant.

1 Select cell G14.

2 In Microsoft Excel for Windows, press CTRL+T, watching the values change each time.

In Microsoft Excel for the Macintosh, press COMMAND+OPTION+T.

Microsoft Excel cycles through the Advertising values.

3 Select cell G15.

4 Press CTRL+T (or COMMAND+OPTION+T) two times, watching the values change each time.

Microsoft Excel cycles through the Salaries values.

5 Repeat steps 1 through 4, setting Advertising back to $4000 and Salaries back to $4700.

  6 Save the ANALYZE worksheet.

In the next exercise, you will learn how to save each combination of Advertising and Salaries values as a scenario.

Using Scenario Manager to Analyze Data

The Scenario Manager command The Scenario Manager command on the Formula menu starts Scenario Manager. With Scenario Manager, you can create and save *scenarios,* which are sets of input data that produce different results. For example, in the preceding exercise, each time you cycled through a set of values for Advertising and Salaries, you were analyzing a different scenario. With Scenario Manager, you can create, name, and save multiple scenarios, and you can view the results of each scenario in your worksheet. You can also create a report that provides a summary of all of the input values and results from the scenarios you have created.

When to use Scenario Manager and the What-If macro Use the What-If macro when you need to cycle through values quickly or share a data sheet among multiple worksheets. Use Scenario Manager when you need to save multiple scenarios as part of your worksheet or when you need to create a report containing your scenarios.

Create a scenario

You will use Scenario Manager to create and name three scenarios of Advertising and Salaries values.

1   From the Formula menu, choose Scenario Manager.

> **Note**   If the Scenario Manager command does not appear on the Formula menu, rerun the Setup program to install Scenario Manager. For more information about adding or removing add-in macros, see "Managing Add-in Commands and Functions" in Chapter 4 in Book 2 of the *Microsoft Excel User's Guide*.

2   In the Changing Cells box, type **Advertising,Salaries**

"Advertising" refers to cell G14, and "Salaries" refers to cell G15. You could also type the cell references or select the cells on the worksheet.

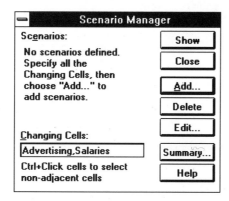

3   Choose the Add button.

The Add Scenario dialog box appears, displaying the current input values for the changing cells.

4   In the Name box, type **Lowest Cost**

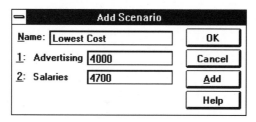

5   Choose the Add button.

6   In the Name box, type **Moderate Cost**

7   In the 1:Advertising and 2:Salaries boxes, type **5000** and **7700,** respectively.

8   Choose the Add button.

9   In the Name box, type **Highest Cost**

10   In the 1:Advertising and 2:Salaries boxes, type **6000** and **7700,** respectively.

11   Choose the OK button and then the Close button.

Your three scenarios are added to the scenario list.

Show a scenario

You will use Scenario Manager to show the scenarios you created in the preceding steps.

1 From the Formula menu, choose Scenario Manager.

2 In the Scenarios box, select Moderate Cost.

3 Choose the Show button.

Microsoft Excel substitutes the values from the Moderate Cost scenario in your worksheet. Your worksheet should look like the following illustration. You may have to move the Scenario Manager dialog box to see the summary of operating income.

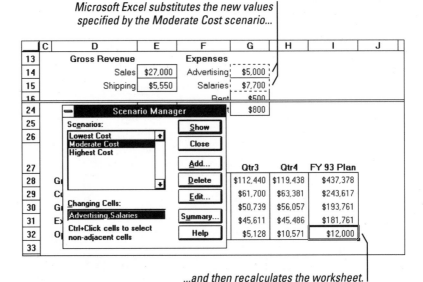

Microsoft Excel substitutes the new values specified by the Moderate Cost scenario...

...and then recalculates the worksheet.

4 Choose the Close button.

5 Save the ANALYZE worksheet.

Editing a scenario   Once you have created a scenario, you can change or add input values. In the Scenario box, select the name of the scenario you want to edit, and then choose the Edit button. To add an input value, insert the new input value in the column of values for that variable.

In the "One Step Further" exercise at the end of this lesson, you will use Scenario Manager to create a summary report of the scenarios you have created.

Using Microsoft Excel Solver

Microsoft Excel Solver is a utility for finding solutions to formulas that have multiple variables and multiple constraints. Microsoft Excel Solver can solve or optimize formulas that involve both linear and nonlinear equations and inequalities.

Microsoft Excel Solver and Scenario Manager can work together. The changing cells you specify with the Scenario Manager command on the Formula menu will be suggested automatically as the changing cells in Solver, and vice versa. Solver can save its solutions as scenarios for display in Scenario Manager. Scenario Manager can also be used to set up initial cell values for Solver's solution process.

Microsoft Excel Step by Step does not include a lesson on Solver, so you may want to go through the tutorial lesson "Learning to Use Microsoft Excel Solver" in Chapter 2 in Book 2 of the *Microsoft Excel User's Guide*.

One Step Further

You can create a report that lists the scenarios you created, showing their input values and any *result cells* that you want to display. A result cell is any cell on your worksheet that is recalculated when you apply a new scenario. Microsoft Excel creates the summary report on a separate worksheet.

In this exercise, you will use Scenario Manager to add one more scenario and then create a summary report, specifying the cell containing total operating income (cell I32) as the result cell. You will then print the report.

1   From the Formula menu, choose Scenario Manager.

2   Add a scenario named "High Advertising."

3   Enter the values 7000 and 4700 for Advertising and Salaries, respectively.

4   After you've added the scenario, choose the Summary button.

5   In the Result Cells box, type **I32**

6   Choose the OK button.

Your scenario report should look similar to the following illustration.

Scenario Summary Report				
	Lowest Cost	Moderate Cost	Highest Cost	High Advertising
Changing Cells:				
Advertising	$4,000	$5,000	$6,000	$7,000
Salaries	$4,700	$7,700	$7,700	$4,700
Result Cells:				
$I$32	$60,000	$12,000	$0	$24,000

7   Print the scenario.

8   Save the ANALYZE worksheet and close all open documents.

You can save the data sheet and summary report with new names if you want, but you will not need them for other lessons.

Lesson Summary

To solve "what-if" problems using	Do this
Data tables	Enter the input values in a row or column. Enter a formula above and to the right of the input values (if they are in a column) or below and to the left of them (if they are in a row). If you are using a two-input table, the formula is placed at the intersection of the row and column of input values. This formula depends on an input cell. Select the range of cells containing the input values, the formula, and room for the calculated values, and then choose the Table command from the Data menu. When prompted, enter the name or reference of the row or column input cell.
Goal seeking	Select the cell containing the formula that you want to reach a specific value. This formula must depend on the values in one or more variable cells. Choose the Goal Seek command from the Formula menu, and specify the variable cell whose value you want to change in order to reach your goal.
The What-If add-in macro	Choose the What If command from the Formula menu. Specify a data sheet or create a new one. If you create a new one, specify the cells you want to vary and the values that will be substituted in those cells. When the variable information has been entered, you can cycle through the variables. In Microsoft Excel for Windows, press CTRL+SHIFT+T to cycle through all variables at once or CTRL+T to cycle through one variable at a time. In Microsoft Excel for the Macintosh, press COMMAND+OPTION+SHIFT+T to cycle through all variables at once or COMMAND+OPTION+T to cycle through one variable at a time.
Scenario Manager	Add one or more scenarios to the list of scenarios by choosing Scenario Manager from the Formula menu and specifying which cells to vary and what the values in those cells should be. You must also name the scenario.

For more information about	See in the *Microsoft Excel User's Guide*
Data tables	Chapter 1, "Analyzing and Calculating Data," in Book 2
Changing data table results to constant values	"Creating and Using an Array Formula" in Chapter 5 in Book 1
Goal seeking, the What-If add-in macro, and Scenario Manager	Chapter 2, "Performing What-If Analysis on a Worksheet Model," in Book 2
Microsoft Excel Solver	"Putting Microsoft Excel Solver to Work" in Chapter 2 in Book 2
Other analysis tools	"Analyzing Statistical or Engineering Data" in Chapter 1 in Book 2

Preview of the Next Lesson

In the next lesson, you will learn how to print a document. You will learn how to change your printer settings, preview a document on the screen, and print a Microsoft Excel document.

Part

4 Printing

Setting Up the Page and Printing

In this lesson, you'll print the BUDGET worksheet. First you'll preview the worksheet to see how it would look if you printed it right away. Then you'll change the page layout, add a header to the page, specify what part of the worksheet you want to print, and specify titles to be printed on every page. After you make these changes, you'll preview the worksheet again before printing it. You'll also use the Report Manager to include different scenarios and views of your data in a single report.

You will learn how to:

- Preview a printed worksheet.
- Set up the page layout.
- Print part of a worksheet.
- Specify titles to be printed on every page.
- Create and print a report.

Estimated lesson time: 25 minutes

Start the lesson

1 Open 11LESSN.

2 Save the file as BUDGET.

3 In Microsoft Excel for Windows, choose the OK button to replace the existing file.

   In Microsoft Excel for the Macintosh, choose the Yes button to replace the existing file.

4 Close any other open windows.

5 Enlarge the document window to fill the workspace.

Setting Up the Document for Printing

You use the Page Setup command on the File menu to change printer settings for a single document.

Note In Microsoft Excel for Windows, you can also change printer settings for all of your applications by choosing the Printer Setup button. For more information, see Appendix A, "Installing and Setting Up Your Printer."

The Page Setup command   With the Page Setup command, you can add headers and
footers, change margins, and turn off gridlines and row and column headings so that
they aren't printed. You can also specify settings such as paper orientation (vertical or
horizontal) and paper size. If you have color in your worksheet, you can print colors
in cells as patterns, or you can print the cells in black and white. Other page setup settings allow you to change the page order and fit your print area into a specified page
width and length. In Microsoft Excel for the Macintosh, you can also specify special
printer effects.

Your Page Setup settings are saved with the document. Use Page Setup again when
you want to make a change.

Change the paper orientation

If you print the BUDGET worksheet horizontally (in landscape orientation), you can
print more columns per page. If your printer does not have a setting for landscape
printing, go to the next section, "Previewing the Printed Worksheet."

1   From the File menu, choose Page Setup.

In Microsoft Excel for Windows, the Page Setup dialog box looks like the
following illustration.

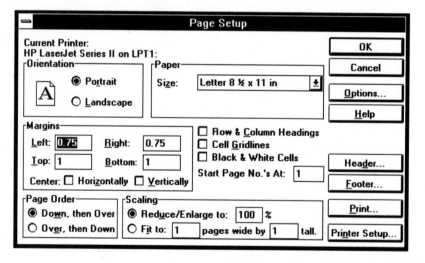

In Microsoft Excel for the Macintosh, the Page Setup dialog box looks like the following illustration.

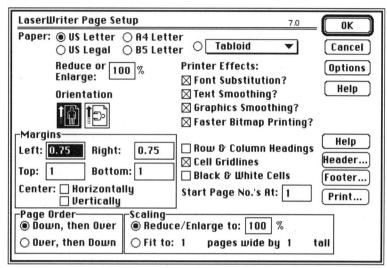

2   Under Orientation, select the Landscape or horizontal option.

3   Change the left and right margins to 1.25.

4   Choose the OK button.

Previewing the Printed Worksheet

You can preview your worksheet on the screen to see how it will look when you print it. By previewing your worksheet first, you can save time and trips to the printer.

The Print Preview command   With the Print Preview command, you can preview a document as it will look when printed. You can change some settings, such as margin and column width, in the preview window. Then you can print the document or return to your document window without printing. You can also preview a document by choosing the Print command from the File menu and selecting the Preview or Print Preview check box.

Preview the printed page

▶ From the File menu, choose Print Preview.

Your worksheet should look like the following illustration.

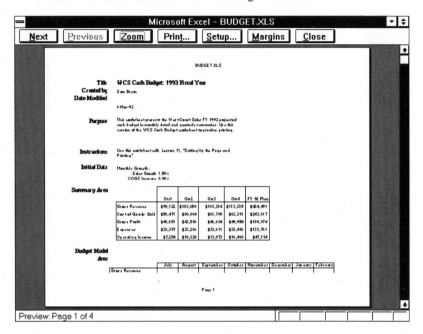

Your worksheet may look slightly different from this, depending on the printer you have selected. The Print Preview command uses the fonts available with your printer.

The Print Preview window   You can use the Zoom, Next, and Previous buttons to look at a part of the page in detail or move to other pages. When you point to the page, the mouse pointer turns into a magnifier. You can click the page with the magnifier to enlarge the page to actual-size view and then click it again to reduce it to the full-page view. Choose the Setup button to change headers, footers, or other settings in the Page Setup dialog box. When you choose the Margins button, the margins and columns appear on your document. You can change margin and column width by dragging the handles.

Setting Up the Page Layout

You can set up the page for printing by changing margins, adding headers and footers, adding print titles, or selecting only the areas on your document that you want to print.

Creating a Header or Footer

You choose the Header or Footer button in the Page Setup dialog box to create headers and footers for your document. When you choose the Header or Footer button in the Page Setup dialog box, the Header or Footer dialog box appears.

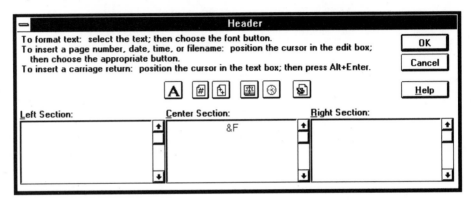

You create a header or footer by typing the text in the Left Section, Center Section, or Right Section text box, depending on where you want the text to appear on your page. You can also enter the page numbers, total pages, date, time, or filename by placing the insertion point where you want the information to appear and then choosing the button corresponding to the type of information you want. To format the text, you select the text you want to format; choose the font button; and apply the font, style, size, or effects that you want.

By default, Microsoft Excel uses the filename as the page header and the page number as the page footer. In the following exercises, you'll create and format a header for the BUDGET worksheet.

Change the header

1   In the Print Preview window, choose the Setup button.

The Page Setup dialog box appears.

2   Choose the Header button.

The Header dialog box appears.

3   In the Center Section box, select "&f".

4   Type **West Coast Sales: FY 1993 Projected Budget**

Note   Don't choose the OK button yet. In the next procedure, you will format the text in the Header dialog box.

Format the header

1 Select the text in the Center Section box.

2 Choose the font button.

3 In Microsoft Excel for Windows, select MS Sans Serif in the Font box.

In Microsoft Excel for the Macintosh, select Helvetica in the Font box.

4 In Microsoft Excel for Windows, select Bold in the Font Style box.

In Microsoft Excel for the Macintosh, select the Bold check box under Style.

5 Choose the OK button in the Font dialog box.

6 Choose the OK button in the Header dialog box.

7 Choose the OK button in the Page Setup dialog box.

8 Choose the Close button to close the print preview window.

Setting the Print Area

The Set Print Area command is like /Print Printer Range in 1-2-3.

Microsoft Excel prints all of your data if you do not specify a print range.

With the Set Print Area command, you can identify the area of the worksheet you want to print. If you don't set a print area, Microsoft Excel prints all of the worksheet that contains data. You can also define nonadjacent selections as the print area.

When you set a print area, Microsoft Excel names your selection Print_Area. To delete the print area, select the entire worksheet and then choose the Remove Print Area command from the Options menu.

Note You can also delete the print area by choosing the Define Name command from the Formula menu, selecting Print_Area in the Names In Sheet box, and then choosing the Delete button.

Select an area of the worksheet to print

Instead of printing the entire worksheet, you will print only the Budget Model Area.

1 Select cells A22:O52.

In Microsoft Excel for Windows, you can also press F5 to choose Goto from the Formula menu, type **a22:o52**, and choose the OK button.

In Microsoft Excel for the Macintosh, you can press COMMAND+G to choose Goto from the Formula menu. Type **a22:o52** and choose the OK button.

2 From the Options menu, choose Set Print Area.

Setting the Print Titles

The Set Print Titles command is like /Print Printer Options Borders in 1-2-3.

With the Set Print Titles command, you can designate row titles and column titles to be printed on each page. The rows you use for column titles or the columns you use for row titles can be anywhere on the worksheet, but the row titles are printed on the left side of a page and the column titles are printed at the top of a page. If your print titles are within the print area, they will only appear once on the page where they first occur.

When you set print titles, Microsoft Excel names your selection Print_Titles. To delete the print titles, choose the Set Print Titles command and delete the references in the Titles For Rows and Titles For Columns boxes.

Note   You can also delete the print titles by choosing the Define Name command from the Formula menu, selecting Print_Titles from the Names In Sheet box, and then choosing the Delete button.

Set columns A through D as the titles for each page

Because all of the Budget Model Area rows fit on one printed page but the columns are printed over two pages, you need to set titles for the rows to be printed on each page. Set columns A through D as the print titles for each page.

1   Select columns A, B, C, and D.

2   From the Options menu, choose Set Print Titles.

$A:$D, meaning columns A through D, appears in the Titles For Rows box.

3   Choose the OK button.

Printing a Worksheet

Now that you've specified how you want the BUDGET worksheet to be printed, you can use the Print command on the File menu or the Print tool on the toolbar to print the document.

The Print command is like /Print Printer Go in 1-2-3.

The Print command   Use the Print command to print your document. In the Print dialog box, you can specify the number of copies and pages to print. You can select the Preview check box in Microsoft Excel for Windows or the Print Preview check box in Microsoft Excel for the Macintosh to display print preview. You can also print the cell notes alone or with the worksheet.

The Print tool   You can also click the Print tool on the toolbar to print your worksheet. When you click the Print tool, the document is immediately printed with the printing and page setup settings you have specified. If you press the SHIFT key when you click the Print tool, the print preview window is displayed.

Preview and print the worksheet

Preview your worksheet once again before printing it.

1 From the File menu, choose Print.

You can also press SHIFT and click the Print tool to display the Print Preview window.

2 Select the Preview check box in Microsoft Excel for Windows or the Print Preview check box in Microsoft Excel for the Macintosh.

3 In Microsoft Excel for Windows, choose the OK button.

In Microsoft Excel for the Macintosh, choose the Print button.

4 Choose the Zoom button or click the worksheet with the magnifier.

Your worksheet should look like the following illustration.

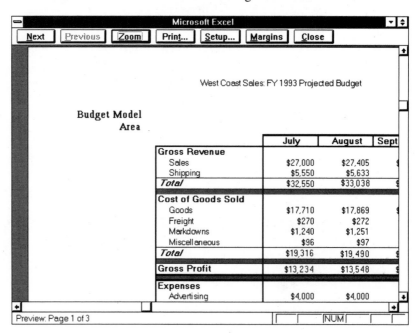

5 Choose the Next button to see the next page.

6 Choose the Print button.

Creating and Printing a Report with the Report Manager

With the Report Manager, you can create reports that include different scenarios and views of your data. You can then edit these reports by changing the scenarios, the views, or the order in which they're presented. Then you can print summary reports containing the scenarios and views that you want.

For more information about creating and naming views of your data, see Lesson 4, "Working with Formatting and Display Features." For more information about creating scenarios of your data, see Lesson 10, "Analyzing Data."

Create a new report

The BUDGET worksheet includes several different views and scenarios. Use these views and scenarios to create a report.

1 From the File menu, choose Print Report.

> **Note** If the Print Report command does not appear on the File menu, rerun the Setup program to install the Report Manager. For more information about adding or removing add-in macros, see "Managing Add-in Commands and Functions" in Chapter 4 in Book 2 of the *Microsoft Excel User's Guide*.

2 Choose the Add button.

The Add Report dialog box appears.

3 In the Report Name box, type **Comparisons**

4 In the View box, select Summary.

5 In the Scenario box, select Projected.

6 Choose the Add button.

The new report section is added to the Current Sections list.

7 In the Scenario box, select Best Case.

8 Choose the Add button.

9 Choose the OK button.

> **Note** In the Add Report and Edit Report dialog boxes, you can use the Move Up and Move Down buttons to change the order of the sections. You can also delete a section by selecting the section and choosing the Delete button. If you want to edit a report, you can select a report from the Reports list, choose the Edit button in the Print Report dialog box, and then make the changes that you want.

Print the report

1   Choose the Print button.

2   Choose the OK button.

Save and close the worksheet

The BUDGET worksheet is complete, so you'll save and close the worksheet. Your page setup settings are saved with the worksheet.

1   Click the Save File tool.

2   From the File menu, choose Close.

Printing a Chart

Printing a chart document is similar to printing a worksheet, except that a chart is always printed on a single page. Also, when a chart is the active document, different options are available in the Page Setup dialog box.

If you print with a one-color printer, Microsoft Excel automatically converts the colors to patterns. Rather than using the default patterns, you may want to use the Patterns command on the Format menu to change the patterns for each data series. That way you'll be better able to distinguish among the different data series. You will learn more about formatting charts in Lesson 14, "Creating and Formatting a Chart."

Printing Worksheet Data and a Chart Together

If you want to print worksheet data and a chart on the same page, you can use the ChartWizard tool on the toolbar to create a chart right on the worksheet. You will learn more about embedding charts in worksheets in Lesson 14, "Creating and Formatting a Chart."

Lesson Summary

To	Do this
Preview a printed worksheet	Use the Print Preview command on the File menu to preview a worksheet before printing it.
Set up the page layout	Use the Page Setup command on the File menu to change the headers on your page, the margins, and the paper orientation for your printed worksheet.
Print part of a worksheet	Use the Set Print Area command on the Options menu to specify a section of a worksheet to be printed.
Specify titles to be printed on every page	Use the Set Print Titles command on the Options menu to specify column or row titles to be printed on each page.
Create and print a report	Use the Print Report command on the File menu to create and print a report.

For more information about	See in the *Microsoft Excel User's Guide*
Setting up your pages and printing	Chapter 16, "Printing," in Book 1
Adding or removing add-in macros	"Managing Add-in Commands and Functions" in Chapter 4 in Book 2

Preview of the Next Lesson

In the next part of this book, you will learn about Microsoft Excel databases. You can set up a database on your worksheet and use it for analyzing your worksheet data. In the next lesson, you will define a database on a worksheet and use the data form to find, add, and delete records.

Setting Up a Database

In this lesson, you'll learn how to set up a database on your worksheet. You'll open the data form and set criteria for viewing certain records. You'll see how a database can help you to manage and analyze data on your worksheet.

In this lesson, you will create a database of personnel records for the WCS Copier Division. You will use this database to add, change, find, sort, and delete records.

You will learn how to:

- Define a database on a worksheet.
- Use the data form to add and change database records.
- Sort data in a database.
- Use the data form to set criteria for selecting database records.
- Use criteria to find database records.
- Delete database records.

Estimated lesson time: 40 minutes

Start the lesson

The 12LESSNA workbook file includes two worksheets: 12COPYRC and 12LESSNB, which you will rename PERSONNL. You will create a worksheet database on PERSONNL and then copy records to it from 12COPYRC.

1 Open the 12LESSNA workbook file.

2 Switch to the 12LESSNB worksheet.

3 Save the worksheet as PERSONNL.

Now you're ready to set up a database on your worksheet.

Setting Up a Database

You can use a database on your worksheet as a tool to organize, update, retrieve, analyze, and summarize large amounts of information. Microsoft Excel worksheet databases are organized in a tabular form. Each row is a *record* of information, and each column is a *field* of information common to all records. The first row of the database contains the *field names*. The parts of a database are shown in the following illustration.

Field names

	C	D	E	F	G	H
13	Last Name	First Name	Position	Department	Salary	Start Date
14	Albert	Max	Group Assist.	Marketing	$21,888	8/16/89
15	Aruda	Felice	Admin. Assist.	Admin	$22,341	3/19/85
16	Beech	Susan	Senior Engineer	Engineering	$56,854	9/13/84
17	Coyne	Dennis	Software Engineer	Engineering	$39,812	10/15/86
18	Davison	Karen	Unit Mgr.	Admin	$77,305	3/4/78
19	Farley	Sam	Group Mgr.	Marketing	$67,512	6/12/80
20	Fein	Caroline	Engineering Mgr.	Engineering	$71,563	7/5/82
21	Goldberg	Malcolm	Product Marketer	Marketing	$43,222	4/29/87
22	Johnson	Miguel	Senior Engineer	Engineering	$54,898	5/19/86
23	Lempert	Alexandra	Research Scientist	R and D	$41,225	9/18/88
24	Raye	Alice	Group Assist.	Engineering	$23,998	12/10/89
25	Richards	Phillip	Cost Accountant	Admin	$39,875	4/22/88
26	Sargent	Evelyn	Product Marketer	Marketing	$46,096	2/23/85
27	Solomon	Ari	Technician	Engineering	$27,543	11/14/89
28	Wells	Jason	Admin. Assist.	Admin	$24,512	2/26/84
29	White	Jessica	Mechanical Engineer	Engineering	$37,888	10/20/87
30						

Record

Once you have organized a database, you can use it to:

- Find and extract records based on criteria you define.

- Analyze data statistically.

- Sort data alphabetically or numerically, by rows or columns, in ascending or descending order.

- Print data organized for specific purposes.

Planning the Database

Before you create your database, plan it carefully. Start by thinking about the reports you will need to generate from the data. For example, a report might include a list of employee earnings and commissions. Next, decide what type of records you will keep. Each record generally contains information about a single person or event. For example, you might keep a record of each sale. You could use these records to generate a report on earned commissions.

Creating the Fields

Once you decide what types of reports and records you will need, create fields for the categories of data that you will use in the report. Make sure to create fields for the smallest units of data you will be analyzing. For example, rather than including one name field, you could include separate fields for first name and last name. Then you could use the same database to generate a sales report listing sales personnel by last name and to create a form letter addressing each salesperson by first name.

Using computed fields   You can create fields that compute values based on the data in other fields. For example, rather than entering the amount of tax withheld, you can enter a formula that will compute the tax withheld based on gross wages.

Enter the field names

1   On the PERSONNL worksheet, select cells C22:H22.

2   Type the field names, as shown in the following illustration. The first one, "Last Name", has already been entered for you.

	C	D	E	F	G	H
22	Last Name	First Name	Position	Department	Salary	Start Date
23						

Format the field names

Now, format the field names so that you can distinguish them from the database records you will be entering.

▶   In the Style box on the toolbar, select the Heading style.

Enter a database record

You can enter records in a database just as you enter any other data on a worksheet, or you can use the data form. Later in this lesson you will use the data form to enter records in the worksheet. Enter the first record by selecting the cells and typing the information.

1   Select cells C23:H23.

2   Type the record, as shown in the following illustration.

	C	D	E	F	G	H
22	Last Name	First Name	Position	Department	Salary	Start Date
23	Price	David	Chief Scientist	R and D	$57,963	1/9/76
24						

The Set Database command is like /Data Query Input in 1-2-3.

The Set Database command   You define the range of cells you want to use as a database with the Set Database command. Select a cell range that includes the field names and any data records you've entered; then choose Set Database from the Data menu. Microsoft Excel names your selection "Database."

Define the worksheet database

Now that you have entered the field names and one data record, use the Set Database command on the Data menu to define this range as a database.

1 Select cells C22:H24.

When you include a blank row after the last record, you can add more records without redefining the database.

2 From the <u>D</u>ata menu, choose Set Data<u>b</u>ase.

Copy records from another worksheet

To save time, you will copy the remaining personnel records from the 12COPYRC worksheet.

1 Switch to the 12COPYRC worksheet.

2 Select cells C14:H29.

 3 Click the Copy tool.

4 Switch to the PERSONNL worksheet.

5 Select cell C24.

6 From the <u>E</u>dit menu, choose <u>I</u>nsert Paste.

7 Choose the OK button.

With the Insert Paste command, you can paste the copied records and insert new rows to contain them at the same time. Because you included a blank record when you defined the database, the database expands to accommodate the pasted records.

Format the database

1 If necessary, use the <u>N</u>umber command on the Forma<u>t</u> menu to format cell G23 for dollars.

 You can also click the Currency Style tool on the Formatting toolbar.

2 To widen any columns that are too narrow, double-click the column heading boundary.

Using the Data Form

The Form command   You use the Form command to display a dialog box that is arranged as a data entry form for the defined database. In this dialog box, which is called the *data form*, you can add, change, find, or delete records. When you add or delete records in the data form, Microsoft Excel adjusts the range named Database.

Use the data form to enter a record

1 From the <u>D</u>ata menu, choose the F<u>o</u>rm command.

2 Choose the New button to display a blank new record.

3 Type the information shown in the following illustration in all the fields in the data form. After each entry, click the next field or press TAB.

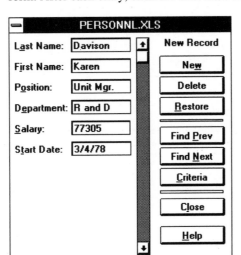

4 Press ENTER to add the record and leave the data form open.

When you add a record by using the data form, Microsoft Excel expands the range named Database to include the new record.

Edit the database with the data form

You can also edit or delete records with the data form. Use the data form to correct the spelling of Caroline Fine's last name.

1 In the data form, use the scroll bar to scroll through the records until Caroline Fein's record appears in the data form.

2 In the Last Name box, type **Fine**

3 Choose the Close button.

The new spelling is reflected in the database range of the worksheet.

Sorting a Database

The Sort command is like /Data Sort in 1-2-3, except that you can also sort columns.

The Sort command   You can use the Sort command to sort database records or other worksheet data. Microsoft Excel sorts the selected records in ascending or descending order according to the contents of a key column, or field, within the selection. You can also use the Sort command whenever you need to sort worksheet data by row or column.

You start sorting database records by selecting the range to be sorted. Make sure that you select only the records and not the field names; otherwise, the field names will be sorted along with the records. Choose the Sort command, specify the sort key (the field you want to sort by), and then choose the Sort button.

With the Sort command, you can sort by three key fields of data at a time. All data is sorted by the first key. The second key sorts records that have identical information in the first key, and the third key sorts records that have identical information in the first two keys.

For example, a three-key sort by department, last name, and first name would sort all records first by department, then by last name within each department, and finally by first name for employees with the same last name, as shown in the following illustration.

	C	D	E	F	G	H	I
13	Last Name	First Name	Position	Department	Salary	Start Date	
14	Aruda	Felice	Admin. Assist.	Admin	$22,341	3/19/85	
15	Richards	Phillip	Cost Accountant	Admin	$39,875	4/22/88	
16	Wells	Jason	Admin. Assist.	Admin	$24,512	2/26/84	
17	Beech	Dennis	Software Engineer	Engineering	$39,812	10/15/86	
18	Beech	Susan	Senior Engineer	Engineering	$56,854	9/13/84	
19	Fine	Caroline	Engineering Mgr.	Engineering	$71,563	7/5/82	

   The Sort tools   If you're sorting by only one field, you can quickly sort the records by selecting them and clicking the Sort Ascending or Sort Descending tool on the Utility toolbar. The column containing the active cell is used as the sort key.

Sort a worksheet database

You will use the Sort Ascending tool on the Utility toolbar to sort the database records. Be sure to include all columns with fields of data; otherwise, the selected fields will be separated from the fields that were not selected. If you make a mistake, click the Undo tool on the Utility toolbar to undo the sort.

1   If the Utility toolbar is not displayed, choose Utility from the toolbar shortcut menu.

2   On the PERSONNL worksheet, select cells C23:H40.

   3   Click the Sort Ascending tool.

The records are sorted by last name in ascending order (from A through Z). Your worksheet should look like the following illustration.

	C	D	E	F	G	H
22	Last Name	First Name	Position	Department	Salary	Start Date
23	Albert	Max	Group Assist.	Marketing	$21,888	8/16/89
24	Aruda	Felice	Admin. Assist.	Admin	$22,341	3/19/85
25	Beech	Susan	Senior Engineer	Engineering	$56,854	9/13/84
26	Coyne	Dennis	Software Engineer	Engineering	$39,812	10/15/86
27	Davison	Karen	Unit Mgr.	R and D	$77,305	3/4/78
28	Farley	Sam	Group Mgr.	Marketing	$67,512	6/12/80
29	Fine	Caroline	Engineering Mgr.	Engineering	$71,563	7/5/82
30	Goldberg	Malcolm	Product Marketer	Marketing	$43,222	4/29/87
31	Johnson	Miguel	Senior Engineer	Engineering	$54,898	5/19/86
32	Lempert	Alexandra	Research Scientist	R and D	$41,225	9/18/88
33	Price	David	Chief Scientist	R and D	$57,963	1/9/76
34	Raye	Alice	Group Assist.	Engineering	$23,998	12/10/89
35	Raye	Alice	Group Assist.	Engineering	$23,998	12/10/89
36	Richards	Phillip	Cost Accountant	Admin	$39,875	4/22/88
37	Sargent	Evelyn	Product Marketer	Marketing	$46,096	2/23/85
38	Solomon	Ari	Technician	Engineering	$27,543	11/14/89
39	Wells	Jason	Admin. Assist.	Admin	$24,512	2/26/84
40	White	Jessica	Mechanical Engineer	Engineering	$37,888	10/20/87
41						

If you will need to return the records to the order in which they were entered, set up the database with an additional field containing a date or number. Sort by this field to return the records to their original sequence.

Sort the records by two key fields

You can use the Sort command to organize the records in different ways. You will now sort the data by department. Within each department, employee records will be sorted in descending order by salary. Employees with the highest salaries within each department will be listed first.

1   With cells C23:H40 still selected, choose <u>S</u>ort from the <u>D</u>ata menu.

2   To enter the first key, select any cell in column F, the Department field.

3   To enter the second key, move to the 2nd Key box and select any cell in column G, the Salary field.

4   Under 2nd Key, select the Descending option button.

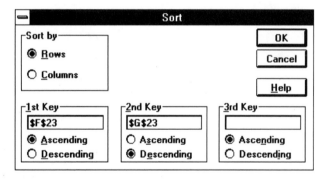

5   Choose the OK button.

The records are sorted in descending order by salary within each department. Your worksheet should look like the following illustration.

	C	D	E	F	G	H
22	**Last Name**	**First Name**	**Position**	**Department**	**Salary**	**Start Date**
23	Richards	Phillip	Cost Accountant	Admin	$39,875	4/22/88
24	Wells	Jason	Admin. Assist.	Admin	$24,512	2/26/84
25	Aruda	Felice	Admin. Assist.	Admin	$22,341	3/19/85
26	Fine	Caroline	Engineering Mgr.	Engineering	$71,563	7/5/82
27	Beech	Susan	Senior Engineer	Engineering	$56,854	9/13/84
28	Johnson	Miguel	Senior Engineer	Engineering	$54,898	5/19/86
29	Coyne	Dennis	Software Engineer	Engineering	$39,812	10/15/86
30	White	Jessica	Mechanical Engineer	Engineering	$37,888	10/20/87
31	Solomon	Ari	Technician	Engineering	$27,543	11/14/89
32	Raye	Alice	Group Assist.	Engineering	$23,998	12/10/89
33	Raye	Alice	Group Assist.	Engineering	$23,998	12/10/89
34	Farley	Sam	Group Mgr.	Marketing	$67,512	6/12/80
35	Sargent	Evelyn	Product Marketer	Marketing	$46,096	2/23/85
36	Goldberg	Malcolm	Product Marketer	Marketing	$43,222	4/29/87
37	Albert	Max	Group Assist.	Marketing	$21,888	8/16/89
38	Davison	Karen	Unit Mgr.	R and D	$77,305	3/4/78
39	Price	David	Chief Scientist	R and D	$57,963	1/9/76
40	Lempert	Alexandra	Research Scientist	R and D	$41,225	9/18/88

If you have a large number of records to sort, you can define a name that refers to database records but not field names. Then you can use the Goto command on the Formula menu to select the records before sorting.

Finding and Deleting Database Records

You can find individual records in your database according to *criteria* that you set. You can set criteria with the data form or with the Set Criteria command on the Data menu. You will use the Set Criteria command in Lesson 13 to set criteria on the worksheet. In the next procedure, you will use the data form to set criteria and find records.

Setting criteria and finding data with the data form   You set criteria by displaying the data form, choosing the Criteria button, and then typing your criteria in the field name boxes. Press ENTER to display the first record that matches your criteria. Choose the Find Prev or Find Next button to display additional records that match your criteria in the data form.

Setting comparison criteria   You can set comparison criteria to find records that match your criteria or fall within the limits you specify. You can enter text strings to match records exactly, or you can use a combination of text strings and operators to set criteria. You can use the following operators.

Operator	Meaning
=	Equal to
>	Greater than
<	Less than
>=	Greater than or equal to
<=	Less than or equal to
<>	Not equal to

To find records in the PERSONNL database, you would enter the following comparison criteria in the data form.

To find	Type
All Marketing Department employees	**Marketing** in the Department box
All employees with salaries greater than $40,000	**>40000** in the Salary box
All employees with salaries less than $50,000	**<50000** in the Salary box
All employees who started on or after 1/1/86	**>=1/1/86** in the Start Date box

To find	Type
All employees who started on or before 4/5/85	**<=4/5/85** in the Start Date box
All employees except for those in the Administrative Department	**<>Admin** in the Department box

Delete a record

A duplicate of Alice Raye's record appears in the worksheet database. You will find and delete the duplicate record.

1   From the Data menu, choose Form.

2   Choose the Criteria button.

3   In the Last Name box, type **Raye**

4   Press ENTER.

The record for Alice Raye appears in the data form.

5   Choose the Find Next button.

The duplicate record is displayed. Alice Raye's records are numbered 10 of 18 and 11 of 18.

6   Choose the Delete button.

A message warns you that the record will be permanently deleted. Deletions cannot be undone.

7   Choose the OK button.

The duplicate record is deleted.

Find records

Find the records for all employees who started working before 1985.

1   Choose the Criteria button.

2   Press BACKSPACE in Microsoft Excel for Windows or DELETE in Microsoft Excel for the Macintosh to delete "Raye" from the Last Name box.

3   In the Start Date field, type **<1/1/1985**

This will find all the employees who started working before January 1, 1985.

4   Press ENTER.

The record for Karen Davison appears in the data form.

5   Choose the Find Next button until you hear a beep.

This means that the last record has been reached. Microsoft Excel starts finding records where it left off after the last search, in which you deleted a duplicate record for Alice Raye. You need to choose Find Prev to view the records at the beginning of the database.

6   Choose the Find Prev button until you've seen all the matching records.

7   Choose the Close button to close the data form.

Save and close the worksheets

Save and close the worksheets. You will use different worksheets for the "One Step Further" exercise.

1   Click the Save File tool.

2   From the File menu, choose Close All.

Remember to hold down the SHIFT key to choose Close All.

3   Choose the No button; you should not have made any changes in 12COPYRC.

One Step Further

The 12STEP worksheet contains the personnel records for the WCS Printer Division. In this exercise, you will rename the worksheet, define the database, add a record, edit a record, find records, sort the records, and print the database.

1   Open the 12STEP worksheet and rename it PRNTPERS.

2   Select all the records, including the field names.

3   Define the database.

4   Display the data form.

5   Find the record for Stephen Alexi.

6   Change the spelling of his first name to Steven.

7   Change his salary to $65,529.

8   Enter the following new record.

In this field	Type
Last Name	**Chu**
First Name	**Steven**
Position	**Group Admin. Assist.**
Department	**Marketing**
Salary	**22500**
Start Date	**12/6/88**

9   Prepare the database to be sorted by selecting all the records.

10 Sort the records by department and by ascending order of start date.

The employees who have been employed the longest will be listed first.

Your worksheet should look like the following illustration.

	C	D	E	F	G	H
13	**Last Name**	**First Name**	**Position**	**Department**	**Salary**	**Start Date**
14	Hodge	Alex	Unit Mgr.	Admin	$79,148	6/22/79
15	Constance	Burt	Admin. Assist.	Admin	$31,995	5/6/83
16	Price	Ellen	Admin. Assist.	Admin	$29,854	8/1/84
17	Wells	Rose	Cost Accountant	Admin	$38,665	4/15/86
18	McKormick	Brad	Lead Engineer	Engineering	$66,900	12/7/77
19	Silverberg	Jay	Lead Engineer	Engineering	$65,777	10/14/78
20	Alexi	Steven	Lead Engineer	Engineering	$65,529	7/18/80
21	Quan	Karen	Engineering Mgr.	Engineering	$75,462	7/7/83
22	Sofer	Ariel	Senior Engineer	Engineering	$55,765	5/19/84
23	Preston	Liza	Mechanical Engineer	Engineering	$41,525	6/5/84
24	Ferngood	Jules	Senior Engineer	Engineering	$54,332	3/22/85
25	Mann	Alyssa	Mechanical Engineer	Engineering	$37,855	1/20/86
26	Lark	Donald	Software Engineer	Engineering	$41,225	7/12/86
27	Dorfberg	Jeremy	Technician	Engineering	$32,400	2/21/87
28	Cash	Mary	Software Engineer	Engineering	$40,100	9/19/87
29	Plant	Allen	Group Admin. Assist.	Engineering	$23,500	5/23/88
30	Smythe	Leslie	Software Engineer	Engineering	$39,500	10/26/88
31	Petry	Robin	Group Admin. Assist.	Engineering	$22,156	9/6/89
32	Taylor	Ralph	Group Mgr.	Marketing	$74,155	5/7/83
33	Cane	Nate	Product Marketer	Marketing	$56,782	2/3/85
34	Wolf	Hilda	Product Marketer	Marketing	$52,995	3/1/86
35	Seidel	Matt	Product Marketer	Marketing	$47,565	3/30/86

11 Define the database as your print area, and then print the database.

12 Save and close the worksheet.

Lesson Summary

To	Do this
Define a database on a worksheet	Enter the field names. Select the field names and any data in subsequent rows, and then choose the Set Database command from the Data menu.
Use the data form to add and change database records	Choose the Form command from the Data menu. Microsoft Excel automatically uses the database field names as labels for the text boxes in the data form.
Sort data in a database	Select the records on the worksheet and use the Sort command on the Data menu to rearrange their order. You can also click one of the Sort tools on the Utility toolbar.
Find database records using the data form	Choose the Form command from the Data menu. Choose the Criteria button and type the criteria in the field name boxes. Choose the Find Next button to find each matching record.
Delete database records using the data form	Choose the Form command from the Data menu. Scroll to the record you want to delete. Choose the Delete button.

For more information about	See in the *Microsoft Excel User's Guide*
Creating databases	Chapter 9, "Creating and Using a Database on a Worksheet," in Book 1

For an online lesson about	Start the tutorial Learning Microsoft Excel and complete this lesson
Databases	"What Is a Database?"

For information about starting an online tutorial lesson, see "Using the Online Tutorials" in "Getting Ready" earlier in this book.

Preview of the Next Lesson

In the next lesson, you will learn more about using a database. You will set criteria on the worksheet to find, extract, summarize, and analyze database records, and you will use the Microsoft Excel ReportWizard to create database reports.

Database Reporting

In this lesson, you will learn ways to analyze database records. You will learn to set criteria on the worksheet and extract database records that meet your criteria. Then you will analyze your data with database functions and use the Crosstab ReportWizard to summarize your worksheet data.

You will learn how to:

- Set criteria on a worksheet.

- Find records in a database that meet your criteria.

- Find and extract records that meet your criteria.

- Analyze data with database functions.

- Analyze and report database information using the Crosstab ReportWizard.

Estimated lesson time: 45 minutes

Start the lesson

The 13LESSN worksheet includes personnel records for all three WCS divisions.

1 Open 13LESSN.

2 Save the worksheet as WCSPRSNL.

Move the database

In this lesson, you will add criteria, data analysis, and extract areas to the worksheet. You will make room for these areas by inserting columns and moving the Database Area to the right.

1 Close any other open worksheets.

2 From the <u>W</u>indow menu, choose <u>A</u>rrange.

3 Choose the OK button.

4 Select cells A17:L78.

Remember, you can use the Goto command on the Formula menu to select a range of cells.

5 From the <u>E</u>dit menu, choose <u>I</u>nsert.

6 Select the Shift Cells Right option button.

7 Choose the OK button.

When you move a database, you need to redefine it.

8 Select cells O18:U78.

9 From the Data menu, choose Set Database.

10 Use the Column Width command on the Format menu to change the column widths so that you can read the cell contents.

Defining a Criteria Range on a Worksheet

In Lesson 12, you set criteria in the data form to find or delete worksheet records. You can also find and delete records by setting criteria on the worksheet. You can use the worksheet criteria range to extract records or analyze records with database functions.

The Set Criteria command is like /Data Query Criteria in 1-2-3.

The Set Criteria command You define the criteria range with the Set Criteria command. To set up a criteria range, copy the database field names to another area of the worksheet. You can also type the field names, but copying them eliminates the chance of typing errors. Select the field names and the cells in the next row and then choose Set Criteria from the Data menu. Microsoft Excel names your selection "Criteria."

Define the criteria range

You will define a criteria range for finding and extracting records from the worksheet database.

1 Select cells O18:U18, the database field names.

 2 Click the Copy tool.

3 Select cell C18.

4 Press ENTER (not RETURN) to paste the data you copied.

5 Select cells C18:I19.

6 From the Data menu, choose Set Criteria.

You have defined the criteria range. Now you will label the area.

Label the criteria area

1 In cell A17, type **Criteria Area**

2 Click the enter box or press ENTER.

 3 In the Style box on the toolbar, select the Title style.

4 From the Format menu, choose Alignment.

5 Under Horizontal, select the Right option button.

6 Select the Wrap Text check box.

7 Choose the OK button.

Your worksheet should look like the following illustration.

	A	B	C	D	E	F	G	H	
17	Criteria Area								
18			Last Name	First Name	Position	Department	Division	Salary	Sta
19									
20									

Enter criteria

Now you will enter criteria in the worksheet to find all employees in the Engineering Department who earn $40,000 or more per year.

1   Select cell F19, the Department criterion cell.

2   Type **Engineering**

3   Click the enter box or press ENTER.

4   Select cell H19, the Salary criterion cell.

5   Type **>=40000**

6   Click the enter box or press ENTER.

The Criteria Area of your worksheet should look like the following illustration.

	A	B	C	D	E	F	G	H	
17	Criteria Area								
18			Last Name	First Name	Position	Department	Division	Salary	Sta
19						Engineering		>=40000	

You defined the criteria range with the Set Criteria command on the Data menu before you entered the criteria. You can change the criteria in the cells once the criteria range has been defined.

Finding Worksheet Database Records

The Find command is like /Data Query Find in 1-2-3. Press ESC to cancel Find mode, just as in 1-2-3.

The Find command   With the Find command, you can select records in the database range that match the criteria in the criteria range. To select the matching records, press the UP ARROW or DOWN ARROW key or click the scroll arrow. To cancel Find mode, choose Exit Find from the Data menu or press the ESC key. In Microsoft Excel for the Macintosh, you can also press COMMAND+PERIOD to cancel Find mode.

The Delete command is like /Data Query Delete in 1-2-3.

The Delete command   With the Delete command, you can delete from the database all records that match the criteria in the criteria range. You should test your criteria with the Find command on the Data menu before you delete records, because you cannot undo the Delete command.

Find the records that match the criteria

Now you will use the Find command on the Data menu to find the records that match your criteria: employees in the Engineering Department who earn $40,000 or more per year.

1   From the Data menu, choose Find.

Microsoft Excel finds the first record that meets these criteria. Your worksheet should look like the following illustration.

	O	P	Q	R	S	T	U
18	Last Name	First Name	Position	Department	Division	Salary	Start Date
19	Able	Aaron	Admin. Assist.	Admin	Fax	$21,789	4/25/89
20	Albert	Max	Group Admin. Assist.	Marketing	Copier	$21,888	8/16/89
21	Alexi	Steven	Lead Engineer	Engineering	Printer	$65,529	7/18/80
22	Aruda	Felice	Admin. Assist.	Admin	Copier	$22,341	3/19/85
23	Asonte	Tony	Group Admin. Assist.	Engineering	Fax	$21,789	8/18/89
24	Barber	Lisa	Product Marketer	Marketing	Fax	$39,854	4/6/85
25	Barth	Bill	Chief Scientist	R and D	Fax	$56,781	7/11/81
26	Beech	Susan	Senior Engineer	Engineering	Copier	$56,854	9/13/84
27	Berg	Bobby	Engineering Mgr.	Engineering	Fax	$71,534	12/7/82
28	Cane	Nate	Product Marketer	Marketing	Printer	$56,782	2/3/85
29	Cash	Mary	Software Engineer	Engineering	Printer	$40,100	9/19/87
30	Chu	Steven	Group Admin. Assist.	Marketing	Printer	$22,500	12/6/88
31	Constance	Burt	Admin. Assist.	Admin	Printer	$31,995	5/6/83
32	Coyne	Dennis	Software Engineer	Engineering	Copier	$39,812	10/15/86
33	Davison	Karen	Unit Mgr.	Admin	Copier	$77,305	3/4/78
34	Dorfberg	Jeremy	Technician	Engineering	Printer	$32,400	2/21/87
35	Farley	Sam	Group Mgr.	Marketing	Copier	$67,512	6/12/80
36	Ferngood	Jules	Senior Engineer	Engineering	Printer	$54,332	3/22/85
37	Fine	Caroline	Engineering Mgr.	Engineering	Copier	$71,563	7/5/82

2   Click the down scroll arrow to view the remaining matching records.

You can also view the matching records by pressing the arrow keys.

3   From the Data menu, choose Exit Find to end the search for records matching your criteria.

You can also end the search by pressing ESC. In Microsoft Excel for the Macintosh, you can also press COMMAND+PERIOD.

Using wildcard characters   You can use the *wildcard characters,* asterisk (*) and question mark (?), to establish criteria for finding and extracting data. Substitute the asterisk (*) when you want to find a string that is a subset of a larger string. For example, typing ***mgr** as the criterion for the Position field will find the records of employees with titles such as Group Marketing Mgr., Engineering Mgr., and so on. Substitute the question mark (?) for a single character in a text string. For example, if you type **Sm?th** in the Last Name field, Microsoft Excel will find the names Smith and Smyth.

Set criteria to match the records of all engineers

You will change the criteria to find the records of all engineers in the worksheet database. First, clear the existing criteria from the criteria range.

1   Select cells F19:H19.

2   From the Edit menu, choose Clear.

3   Choose the OK button.

4   Select cell E19, the Position criterion.

5   Type ***Engineer**

6   Click the enter box or press ENTER.

The Criteria Area on your worksheet should look like the following illustration.

	C	D	E	F	G	H	I
17							
18	Last Name	First Name	Position	Department	Division	Salary	Start Date
19			*Engineer				
20							

You will use this criterion to extract database records in the next exercise.

Extracting Worksheet Database Records

You can find and copy records from a worksheet database to another cell range called an *extract* range.

The Extract command is like /Data Query Extract in 1-2-3, except that you can either select the output range or define it with the Set Extract command.

The Extract command   With the Extract command, you can copy, or *extract*, the database records that match your criteria into a separate extract range or onto a separate worksheet. You can do this in two ways. You can copy the database field names to your extract range, select the field names, and choose Extract from the Data menu. Or you can define the extract range in advance with the Set Extract command on the Data menu.

The Set Extract command is like /Data Query Output in 1-2-3.

The Set Extract command   If you use the Set Extract command to define the extract range, you don't need to select the extract range every time you extract data. Select the extract range and choose Set Extract from the Data menu, and then choose Extract from the Data menu when you are ready. This command is especially useful if you need to extract data while you are working in another part of a large database.

Extract the records for all engineers

You'll use the criteria set in the previous procedure to find and extract all the records of West Coast Sales engineers. First you will copy the first five field names from the database to the extract range. Don't include the Salary or Start Date field name.

1 Select cells C18:G18.

2 Click the Copy tool.

3 Select cell C23.

4 Press ENTER (not RETURN) to paste the field names.

The pasted field names should still be selected.

5 From the Data menu, choose Extract.

6 Select the Unique Records Only check box.

Microsoft Excel will extract only the first of any duplicate records.

7 Choose the OK button.

Only the data for the fields that you selected is extracted. The Extract command finds all records that match the criteria and copies them to the extract range. Your worksheet should look like the following illustration.

	A	B	C	D	E	F	G
17	**Criteria Area**						
18			Last Name	First Name	Position	Department	Division
19					*Engineer		
20							
21							
22							
23			Last Name	First Name	Position	Department	Division
24			Alexi	Steven	Lead Engineer	Engineering	Printer
25			Beech	Susan	Senior Engineer	Engineering	Copier
26			Berg	Bobby	Engineering Mgr.	Engineering	Fax
27			Cash	Mary	Software Engineer	Engineering	Printer
28			Coyne	Dennis	Software Engineer	Engineering	Copier
29			Ferngood	Jules	Senior Engineer	Engineering	Printer
30			Fine	Caroline	Engineering Mgr.	Engineering	Copier
31			Johnson	Miguel	Senior Engineer	Engineering	Copier
32			Lark	Donald	Software Engineer	Engineering	Printer
33			Lin	Michael	Software Engineer	Engineering	Fax
34			Mann	Alyssa	Mechanical Engineer	Engineering	Printer
35			McKormick	Brad	Lead Engineer	Engineering	Printer
36			North	Roberta	Mechanical Engineer	Engineering	Fax
37			Preston	Liza	Mechanical Engineer	Engineering	Printer
38			Quan	Karen	Engineering Mgr.	Engineering	Printer
39			Silverberg	Jay	Lead Engineer	Engineering	Printer
40			Smythe	Leslie	Software Engineer	Engineering	Printer
41			Sofer	Ariel	Senior Engineer	Engineering	Printer
42			Weston	Sam	Senior Engineer	Engineering	Fax
43			White	Jessica	Mechanical Engineer	Engineering	Copier
44							

Rather than selecting only the field names for the extract range, you can select enough rows to accommodate all the extracted records. Only the cells within the selection are cleared before the records are copied. When you select only the field names, all subsequent rows below the field names are cleared before the records are copied. When you set up your worksheet, you should avoid entering data below databases and extract areas.

Combining criteria   You can also combine criteria. You already used two criteria in a criteria range to select all members of the Engineering Department who earn more than $40,000 per year. If you add a second row to your criteria range, Microsoft Excel finds records that match the criteria in the first row or the second row. You can also combine criteria by entering a field name twice in the criteria range and specifying two criteria for the same field.

Extract records that meet either criterion

A meeting is scheduled for all administrative personnel in the Copier Division. The meeting will include all members of the Administrative Department, but only the group administrative assistants from the other departments within the Copier Division. You need to set up criteria to find employees who are members of the Administrative Department, or whose job title is "Group Admin. Assist."

1   Select cell E19.

2   From the Edit menu, choose Clear.

3   Choose the OK button.

4   In the Criteria Area, type the information included in the following illustration.

	A	B	C	D	E	F	G
17	**Criteria Area**						
18			Last Name	First Name	Position	Department	Division
19						Admin	Copier
20					*Admin		Copier
21							

These criteria will find employees of the Copier Division who belong to the Administrative Department, or whose title includes "Admin."

5   Select cells C18:I20.

6   From the Data menu, choose Set Criteria.

Set the extract range and extract the records

1   Select cells C23:G23.

2   From the Data menu, choose Set Extract.

3   From the Data menu, choose Extract.

4   Choose the OK button.

Your worksheet should look like the following illustration.

	C	D	E	F	G
23	Last Name	First Name	Position	Department	Division
24	Albert	Max	Group Admin.Assist.	Marketing	Copier
25	Aruda	Felice	Admin.Assist.	Admin	Copier
26	Davison	Karen	Unit Mgr.	Admin	Copier
27	Raye	Alice	Group Admin.Assist.	Engineering	Copier
28	Richards	Phillip	Cost Accountant	Admin	Copier
29	Wells	Jason	Admin.Assist.	Admin	Copier
30					

Label the extract area

1   Select cell A22.

2   Type **Extract Area**

3   Click the enter box or press ENTER.

4   From the Style box on the toolbar, select the Title style.

Analyzing Data with Database Functions

Using database functions to summarize information   With database functions such as DSUM, DCOUNT, and DAVERAGE, you can summarize worksheet data from a database. You can use the Paste Function command on the Formula menu to paste a database function into a cell.

The arguments for each database function are the same: (*database, field, criteria*). The *database* argument can be the name Database, another named range, or a reference to a range. The *field* argument can be the field name in quotation marks, the field number, or the cell reference of the field name. The *criteria* argument can be the name Criteria, another named range, or a reference to a range.

Insert rows for an analysis area

Before you analyze the database, you will insert a Data Analysis Area. You will insert a range of cells rather than entire rows to avoid inserting rows between the records in the Database Area, which is out of sight to the right of the Criteria Area and the Extract Area.

1   Select cells A22:G40.

2   From the Edit menu, choose Insert.

3   Select the Shift Cells Down option button.

4   Choose the OK button.

5   Scroll to the right until you can see the database.

You inserted cells to move the Extract Area down, but you did not affect the database.

Use the DSUM function in a formula

You can create a formula that sums the salaries for the employees who meet the criteria.

1 In cells A23 and C25, type and format the labels, as shown in the following illustration.

	A	B	C	D
	Data			
	Analysis			
23	**Area**			
24				
25			Admin Salaries	
26				

2 Select cell D25.

3 From the Formula menu, choose Paste Function.

4 In the Function Category box, select Database.

5 In the Paste Function box, select DSUM.

6 Choose the OK button.

7 Select the *field* argument in the formula bar.

8 Type **"Salary"**

Make sure to type the quotation marks around "Salary".

9 Click the enter box or press ENTER.

10 In the Style box on the toolbar, select the Currency 0 Decimals style.

The total of administrative salaries, $209,919, appears in cell D25.

Change the criterion and calculate all engineer salaries

1 Select cell C25.

2 Type **Engineer Salaries**

3 Click the enter box or press ENTER.

You can drag the column heading boundary to widen the column.

4 Select cells E19:G20.

5 From the Edit menu, choose Clear to clear the criteria from these cells.

6 Choose the OK button.

7 Select cell E19.

8 Type ***Engineer**

9 Click the enter box or press ENTER.

You need to redefine the criteria so as not to include a blank row, which would calculate all salaries.

10 Select cells C18:I19.

11 From the Data menu, choose Set Criteria.

The total of salaries for the Engineering departments in all three divisions, $1,051,305, appears in cell D25.

Analyzing and Reporting Data with the Crosstab ReportWizard

The Crosstab command is like /Data Table 2 in 1-2-3.

The Crosstab command   The Crosstab command starts the Microsoft Excel Crosstab ReportWizard. The ReportWizard is a utility that guides you through the steps to create a cross-tabulation table, or *crosstab table*. With a crosstab table, you can organize the database information into categories, and then calculate, analyze, and compare the information in the ways you specify.

You use the ReportWizard to select the database field names you want used in the *row categories* and *column categories* in the crosstab table. The values from the selected row categories will appear along the left side of the crosstab table, and the values from the selected column categories will appear along the top of the crosstab table. You can also specify a *value field*. Microsoft Excel summarizes the values in the value fields that you select and displays the results in the cells of the crosstab table.

Each screen in the ReportWizard prompts you for the information needed to create the crosstab table, as shown in the following illustration. If you do not understand a particular screen, you can choose the Explain button to get more information.

The Crosstab ReportWizard prompts you for the information needed for the crosstab table.

Crosstab ReportWizard - Introduction

A cross tabulation table (crosstab) is a report that groups data from a database into categories and summarizes, analyzes, or compares the data in ways you specify.

What would you like to do?

Create a New Crosstab

Recalculate Current Crosstab

Modify Current Crosstab

Cancel

The data for a crosstab table comes from an internal or external database defined with the Set Database command. If criteria are set for the database, only values matching the criteria will appear in the crosstab table.

Explain

Choose the Explain button for detailed information about each screen.

You will use the ReportWizard to calculate the sum of salaries for each department within each division and display the results in a table.

Clear the criterion

Clear the criteria area so that the Crosstab ReportWizard will calculate the sum of salaries for all employees, not just the salaries of engineers.

1 Select cell E19.

2 From the Edit menu, choose Clear.

3 Choose the OK button.

Summarize department salaries by division

1 From the Data menu, choose Crosstab.

> **Note** If the Crosstab command does not appear on the Data menu, rerun the Setup program to install the Crosstab ReportWizard. For more information about adding or removing add-in macros, see "Managing Add-in Commands and Functions" in Chapter 4 in Book 2 of the *Microsoft Excel User's Guide*.

2 Choose the Create A New Crosstab button.

3 In the Fields In Database box, select Department. This specifies that each department is a row category.

4 Choose the Add button and then the Next button.

5 In the Fields In Database box, select Division. This specifies that each division is a column category.

6 Choose the Add button and then the Next button.

7 In the Fields In Database box, select Salary. This specifies that you're calculating salaries.

The ReportWizard assumes that you want the sum of the salaries, as the Salaries field contains numbers.

8 Choose the Add button and then the Next button.

9 Choose the Create It button.

The ReportWizard creates the report on a new worksheet, as shown in the following illustration.

	A	B	C	D	E	F	G	H
1	Sum of Salary	Division						
2	Department	Copier	Fax	Printer	Grand total			
3	Admin	164033	133694	179662	477389			
4	Engineering	312556	255564	662026	1230146			
5	Marketing	178718	106313	322198	607229			
6	R and D	99208	98116	215118	412442			
7	Grand total	754515	593687	1379004	2727206			
8								
9								
10								
11								
12								
13								
14								
15								

The ReportWizard also creates an outline. You can collapse the outline to see the salaries only by division or only by department. For more information about outlines, see Lesson 9, "Worksheet Outlining and Data Consolidation."

10 Format the crosstab table by adding titles, text formatting, and borders, and turn off the display of gridlines on the worksheet.

You can use the completed table shown in the following illustration as an example.

Sum of Salary	Division			
Department	*Copier*	*Fax*	*Printer*	*Grand total*
Admin	$164,033	$133,694	$179,662	$477,389
Engineering	$312,556	$255,564	$662,026	$1,230,146
Marketing	$178,718	$106,313	$322,198	$607,229
R and D	$99,208	$98,116	$215,118	$412,442
Grand total	$754,515	$593,687	$1,379,004	$2,727,206

11 Click the Save File tool and save the worksheet as SALARY.

Displaying more than one crosstab table on a worksheet   A worksheet can contain only one crosstab table. That is why the ReportWizard usually opens a new worksheet before creating the table, as you saw in the preceding exercise. If you want your worksheet to contain more than one crosstab table, you can use the Camera tool on the Utility toolbar to copy pictures of crosstab tables from different worksheets to a single worksheet.

Copy the crosstab table

You will use the camera tool to copy the crosstab table you just created to the WCSPRSNL worksheet.

1 If the Utility toolbar is not displayed, choose Utility from the toolbar shortcut menu.

2 On the SALARY worksheet, the table should still be selected. If it is not, select cells A1:E7.

3 Click the Camera tool.

4 Switch to the WCSPRSNL worksheet.

5 Point to the upper-left corner of cell C25 and click. Your worksheet should look like the following illustration.

	A	B	C	D	E	F	G	H	I
21									
22									
23	**Data Analysis Area**								
24									
25			Sum of Salary			*Division*			
26			*Department*	*Copier*	*Fax*	*Printer*	*Grand total*		
27			Admin	$164,033	$133,694	$179,662	$477,389		
28			Engineering	$312,556	$255,564	$662,026	$1,230,146		
29			Marketing	$178,718	$106,313	$322,198	$607,229		
30			R and D	$99,208	$98,116	$215,118	$412,442		
31			Grand total	$754,515	$593,687	$1,379,004	$2,727,206		
32									
33									
34									

Changing the ReportWizard's Options

The Crosstab ReportWizard provides options that you can use to customize your crosstab table.

Specifying additional ways to report and analyze row and column categories When you select row and column categories in the Crosstab ReportWizard, you can choose the Options button and select additional ways to limit and group the records that you want chosen.

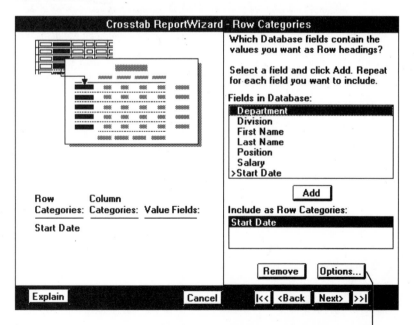

Choose the Options button to analyze row and column categories in different ways.

For example, if the row categories are starting dates, with the In Groups Of option you could group data by month for a budget report or by quarters for a quarterly report. You can limit the records that you want chosen by entering ranges for time, numeric values, or dates in the Starting At and Ending At boxes.

If the row categories are dates...

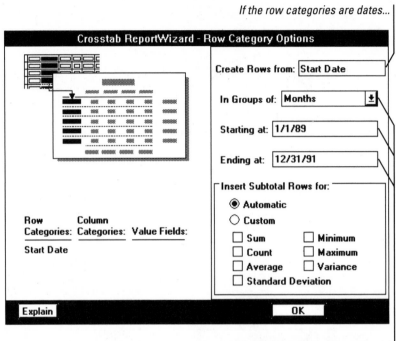

...you can group them by month and specify starting and ending dates.

Specifying additional ways to analyze and calculate value fields   When you select value fields in the Crosstab ReportWizard, you can choose the Options button and select additional ways to analyze, calculate, and report the values that appear in the crosstab table cells. For each value field, you can choose an operation to summarize the data. Your choices for summarizing the row and column categories by the value fields include sum, average, minimum, maximum, standard deviation, and variance.

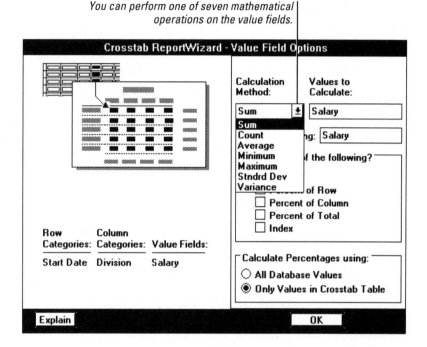

You can perform one of seven mathematical operations on the value fields.

The default operation is SUM if the value field is numeric. If the value field is a text field, the ReportWizard counts the number of matching records. You will use the ReportWizard to count records in the next exercise.

Save the worksheet

You will continue to use the WCSPRSNL worksheet in the "One Step Further" exercise.

 ▶ Click the Save File tool.

One Step Further

In this lesson, you used the Crosstab ReportWizard to create a crosstab table showing the sum of the salaries for each department in each division. The table was created on a new worksheet, and you used the Camera tool to place a picture of the table on the WCSPRSNL worksheet.

Now you will use the Crosstab ReportWizard to calculate the number of employees in each department within each division. You will place the actual table on the WCSPRSNL worksheet, instead of creating a new worksheet and then taking a picture of the crosstab table. Remember, a worksheet can contain only one crosstab table.

You want to count the number of employee records in the database. When the ReportWizard prompts you for a value field, you must specify a field for each employee record that contains text. Remember, the ReportWizard usually calculates the sum of value fields if the value field you specify is a number field; it counts the value fields if the field you specify is a text field. The Last Name field meets these criteria.

1 Select cell C33.

2 From the Data menu, choose Crosstab.

3 Choose the Create A New Crosstab button.

4 Select Department as the row category.

5 Choose the Add button and then the Next button.

6 Select Division as the column category.

7 Choose the Add button and then the Next button.

8 Select Last Name as the value field. This specifies the value field as a text field.

9 Choose the Add button and then the Next button.

10 Choose the Set Table Creation Options button.

11 Select the No option button under the prompt "Create an outline in Microsoft Excel for the Crosstab table?"

12 Select the No option button under the prompt "Create the crosstab table on a new worksheet?"

13 Choose the OK button.

14 Choose the Create It button.

15 Format the crosstab table by adding titles, text formatting, and borders. Use the completed table shown in the following illustration as an example.

	A	B	C	D	E	F	G	H
23	**Data Analysis Area**							
24								
25		Sum of Salary			*Division*			
26		*Department*		*Copier*	*Fax*	*Printer*	*Grand total*	
27		Admin		$164,033	$133,694	$179,662	$477,389	
28		Engineering		$312,556	$255,564	$662,026	$1,230,146	
29		Marketing		$178,718	$106,313	$322,198	$607,229	
30		R and D		$99,208	$98,116	$215,118	$412,442	
31		Grand total		$754,515	$593,687	$1,379,004	$2,727,206	
32								
33		Count of Last Name			*Division*			
34		*Department*		*Copier*	*Fax*	*Printer*	*Grand total*	
35		Admin		4	3	4	11	
36		Engineering		7	6	14	27	
37		Marketing		4	2	7	13	
38		R and D		2	2	5	9	
39		Grand total		17	13	30	60	
40								

16 Print the Data Analysis Area.

17 Save and close the worksheet when you are finished.

Lesson Summary

To	Do this
Set criteria on a worksheet	Copy field names from the worksheet database to another cell range. Select the pasted field names and the following row, and choose the Set Criteria command from the Data menu.
Find records in a database	After setting the criteria range, choose the Find command from the Data menu. Press the UP ARROW or DOWN ARROW key or click the scroll arrow to select the matching records.
Delete records from a database	After setting the criteria range, choose the Delete command from the Data menu.
Extract records from a database	After setting the criteria range, copy the database field names to your extract range. Select the extract range and choose the Set Extract command from the Data menu. Then choose the Extract command from the Data menu.

To	Do this
Analyze data with database functions	After setting the criteria range, choose the Paste Function command from the Formula menu and select an appropriate database funtion. The first argument to the database functions is usually Database; the second is a field name enclosed in quotation marks; the third is usually Criteria.
Create a crosstab table	Choose the Crosstab command from the Data menu. Follow the instructions in the Crosstab ReportWizard to specify row categories, column categories, and value fields.

For more information about	See in the *Microsoft Excel User's Guide*
Database reporting	Chapter 10, "Analyzing and Reporting Database Information," in Book 1

Preview of the Next Lesson

In the next lesson, you will learn to display information graphically. You will learn to create a chart as a separate document or embed a chart in your worksheet to create effective reports and presentations.

Part

6

Creating Charts and Presentations

Creating and Formatting a Chart

A chart is like a graph in 1-2-3, except that a chart can be a separate document or be embedded in the worksheet.

In this lesson, you will learn how to display worksheet data in a chart. You can create the chart as a separate document or embed it in your worksheet. You will choose the chart type that best presents your data, add text for the chart title, and label the chart axes. You will learn how to select chart items so that you can move and format them. You will change the font and pattern of items and add new items to the chart.

You'll also save your customized chart formatting in a template file, which you can use to create similar charts.

You will learn how to:

- Select worksheet data to create a new chart.
- Embed a chart in a worksheet with the ChartWizard.
- Create a separate chart document.
- Add chart gridlines.
- Select, move, and size chart items with the mouse or the keyboard.
- Change fonts and patterns of chart items.
- Add an arrow to a chart.
- Add unattached text to a chart.
- Save a chart as a template.

Estimated lesson time: 55 minutes

Start the lesson

1 Open the 14LESSN worksheet.
2 Save the worksheet as SALEHIST.

Selecting Worksheet Data

As with other Microsoft Excel actions, the data you select before you create a chart determines what appears in the chart.

Select the worksheet data for the chart

Your chart will compare annual sales for the company and the entire industry from 1982 to 1991. Select the worksheet data to include in the chart, omitting the 1992 data for now.

▶ Select cells C9:E19.

Your worksheet should look like the following illustration.

	A	B	C	D	E	F	G	H
1	Title		WCS Ten-Year Sales History					
2	Created by		Sam Bryan					
3	Date Modified		17-Jun-92					
4								
5	Purpose		This worksheet summarizes West Coast Sales' gross revenue					
6			for the previous 10 years.					
7								
8	Sales History							
9			Year	Company	Industry			
10			1982	$62,947	$1,210,000			
11			1983	$69,941	$1,230,000			
12			1984	$93,254	$1,260,000			
13			1985	$124,339	$1,300,000			
14			1986	$138,155	$1,350,000			
15			1987	$162,535	$1,380,000			
16			1988	$205,740	$1,370,000			
17			1989	$233,796	$1,400,000			
18			1990	$320,268	$1,500,000			
19			1991	$363,941	$1,690,000			
20			1992	$424,491	$2,000,000			

Creating a New Chart

You can embed a chart in your worksheet with the ChartWizard tool or create a chart document with the New command on the File menu.

To create a new chart, you first select the worksheet data you want to display in the chart, and then you create a new chart by clicking the ChartWizard tool or by choosing the New command from the File menu.

The ChartWizard tool   The ChartWizard tool displays the ChartWizard, an online assistant that guides you through the steps needed to embed a chart in your worksheet. Embedded charts are saved and printed with the worksheet and always reflect the latest worksheet data. You must have a mouse to use the ChartWizard tool.

ChartWizard tool

Create a chart with the ChartWizard tool

With your worksheet data selected, use the ChartWizard tool to create an embedded chart.

   1   Click the ChartWizard tool.

The mouse pointer turns into a cross hair.

2   Point to cell A22.

3   Drag the dotted box to cell G40.

When you release the mouse button, Microsoft Excel displays the ChartWizard.

4   The range of data that you selected is already entered, so choose the Next button to move to the next step.

The ChartWizard looks like the following illustration.

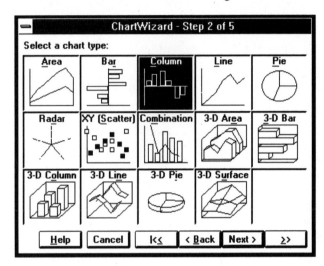

Microsoft Excel has 8 two-dimensional (2-D) chart types and 6 three-dimensional (3-D) chart types.

2-D chart types	3-D chart types
Area	3-D area
Bar	3-D bar
Column	3-D column
Line	3-D line
Pie	3-D pie
Radar	3-D surface
XY (scatter)	
Combination	

When you choose a chart type, a gallery appears showing the available formats for that chart type.

Combination charts   Combination charts have two value axes so that you can compare trends.

Pie charts and xy charts   Use a pie chart when you have only one data series. An xy (scatter) chart is used to plot values when you expect to see a relationship between values in one data series and values in another data series. An xy chart has no categories. You'll create an xy chart in Lesson 15, "Editing Chart Data Series."

3-D charts   Use three-dimensional (3-D) charts to show relationships between two categories of information and one set of values. A 3-D chart has an additional axis. The z-axis is the horizontal value axis, the category labels are plotted along the x-axis, and the series names are plotted along the y-axis. You will create a 3-D column chart in the "One Step Further" exercise at the end of this lesson.

Gallery menu   You can also change the chart type after you create a chart by choosing a command from the Gallery menu. When you choose a chart type from the Gallery menu, you'll see the same gallery dialog box as in the ChartWizard.

Change to a combination chart

You can use a combination of two chart types to compare the trends in your data.

1   Select the Combination chart type.

2   Choose the Next button.

3   With the combination chart gallery displayed, select format 2.

4   Choose the Next button.

   Your chart appears in the Sample Chart box.

Data series and categories   When you create a new chart with the ChartWizard tool, you can classify your selected worksheet data into data series and categories. The categories are the labels that appear along the x-axis. The bars or markers of the same color or pattern represent a data series.

In general, Microsoft Excel defines data series and categories according to the number of rows and columns in your worksheet selection. Unless you specify otherwise, Microsoft Excel assumes that you want fewer data series than categories.

In this case, you will define the data in column D as the "Company" data series and the data in column E as the "Industry" data series. The selected years in column C will be categories.

You'll learn how to change the data series and categories of an existing chart with the ChartWizard tool in Lesson 15, "Editing Chart Data Series."

Specify data series and categories

1   Under Data Series In, select the Rows option button.

   The sample chart now plots the differences among the years between company and industry. The legend changes to list the row labels.

2   Under Data Series In, select the Columns option button.

   The sample chart now plots the differences between company and industry over the years. The legend changes to list the column labels.

3   Choose the Next button.

The Add Legend command is like /Graph Options Legend in 1-2-3.

Adding a legend   When you add a legend to your chart, Microsoft Excel automatically uses your data series names for the legend. You can add a legend while creating a chart with the ChartWizard. You can also add a legend with the Legend tool on the Chart toolbar or the Add Legend command on the Chart menu. By default, the legend appears to the right of the plot area. You'll learn how to move the legend later in this lesson.

Deleting a legend   You can have only one chart legend. After you add a legend, the Add Legend command changes to the Delete Legend command. When you choose Delete Legend from the Chart menu to remove the legend, Add Legend appears in the menu again. You can also delete the legend with the Legend tool or the Clear command on the Edit menu.

The Attach Text command is like /Graph Options Titles and /Graph Options Data-Labels in 1-2-3.

Adding a chart title   You can add a title while creating the chart with the ChartWizard or by choosing the Attach Text command. In addition to chart titles, you can use this command to add titles to the axes and the data points. After you add the text, you can edit it in the formula bar. When you add a chart title or an axis title, the text is attached to a specific part of the chart and can't be moved. You'll learn how to add unattached text to a chart later in this lesson.

Add titles to the chart

1   In the Chart Title box, type **Company vs. Industry-Wide Sales**

2   In the Category (X) box, type **Year**

3   In the Value (Y) box, type **Company**

4   Choose the OK button.

Your chart should look like the following illustration.

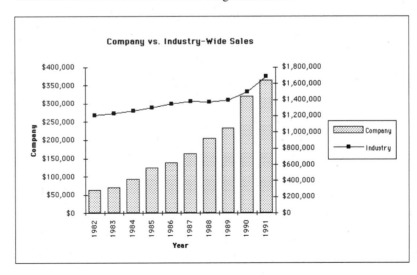

Adding Gridlines

The Chart toolbar   When an embedded chart is selected or a chart window is active, the Chart toolbar is displayed automatically. You can use the Chart toolbar to edit an existing chart or to create an embedded chart on the active worksheet. The Chart toolbar contains tools for the most commonly used formats for each chart type and for common formatting tasks, such as adding a legend.

The Horizontal Gridlines tool   With the Horizontal Gridlines tool on the Chart toolbar, you can change the display of major gridlines for the y-axis.

Add major gridlines to the y-axis

▶   Click the Horizontal Gridlines tool on the Chart toolbar.

Your chart should look like the following illustration.

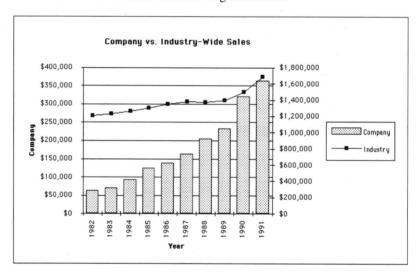

The Gridlines command is like /Graph Options Grid in 1-2-3.

You can control the display of major and minor gridlines for both axes with the Gridlines command on the Chart menu.

Creating a Chart Document

If you decide you want to work with this chart in a separate document, you can display it as a separate document or use the New command on the File menu to create a new chart document with the same data. You will create a worksheet presentation using worksheet objects and embedded charts in Lesson 16, "Creating a Presentation Using Charts and Graphics."

Create a new chart document

You can display an embedded chart in its own chart window. Then you can save it as a separate document.

1   Double-click the embedded chart.

The chart appears in its own window.

2   Enlarge the chart window to fill the screen.

The chart window   The entire chart window is the *chart area*. The rectangle defined by the two axes is the *plot area*. On your chart, the vertical (y) axis is the value axis; it displays dollar values. The horizontal (x) axis is the category axis; it displays years as category names.

Selecting Chart Items

You don't work directly with a graph in 1-2-3, so the idea of selecting chart items may be new to you.

You select the chart item you want to act on before you choose a command, just as you select the worksheet cells you want to act on before choosing a command. You can select chart items with the mouse or the keyboard. A selected chart item is surrounded with white or black selection squares. Black selection squares are handles you can drag to move the item. White selection squares indicate that the item can't be moved.

Selecting a chart item with the mouse   To select a chart item with the mouse, click the item.

Selecting a chart item with the keyboard   To select a chart item with the keyboard, use the arrow keys. You can press the LEFT ARROW or RIGHT ARROW key to move to any individual item. You can also press the UP ARROW or DOWN ARROW key to move between classes of items, and then press the LEFT ARROW or RIGHT ARROW key to move to the individual item you want. Microsoft Excel groups chart items into the following classes:

- Chart area
- Plot area
- Legend
- Axes
- Chart text

- Chart arrows
- Gridlines
- First data series
- Second data series, and so on

Moving and Formatting the Legend

The Legend command   You can position a legend in one of five places on a chart with the Legend command. The horizontal or vertical orientation of the legend depends on its position. In the Legend dialog box, you can choose the Patterns button or the Font button to open another dialog box and format the legend.

Moving the legend with the mouse   You can move a legend anywhere on the chart by dragging it with the mouse. If you drag the legend to the left or right side of the chart, the legend will be oriented vertically. If you drag the legend above or below the chart, the legend will be oriented horizontally.

Move the legend

1   Click the legend to select it.

2   From the Format menu, choose Legend.

3   Select the Bottom option button.

Don't choose the OK button yet.

Choosing buttons to bypass the Format menu   You can move directly from one formatting dialog box to another by choosing buttons in the dialog box. You can save time by choosing a button instead of choosing another command from the menu.

Change the legend pattern

Remove the legend border and change the legend color.

1   In the Legend dialog box, choose the Patterns button.

2   Under Border, select the None option button.

3   Under Area, select the third pattern from the Pattern list.

Don't choose the OK button yet.

Change the legend font

You'll change the font, size, and color of the text in the legend.

1 Choose the Font button.

2 In the Font box, select MS Serif in Microsoft Excel for Windows or Times in Microsoft Excel for the Macintosh.

3 In Microsoft Excel for Windows, select Bold in the Font Style box.

In Microsoft Excel for the Macintosh, select the Bold check box under Style.

4 In the Size box, select 12.

5 In the Color list, select Blue.

6 Choose the OK button.

Your chart should look like the following illustration.

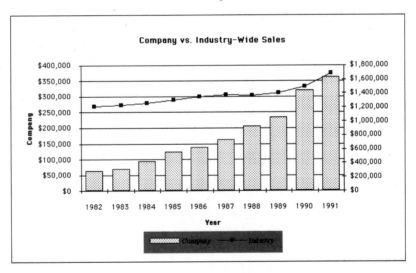

Formatting the Chart Area

The Select Chart command   You can use the mouse, the arrow keys, or the Select Chart command to select the chart area. You select the chart area when you want to change fonts or patterns for the chart, clear formats, or copy chart attributes to another chart.

Apply a shadow border and a different pattern to the chart area

You'll create a shadow border around the entire chart and change the color of the chart to match that of the legend.

1   From the Chart menu, choose Select Chart.

2   From the Format menu, choose Patterns.

3   In the Weight list, select the third line weight.

4   Under Border, select the Shadow check box.

5   Under Area, select the third pattern from the Pattern list.

6   Choose the OK button.

Your chart should look like the following illustration.

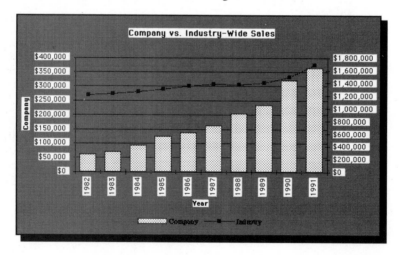

Formatting the Plot Area

The Select Plot Area command   You can use the mouse, the arrow keys, or the Select Plot Area command to select the plot area. You select the plot area before formatting it with the Patterns command on the Format menu.

Change the color of the plot area

You'll change the color of the plot area to make the plotted data stand out from the rest of the chart.

1   From the Chart menu, choose Select Plot Area.

2   From the Format menu, choose Patterns.

3   Under Area, select white from the Foreground list.

4   Choose the OK button.

Your chart should look like the following illustration.

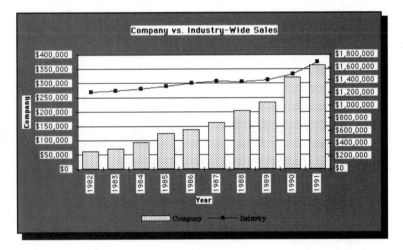

Formatting the Text

Change the font of the y-axis label

You'll use the Font command on the Format menu to change the font and color of the y-axis label.

1 Select the y-axis label, "Company."

2 From the Format menu, choose Font.

3 In the Font box, select MS Serif in Microsoft Excel for Windows or Times in Microsoft Excel for the Macintosh.

4 In the Size box, select 12.

5 In the Color list, select Blue.

6 Choose the OK button.

Repeat the format for the x-axis label

You can use the Repeat Font command on the Edit menu to repeat your formatting for the x-axis label.

1 Select the x-axis label, "Year."

2 From the Edit menu, choose Repeat Font.

Your chart should look like the following illustration.

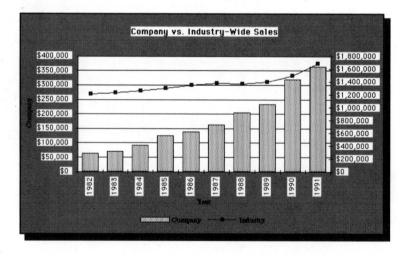

Change the font and pattern of the chart title

You can use the Repeat Font command on the Edit menu again to repeat your formatting changes for the chart title. Use the Font command on the Format menu to increase the font size to 14 points. Then choose the Patterns button to add a border around the chart title and change its color.

1   Select the chart title, "Company vs. Industry-Wide Sales."

2   From the Edit menu, choose Repeat Font.

3   From the Format menu, choose Font.

4   In the Size box, select 14.

5   Choose the Patterns button.

6   Under Border, select the Shadow check box.

7   Under Area, select white from the Foreground list.

8   Choose the OK button.

Your chart should look like the following illustration.

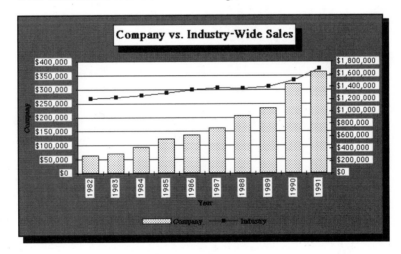

Saving the Chart as a Template

You can save your chart settings and formatting in a chart template so that you can create other charts later without going through all the formatting steps. You will use SALESCH as a template to create other charts in later lessons.

Saving a chart template   You save a chart as a template with the Save As command on the File menu. If you use a template frequently, you can have its name appear in the New dialog box. In Microsoft Excel for Windows, save the template in the XLSTART directory. In Microsoft Excel for the Macintosh, save the template in the EXCEL STARTUP Folder(4). The template will appear in the New dialog box the next time you open it.

Save a chart template in Microsoft Excel for Windows

1   From the File menu, choose Save As.

2   In the File Name box, type SALESTMP.

3   In the Save File As Type list, select Template.

4   Choose the OK button.

Microsoft Excel saves a copy of your chart on the disk as a template. You are still working with your embedded chart, open in a chart window.

Now you'll be able to reuse your chart settings and formatting by opening the SALESTMP template.

Save a chart template in Microsoft Excel for the Macintosh

1   From the File menu, choose Save As.

2   In the Save File As box, type SALESTMP.

3   Choose the Options button.

4   In the File Format list, select Template.

5   Choose the OK button to save the format.

6   Choose the Save button.

Microsoft Excel saves a copy of your chart on the disk as a template. You are still working with your embedded chart, which is open in a chart window.

Now you'll be able to reuse your chart settings and formatting by opening the SALESTMP template.

Adding an Arrow

You can add one or more arrows to a chart to point out important information. You can move, size, and format the arrows to give them the appearance you want.

Adding an arrow   You can add an arrow to the active chart window with the Arrow tool on the Chart toolbar or the Add Arrow command on the Chart menu.

Deleting an arrow   You can delete the selected arrow from the active chart window with the Delete Arrow command on the Chart menu or the Clear command on the Edit menu.

You'll add an arrow to your chart to highlight your company's gains in percentage of market share.

Add an arrow

▶ Click the Arrow tool on the Chart toolbar.

You need to move, size, and format the arrow.

Moving and sizing an arrow with the mouse   To change the orientation and length of an arrow, drag either of its end points. You can rotate the arrow and change its length in one step. To move the entire arrow, drag the shaft.

Moving and sizing an arrow with the keyboard   To size an arrow, select it and choose the Size command from the Format menu. Use the arrow keys to change the orientation and length, and then press ENTER. To move the entire arrow, select it and choose the Move command from the Format menu. Use the arrow keys to position the arrow, and then press ENTER.

Size the arrow

Shorten the arrow and rotate it so that it points to the left.

▶ Drag the handle at the arrow point clockwise, up and to the left. It should point to about 8 o'clock.

You still need to move the arrow.

Move the arrow

▶ Drag the arrow to the right by the shaft until it points to the 1991 sales data.

Format the arrow

You will use the Patterns command on the Format menu to change the color and weight of the arrow.

1 Double-click the arrow to display the Patterns dialog box.

You can also choose the Patterns command from the Format menu.

2 Under Line, select the second line weight in the Weight list.

3 In the Color list, select blue.

4 Choose the OK button.

Your chart should look like the following illustration.

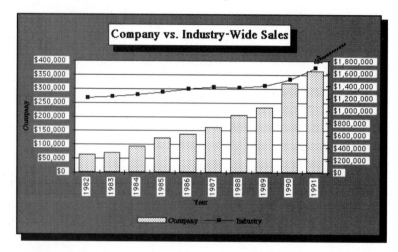

Formatting Text

The Text Box tool   To add text anywhere on a chart, use the Text Box tool on the Chart toolbar. You can move the text anywhere in the chart and format it just as you would format any other text.

Add unattached text

You'll add the text "Market share gain" to the chart and use it to label the arrow.

 1 Click the Text Box tool in the Chart toolbar.

The word "Text" appears in the chart.

2 Type **Market share gain**

3 Click the enter box or press ENTER.

Your typing replaces the word "Text."

4 Drag the text box above the arrow.

Format the text

Change the color, size, and style of the text with the Font command on the Format menu.

1   Select the text box, if it is not still selected.

2   From the Format menu, choose Font.

3   In Microsoft Excel for Windows, select Italic in the Font Style box.

   In Microsoft Excel for the Macintosh, select the Italic check box under Style.

4   In the Size box, select 8 in Microsoft Excel for Windows, or 9 in Microsoft Excel for the Macintosh.

5   In the Color list, select Blue.

6   Choose the Patterns button.

7   In the Foreground list, select white.

8   Choose the OK button.

Your finished chart should look like the following illustration.

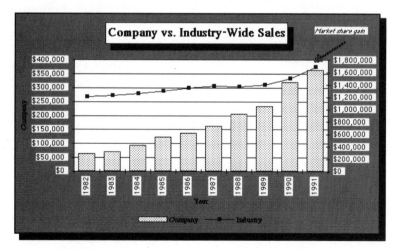

Save and close your document

Save and close the document.

1   Switch to SALEHIST.

   Your changes are reflected in the embedded chart in the worksheet.

2   From the File menu, choose Close.

3   Choose the Yes button to save your changes.

One Step Further

In this exercise, you will create two charts from crosstab tables summarizing database records. You created the tables in the previous lesson to compare the number of employees and the total of salaries for each department within the Fax, Copier, and Printer divisions of West Coast Sales. You will create a 3-D column chart for each table. To change the size of the chart, resize the chart window. You will also format the Salary chart.

1   Open the 14STEP worksheet.

2   Select cells D25:G29.

3   Click the ChartWizard tool.

4   Draw the chart in cells I25:M36.

5   Change the chart type to a 3-D column chart with gridlines (format 6).

6   Add a legend to the chart.

7   Add the chart title "Departmental Salaries" and choose the OK button.

8   Open the chart in its own window, and save the chart with the name SALARYCH.

9   On the 14STEP worksheet, select cells D33:G37.

10   Repeat steps 3 through 7, drawing the chart in cells I38:M49 and titling the chart "Number of Departmental Employees." Don't choose the OK button yet.

11   Label the category (x) axis "Departments."

12   Label the value (z) axis "Salaries."

13   Label the series (y) axis "Divisions" and choose the OK button.

14   Open the chart in its own window, and save the chart with the name EMPLOYCH.

15   Add an arrow that points to the Printer R and D column and another that points to the Printer Engineering column.

16   Add the following unattached text with the Text Box tool:

The Printer division currently markets more products than the other two divisions combined.

17   Drag the text box to the upper-right corner of the chart. Use the handles to resize the box if necessary.

18   Format the text as blue MS Sans Serif 8-point italic (Helvetica 9-point italic in Microsoft Excel for the Macintosh), with a shadow border and a white foreground.

19   Move both arrows to point to the unattached text.

20   Select the chart area and format it with a shadow border and a light gray foreground.

You can compare the 14SALARY and 14EMPLOY charts with your results. Save and close the charts when you are finished.

Lesson Summary

To	Do this
Select worksheet data to create a new chart	Select the range of cells that includes the information you want to plot in a chart.
Embed a chart in a worksheet	Click the ChartWizard tool and drag the mouse pointer across the worksheet. Follow the instructions in the ChartWizard to complete the chart.
Create a separate chart document	Double-click an embedded chart to open it in its own window; then save it as a separate document. You can also choose the New command and select Chart.
Change the chart type	Select an appropriate chart type for your data with the ChartWizard or the Gallery menu.
Add a chart legend	Use the Legend tool on the Chart toolbar or the Add Legend command on the Chart menu to add a legend to your chart.
Add a title to the chart	Use the Attach Text command on the Chart menu to add a title to the chart and label the axes.
Add chart gridlines	Use the Horizontal Gridlines tool on the Chart toolbar to add gridlines to your chart.
Select chart items with the mouse	Click the chart area, plot area, text, and chart items such as the legend before moving, sizing, and formatting them.
Change fonts and patterns of chart items	Use the Font and Patterns commands on the Format menu to format chart items and text. Double-click a chart item to open the Patterns dialog box.
Move and size chart items	Drag the item by the border to move it and by the handle to size it.
Add an arrow to a chart	Click the Arrow tool on the Chart toolbar.
Add unattached text to a chart	Click the Text Box tool on the Chart toolbar to add text anywhere on a chart.
Save chart settings and formatting in a chart template	Use the Save As command on the File menu.

For more information about	See in the *Microsoft Excel User's Guide*
Creating a chart	Chapter 12, "Creating a Chart," in Book 1
Formatting a chart	Chapter 14, "Formatting a Chart," in Book 1

For an online lesson about	Start the tutorial Learning Microsoft Excel and complete this lesson
Creating and formatting a chart	"What Is a Chart?"
Using the ChartWizard and the Chart toolbar to create and edit a chart	"Using a Chart"

For information about starting an online tutorial, see "Using the Online Tutorials" in "Getting Ready" earlier in this book.

Preview of the Next Lesson

In the next lesson, you'll learn how to change the contents of an existing chart by editing chart data series. You'll add worksheet data to an existing chart. You'll also create an xy (scatter) chart.

Editing Chart Data Series

In this lesson, you will edit the series formula to change, add, and delete the data in your chart. You will also create an xy (scatter) chart to show the relationship between two data series.

You will learn how to:

- Select a data series on a chart.
- Edit a series formula to plot different data in a chart.
- Add a data series to a chart or delete it from a chart.
- Create an xy (scatter) chart.

Estimated lesson time: 45 minutes

Start the lesson

In this lesson, you will create charts using chart templates and the data in the SALEHIST and STOCK worksheets.

1 Open the 15LESSN workbook file.

The 15LESSNB worksheet should be active.

2 Save the worksheet as STOCK.

3 Switch to the 15LESSNA worksheet.

4 Save the worksheet as SALEHIST.

Using a Chart Template

Create a chart from a template

The legend was removed from the SALESTMP template file to create the 15SALECH template file. Use the 15SALECH template file to create a chart showing only the company sales from 1982 to 1991.

1 On the SALEHIST worksheet, select cells C9:D19.

2 Open the 15SALECH template file.

3 Save the chart as SALECHRT.

4 Enlarge the chart window to fill the workspace.

Your chart should look like the following illustration.

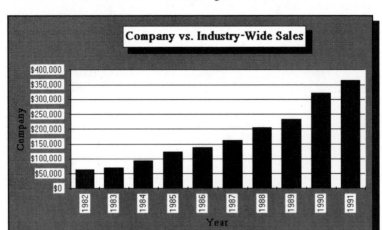

Selecting a Data Series

A chart data series is like a graph data range in 1-2-3.

You can select a data series on a chart by selecting any of its data markers. When you select a data series, the data series formula is displayed in the formula bar.

Select the company data series

▶ Click one of the columns on the chart.

The series formula appears in the formula bar. In Microsoft Excel for the Macintosh, the filenames in the formula bar will not have the .XLS extension.

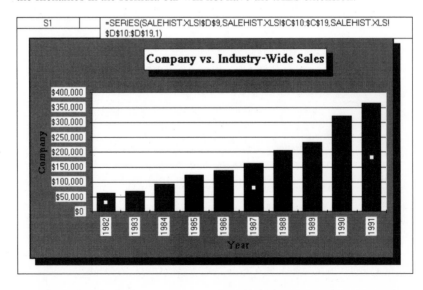

Parts of a series formula The following illustration provides a closer look at the series formula you see in the formula bar.

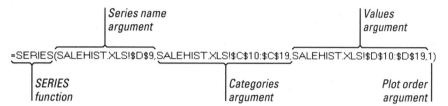

The SERIES function is used to build the series formula. It is used only on charts. The arguments to the SERIES function are external references to the worksheet cells that contain the data. The arguments are:

- **Series name** This is the company data series, and cell D9 on the SALEHIST worksheet contains the name "Company."

- **Categories** This argument refers to the cells on the SALEHIST worksheet that contain the years 1982 through 1991.

- **Values** This argument refers to the cells on the SALEHIST worksheet that contain the company sales data.

- **Plot order** This is the order in which the data series is plotted on the chart. Because you have only one data series, the plot order argument is 1.

Adding a Data Series

Using the ChartWizard to add data series or points is like respecifying the ranges in /Graph XABCDE in 1-2-3.

You add a data series to a chart by clicking the ChartWizard tool and changing the selected range on the worksheet to include another data series.

The ChartWizard tool You can use the ChartWizard tool to edit an existing embedded chart or a chart document. Before you can use the ChartWizard tool to edit a chart, you must open the worksheet that contains the chart data. The ChartWizard tool is on the Standard toolbar and the Chart toolbar.

The Edit Series command You can also use the Edit Series command on the Chart menu to enter, edit, or delete a data series in a chart. To edit a series, you select the series in the Series box and make the changes in the Name, X, Y, Z, and Plot Order boxes.

Add the industry data series to the chart

1 Click the ChartWizard tool.

The ChartWizard switches to the SALEHIST worksheet.

2 In the Range box, change the selected range to $C$9:$E$19. You can edit the range in the box or select the range in the worksheet.

In Microsoft Excel for Windows, the full reference should be SALEHIST.XLS!$C$9:$E$19. In Microsoft Excel for the Macintosh, the reference should be SALEHIST!$C$9:$E$19.

3 Choose the ›› button.

Your chart should look like the following illustration.

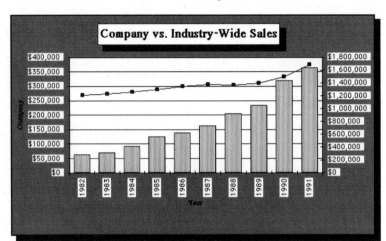

Adding Points to Existing Data Series

You can use the ChartWizard tool to add points to an existing data series. You just change the selection on the worksheet. You can also use the Edit Series command to edit the data series in a dialog box.

Add the 1992 data

You'll use the ChartWizard tool to include the cells that contain the company sales for 1992.

1 Click the ChartWizard tool.

The ChartWizard switches to the SALEHIST worksheet.

2 In the Range box, change the range to $C$9:$E$20.

In Microsoft Excel for Windows, the full reference should be SALEHIST.XLS!$C$9:$E$20. In Microsoft Excel for the Macintosh, the reference should be SALEHIST!$C$9:$E$20.

3 Choose the ›› button.

The 1992 sales figures are added to the chart. Your chart should look like the following illustration.

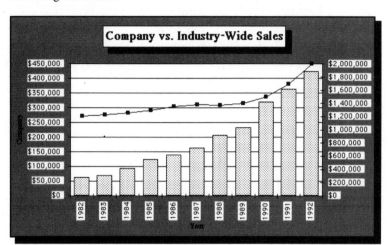

Deleting and Moving a Data Series

You can delete a data series from a chart by using the Delete button in the Edit Series dialog box or by selecting the series formula in the formula bar and choosing the Clear command from the Edit menu. You can also use the Cut and Paste commands on the Edit menu to move a data series to another chart.

Save and close the chart and its supporting worksheet

You have finished the SALEHIST worksheet and the SALECHRT chart. Next, you'll create an xy (scatter) chart using the STOCK worksheet.

 1 Click the Save File tool on the Standard toolbar.

2 From the File menu, choose Close.

The SALEHIST worksheet should now be active.

3 From the File menu, choose Close.

4 Switch to the STOCK worksheet.

Creating an XY (Scatter) Chart

An xy (scatter) chart is like an XY graph in 1-2-3.

An xy (scatter) chart is different from other charts because it has two sets of values and no categories.

You use an xy chart to plot two sets of numbers to see the relationship between them. One easy way to create an xy chart is to select only rows or columns of data.

The New command   You can create a separate chart document by selecting the data you want to plot and choosing the New command from the File menu. You can then use the commands on the Chart, Format, and Gallery menus to change the chart type and format the chart. You can still edit the chart with the ChartWizard as you do any chart.

Create an xy chart

You will create an xy chart that examines the relationship between the Dow Jones Industrial Averages and the fair market value of West Coast Sales stock. The STOCK worksheet should be active.

1   From the Formula menu, choose Goto.

2   Select "Dow_vs_WCS."

3   Choose the OK button.

4   From the File menu, choose New.

5   Select Chart.

6   Choose the OK button.

7   Under First Column Contains, select the Category (X) Axis Labels option button.

8   Choose the OK button.

Your chart should look like the following illustration.

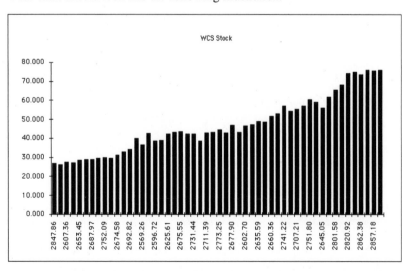

Save the chart

1 Click the Save File tool.

2 Save the chart as STOCKXY.

Change the chart format

The XY (Scatter) command on the Gallery menu is like /Graph Type XY in 1-2-3.

1 From the Gallery menu, choose XY (Scatter).

2 In the XY (Scatter) gallery, select format 3.

3 Choose the OK button.

Your chart should look like the following illustration.

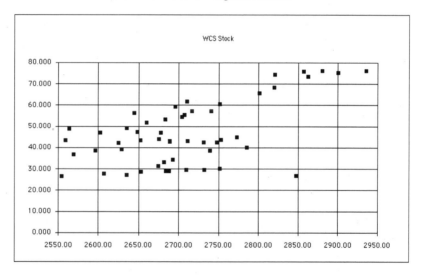

Edit the chart title

When you created the chart, Microsoft Excel used the name of the y-axis data series as the chart title. You will select and edit the chart title.

1 Select the chart title.

2 In the formula bar, position the insertion point after "WCS Stock."

3 Type **vs. Dow Jones Industrial Averages**

4 Click the enter box or press ENTER.

Format the chart title

1 From the Format menu, choose Font.

2 In the Font box, select MS Serif in Microsoft Excel for Windows or Times in Microsoft Excel for the Macintosh.

3 In Microsoft Excel for Windows, select Bold under Font Style.

In Microsoft Excel for the Macintosh, select the Bold check box under Style.

4 In the Size box, select 12.

5 Choose the Patterns button.

6 Under Border, select the Automatic option button.

7 Select the Shadow check box.

8 Choose the OK button.

Attach text to the y-axis

1 From the Chart menu, choose Attach Text.

2 Under Attach Text To, select the Value (Y) Axis option button.

3 Choose the OK button.

4 In the formula bar, type **WCS Stock Prices**

5 Click the enter box or press ENTER.

Attach text to the x-axis

1 From the Chart menu, choose Attach Text.

2 Under Attach Text To, select the Category (X) Axis option button.

3 Choose the OK button.

4 In the formula bar, type **Dow Jones Industrial Averages**

5 Click the enter box or press ENTER.

Your finished xy chart should look like the following illustration.

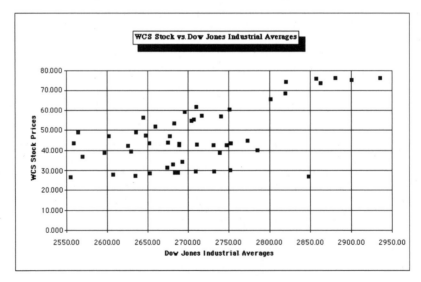

Printing the chart When you print a chart, the options in the Page Setup dialog box change. To see the Page Setup dialog box, choose Page Setup from the File menu. There are no options for printing gridlines and row and column headings, and there's an extra option for setting the size of your printed chart.

Save and close the chart

You will use the STOCK worksheet for the "One Step Further" exercise.

1   Click the Save File tool.

2   From the File menu, choose Close.

One Step Further

In this exercise, you will create a chart using the date as the x-axis to compare the performance of the West Coast Sales stock with the Dow Jones Industrial Averages. You will use the combination chart template that you created in Lesson 14. You will select all three data series on the STOCK worksheet, open the chart template, edit the data series so that West Coast Sales stock prices are on the left, and then change the title and the attached text to reflect the data series you are currently using with the template.

1   With the STOCK worksheet active, use the Goto command on the Formula menu to select Week_Dow_WCS, the area that you will plot in a chart.

2   Open the 15SALECH template file.

3   Save the chart as STOCKCHT.

4   From the Chart menu, choose Edit Series.

5   Change the plot order of the WCS_Stock series to 1.

6   Change the chart title to "WCS Stock vs. Dow Jones Performance, 7/91-7/92."

7   Change the y-axis label to "WCS Stock Prices."

8   Change the x-axis label to "Week Ending."

9   Change the chart type to combination chart format 3.

10 Use arrows and text boxes to label the WCS Stock and Dow Jones Industrial Averages data series.

   You can use the Add Legend command on the Chart menu to help you identify the data marker that represents each data series. Use the Delete Legend command on the Chart menu to delete the legend when you are finished.

Your finished chart should look like the following illustration.

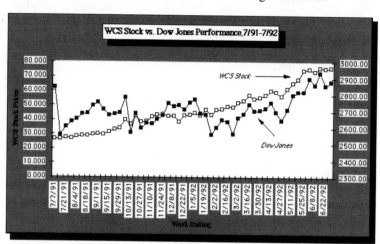

Save and close the chart and close the worksheet when you are finished.

Lesson Summary

To	Do this
Select a data series on a chart	Select a data series by selecting a marker on the chart.
Edit a data series formula to show different data in a chart	Click the ChartWizard tool and specify the new range.
Add or delete a data series from a chart	Click the ChartWizard tool and specify the new range, or use the Edit Series command on the Chart menu.
Create an xy (scatter) chart	Select two columns of data on a work-sheet and specify the first column for the x-axis. Then choose the XY (Scatter) command from the Gallery menu to change the chart type.

For more information about	See in the *Microsoft Excel User's Guide*
Editing a data series	Chapter 13, "Editing a Chart," in Book 1

Preview of the Next Lesson

In the next lesson, you'll format a worksheet with graphics and embedded charts for a presentation. You'll also create slides containing Microsoft Excel worksheet data and charts and run the slides as a slide show.

Creating a Presentation Using Charts and Graphics

In this lesson, you will create a worksheet presentation that combines worksheet data, embedded charts, graphic objects, and text boxes. Combining graphic objects and charts with worksheet data helps you to create a more effective presentation. You will also create a slide show presentation.

You will learn how to:

- Add graphic objects to a worksheet.
- Format graphic objects.
- Add text boxes to a worksheet.
- Create a picture chart.
- Create a slide show.

Estimated lesson time: 45 minutes

Start the lesson

You will use the 16LESSN worksheet to create a presentation that depicts the Printer division market share increase since 1982.

1   Open the 16LESSN worksheet.

2   Save the file as PRESENT.

Wrap the column title text

The Market Share title is wider than the data in the Market Share column. You will adjust the column width and then wrap the Market Share column title text to improve the worksheet's appearance.

1   Select cell E13.

2   From the Forma_t menu, choose _Alignment.

3   Select the Wrap Text check box.

4   Choose the OK button.

Your worksheet should look like the following illustration.

	A	B	C	D	E	F	G	H	I
1	**West Coast Sales Technologies**								
2	**Printer Division**								
3									
4	*A decade of growth*								
5									
6									
7									
8									
9									
10									
11									
12									
13		Year	Company	Industry	Market Share				
14		1982	$62,947	$1,210,000	4.94%				
15		1983	$69,941	$1,230,000	5.38%				
16		1984	$93,254	$1,260,000	6.89%				
17		1985	$124,339	$1,300,000	8.73%				
18		1986	$138,155	$1,350,000	9.28%				
19		1987	$162,535	$1,380,000	10.54%				
20		1988	$205,740	$1,370,000	13.06%				
21		1989	$233,796	$1,400,000	14.31%				
22		1990	$320,268	$1,500,000	17.59%				
23		1991	$363,941	$1,690,000	17.72%				
24		1992	$423,187	$2,000,000	17.46%				
25									
26									
27									
28									

Laying Out a Worksheet with Charts

You added a chart to a worksheet in Lesson 14. In this lesson, you'll add two 3-D pie charts to the worksheet to emphasize the company's increase in market share. To lay out the page properly, you'll use the worksheet gridlines to guide the size and placement of your charts. You'll also use the Set Preferred command on the Gallery menu to create a second pie chart that is formatted the same way as the first chart.

Display gridlines on the worksheet

Use gridlines as a guide for creating objects.

1 From the Options menu, choose Display.

2 Under Cells, select the Gridlines check box.

3 Choose the OK button.

Embed a chart in the worksheet

1 Select cells C14:D14.

2 Click the ChartWizard tool on the Standard toolbar.

3 Hold down ALT in Microsoft Excel for Windows or COMMAND in Microsoft Excel for the Macintosh, and drag from cell G14 to cell I24.

Pressing ALT or COMMAND while dragging aligns an object with the worksheet grid.

4 To verify the range of data that you selected and to move to the next screen, choose the Next button.

5 Select the 3-D Pie chart type, and then choose the Next button.

6 Select format 3 to format the pie chart with the first slice exploded, and then choose the Next button.

7 The option buttons for the data series are already selected, so choose the Next button.

8 In the Chart Title box, type **Fiscal Year 1982**

9 Choose the OK button.

Your chart should look like the following illustration.

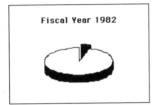

Open the embedded chart

To edit any chart item, such as the chart title, you must open the chart in its own window.

▶ Double-click the embedded chart.

Your chart appears in a chart window.

Format the chart title

1 Select the chart title.

2 From the Format menu, choose Font.

3 In Microsoft Excel for Windows, select Bold Italic in the Font Style box.

In Microsoft Excel for the Macintosh, select the Bold and Italic check boxes under Style.

4 In the Size box, select 10.

5 Choose the Patterns button.

6 Under Border, select the Shadow check box.

7 Under Area, select the third pattern in the Pattern list.

8 Choose the OK button.

Format the industry data point

You will change the pattern of the pie section that represents the industry.

1 Double-click the large pie section—the data point representing the industry—to display the Patterns dialog box.

2 Under Area, select the fourth pattern option in the Pattern list.

3 In the Foreground list, select cyan. Cyan is the eighth option in the list.

4 Choose the OK button.

Format the company data point

Now you will change the pattern of the pie section that represents the company.

1 Double-click the small slice of the pie—the data point representing the company—to display the Patterns dialog box.

2 Under Area, select the third pattern in the Pattern list.

3 Choose the OK button.

Your chart should look like the following illustration.

The preferred chart type   The preferred chart type is the chart type that appears when you create a new chart with the Preferred Chart tool or with the New command on the File menu. The default Microsoft Excel preferred chart type is a column chart. If you create another type of chart that you want to use again in the same session, you can save time by creating and saving your own preferred chart type.

You can save all of your chart formatting, including titles, with your preferred chart; thus, you can quickly produce several charts that are formatted alike.

The Set Preferred command   With the Set Preferred command, you can change the default format that Microsoft Excel uses when you create a new chart. To change the preferred chart format, format the active chart the way you want it, and then choose Set Preferred from the Gallery menu.

The Preferred Chart tool   With the Preferred Chart tool, you can change the active chart to the preferred chart format or create charts in the preferred chart format. If you change the active chart and then decide you want to return to the default chart format, click the Preferred Chart tool on the Chart toolbar.

Preferred Chart tool

Set the preferred chart type

You created a 3-D pie chart that represents the company's market share for 1982. Rather than repeating all of the formatting procedures, set the active chart as the preferred chart type. When you create your next chart, the chart type and formatting will already be set.

▶ From the Gallery menu, choose Set Preferred.

Close the chart window

You've finished creating the first chart. Now you will add another pie chart to the worksheet.

▶ Close the chart window.

Embed a second pie chart in the worksheet

You will create a pie chart representing the 1992 data series. It will use the same chart type and formatting as the Fiscal Year 1982 chart. Create the new chart and edit the chart title.

1   Select cells C24:D24.

2   From the toolbar shortcut menu, choose Chart.

3   Click the Preferred Chart tool on the Chart toolbar.

4   Hold down ALT in Microsoft Excel for Windows or COMMAND in Microsoft Excel for the Macintosh, and drag from cell G26 to cell I36.

5   Double-click the embedded chart to open a chart window.

6   Select the chart title.

7   In the formula bar, change the title to **Fiscal Year 1992**

8   Click the enter box or press ENTER.

9   Close the chart window.

Your worksheet should look like the following illustration.

	A	B	C	D	E	F	G	H	I
13		Year	Company	Industry	Market Share				
14		1982	$62,947	$1,210,000	4.94%				
15		1983	$69,941	$1,230,000	5.38%				
16		1984	$93,254	$1,260,000	6.89%				
17		1985	$124,339	$1,300,000	8.73%				
18		1986	$138,155	$1,350,000	9.28%				
19		1987	$162,535	$1,380,000	10.54%				
20		1988	$205,740	$1,370,000	13.06%				
21		1989	$233,796	$1,400,000	14.31%				
22		1990	$320,268	$1,500,000	17.59%				
23		1991	$363,941	$1,690,000	17.72%				
24		1992	$423,187	$2,000,000	17.46%				
25									
26									
27									
28									
29									
30									
31									
32									
33									
34									
35									
36									
37									

Move the charts on the worksheet

You will rearrange the charts on the worksheet to make room for text boxes and arrows. Select the charts and drag them where you want them. Use the worksheet gridlines as guides for placing the charts.

1   Select the Fiscal Year 1982 chart.

2   Hold down ALT in Microsoft Excel for Windows or COMMAND in Microsoft Excel for the Macintosh, and drag the chart to cell G6.

The chart should be in the cell range G6:I15.

3   Select the Fiscal Year 1992 chart.

4   Hold down ALT in Microsoft Excel for Windows or COMMAND in Microsoft Excel for the Macintosh, and drag the chart to cell G23.

The chart should be within the cell range G23:I33.

The Selection tool   You can use the Selection tool on the Drawing toolbar to select multiple worksheet objects at once. Click the Selection tool, point to the first object you want to select, and then drag the pointer over the remaining objects you want in the selection. Each object must be entirely surrounded by the selection rectangle to be selected. Each selected object is marked by selection squares. To cancel the Selection tool, click the tool again.

| Selection tool

Display the Drawing toolbar

▶ From the toolbar shortcut menu, choose Drawing.

Remove the chart borders

You want the 3-D pie charts to appear on the worksheet without borders.

1 Click the Selection tool on the Drawing toolbar.

2 Point above and to the left of the Fiscal Year 1982 chart, and drag down below the Fiscal Year 1992 chart, so that both charts are enclosed by the selection rectangle.

 Both charts are surrounded by selection handles.

3 Click the Selection tool again.

4 From the Format menu, choose Patterns.

5 Under Border, select the None option button.

6 Choose the OK button.

Turn off the gridlines

1 From the Options menu, choose Display.

2 Under Cells, clear the Gridlines check box.

3 Choose the OK button.

Your worksheet should look like the following illustration.

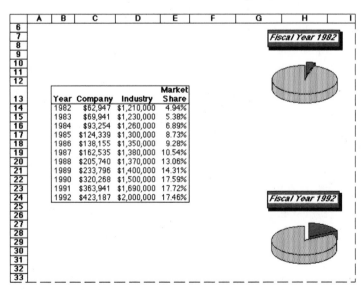

Drawing Lines and Shapes on the Worksheet

Drawing graphic objects   You can add emphasis to your worksheet or macro sheet with graphic objects such as straight lines, arrows, ovals, rectangles, polygons, and arcs. With the Arrow tool on the Drawing toolbar, you can point to cells, charts, other graphic objects, or copied pictures. You can also draw filled ovals, rectangles, polygons, and arcs with the tools on the Drawing toolbar and then change the color and pattern of the filling to highlight certain areas of the document.

In the previous exercise, you learned how to align graphic objects with the worksheet grid. You can also restrict a graphic object to certain shapes by pressing the SHIFT key while drawing the object.

To draw a	Press the SHIFT key while drawing a
Square	Rectangle
Circle	Oval
Horizontal, vertical, or 45-degree-angle line	Line

Formatting object placement   You can use the Object Placement command on the Format menu to align an object on the worksheet. You can use this command to maintain an object's position relative to the cells at the upper-left and lower-right corners, to move the object with the cell under its upper-left corner without changing size, or to fix the object's position so that it doesn't move with the cells at all.

Add arrows to the worksheet

The arrows will point from the 1982 and 1992 worksheet data to the pie charts representing that data.

1   Click the Arrow tool on the Drawing toolbar or the Chart toolbar.

2   Drag from the right border of cell E14, the 1982 data, to the left of the pie slice on the Fiscal Year 1982 pie chart.

Your worksheet should look like the following illustration.

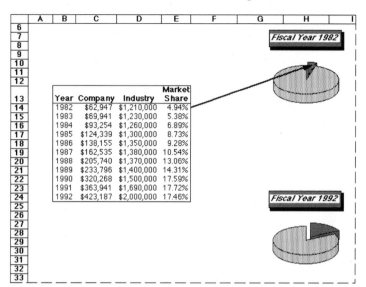

Copy the arrow

You will copy and paste a second arrow into the worksheet. To do this, press CTRL in Microsoft Excel for Windows or OPTION in Microsoft Excel in the Macintosh, and drag either end of the arrow where you want it to point. In this procedure, you will copy the arrow and move it between the 1992 data series and the Fiscal Year 1992 chart.

1   If the arrow is not still selected, click it.

2   In Microsoft Excel for Windows, press CTRL and drag the arrow by the shaft to the right border of cell E24.

   In Microsoft Excel for the Macintosh, press OPTION and drag the arrow by the shaft to the right border of cell E24.

3   Drag the handle at the arrowhead to the left of the pie slice on the Fiscal Year 1992 pie chart.

Your worksheet should look like the following illustration.

	A	B	C	D	E	F	G	H	I

Market
Year Company Industry Share
1982 $62,947 $1,210,000 4.94%
1983 $69,941 $1,230,000 5.38%
1984 $93,254 $1,260,000 6.89%
1985 $124,339 $1,300,000 8.73%
1986 $138,155 $1,350,000 9.28%
1987 $162,535 $1,380,000 10.54%
1988 $205,740 $1,370,000 13.06%
1989 $233,796 $1,400,000 14.31%
1990 $320,268 $1,500,000 17.59%
1991 $363,941 $1,690,000 17.72%
1992 $423,187 $2,000,000 17.46%

Fiscal Year 1982

Fiscal Year 1992

Adding Text Boxes to the Worksheet

You can use text boxes to add titles, footnotes, and comments about cell data.

Adding text boxes   You use the Text Box tool on the Utility toolbar or the Chart toolbar to draw text boxes on your worksheet. Draw a text box just as you draw any other graphic object, by clicking the tool and dragging across the worksheet. To add text to the text box, click inside the text box and type the text. You can change the font, style, size, and color of the text with the formatting tools or with the Font command on the Format menu. One text box can contain multiple fonts, styles, and colors. You can also use the Patterns command on the Format menu to change the fill pattern or borders of a text box.

Add a text box to the worksheet

Use a text box to add a title to the worksheet data.

1   Click the Text Box tool on the Drawing toolbar or the Chart toolbar.

2   Hold down ALT in Microsoft Excel for Windows or COMMAND in Microsoft Excel for the Macintosh, and drag from the upper-left corner of cell B9 to the lower-right corner of cell F11.

3   If the insertion point is not in the text box, click inside the text box.

4   Type **Printer Division Revenues**

Format the title

1 Select the text you just typed.

2 From the Forma̱t menu, choose Ḟont.

3 In Microsoft Excel for Windows, select Bold Italic in the Font Style box.

In Microsoft Excel for the Macintosh, select the Bold and Italic check boxes under Style.

4 In the Size box, select 14.

5 In the Color list, select Dark Blue.

6 Choose the OK button.

Your worksheet should look like the following illustration.

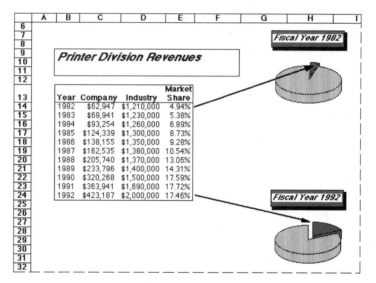

Format the text box

You will format the border and the fill pattern of the text box so that the title will stand out.

1 Double-click the border of the "Printer Division Revenues" text box to display the Patterns dialog box.

2 Under Border, select the second option in the Weight list.

3 Select the Round Corners check box.

4 Under Fill, select the third pattern in the Pattern list.

5 Choose the Text button.

6 Under Horizontal, select the Center option button.

7 Under Vertical, select the Center option button.

8 Choose the OK button.

9 With the text box still selected, drag the handle on the right side of the box to the left so that the box aligns with the border of the table below it.

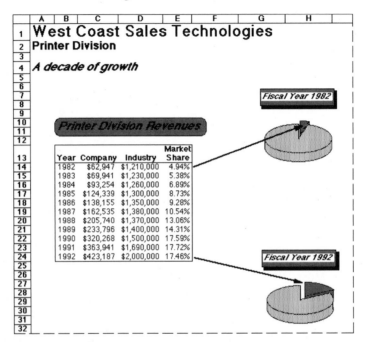

Add footnotes to the revenue table

1 Click the Text Box tool on the Drawing toolbar or the Chart toolbar.

2 Hold down ALT in Microsoft Excel for Windows or COMMAND in Microsoft Excel for the Macintosh, and drag from cell B26 to cell F28.

3 In the text box, type the following text:

* Revenue in thousands of dollars

* Industry figures exclusive of WCS revenues

Format the footnotes

1 Select the text you just entered.

2 From the Format menu, choose Font.

3 In Microsoft Excel for Windows, select Italic in the Font Style box.

In Microsoft Excel for the Macintosh, select the Italic check box under Style.

4 In the Color list, select Dark Blue.

5 Choose the Patterns button.

6 Under Border, select the None option button.

7 Choose the OK button.

Your worksheet should look like the following illustration.

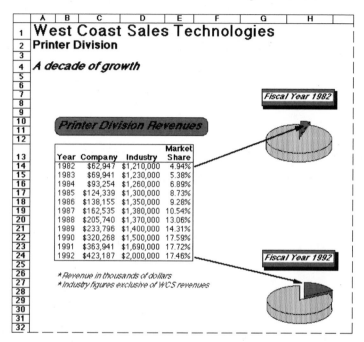

Save the worksheet

▶ Click the Save File tool on the Standard toolbar.

Set up the page to print the worksheet

You will use the Page Setup command on the File menu to set up the page for printing.

1 From the File menu, choose Page Setup.

2 Under Orientation, select the Landscape (horizontal) option.

3 Choose the Header button.

4 In the Center Section box, delete "&f".

5 Choose the OK button.

6 Choose the Footer button.

7 Move to the Right Section box.

8 Choose the date button.

9 Choose the OK button in the Footer dialog box.

10 Choose the OK button in the Page Setup dialog box.

Preview the worksheet before printing

You will use the Print Preview command on the File menu to see how the document will look when printed.

1 From the File menu, choose Print Preview.

The print preview window should look like the following illustration. Yours may look slightly different, depending on the printer driver you have installed.

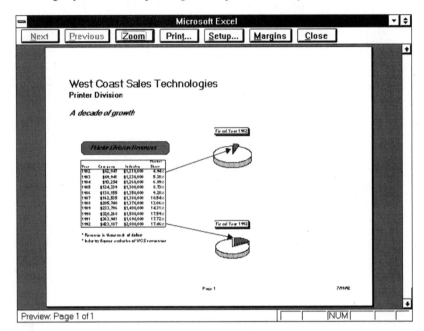

2 If you want to print the worksheet now, choose the Print button.

Otherwise, choose the Close button to close the preview window.

Creating Picture Charts

You can use pictures as data markers in Microsoft Excel charts. You can use graphics drawn in Microsoft Excel or pictures copied from other applications.

Using pictures as data markers   You can create unique charts by using pictures as data markers. Select a picture and choose the Copy command from the Edit menu. Open your chart, select a data marker, and then choose the Paste command from the Edit menu. The data series marker is replaced with the picture.

Formatting a data marker picture   You can format the picture data markers as stacked or stretched. Use the Stretch option to stretch or shrink the picture to show different values; use the Stack option to stack copies of the picture to represent different values;

or use the Stack And Scale option to stack copies of the picture and scale each picture to a value that you specify.

Create a new chart

You will create a picture chart to use with the worksheet that you just formatted. You will use the data in the PRESENT worksheet to create a combination chart with the 16SALECH chart template.

1   On the PRESENT worksheet, select cells B13:D24.

2   Open the 16SALECH template file.

3   Save the chart as PRINTCH.

Copy a picture to the company data marker

You will replace the company data marker with a picture. To do this, you will copy a picture from another worksheet, 16PRTART, and paste it into the PRINTCH chart.

1   Open the 16PRTART worksheet.

2   On the 16PRTART worksheet, select the picture labeled Graphic.

3   Click the Copy tool on the Standard toolbar.

4   Switch to the PRINTCH chart.

5   Select the Company data markers (the column markers).

6   From the Edit menu, choose Paste.

The printer graphic replaces the company data markers. Your chart should look like the following illustration.

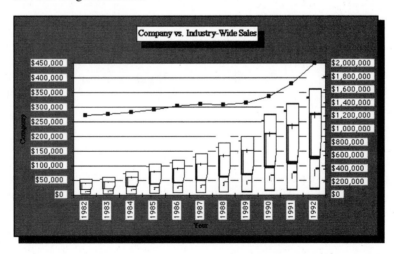

Format the data marker pictures

Use the Patterns command on the Format menu to stack and scale the data marker
pictures.

1   Double-click a Company data marker to display the Patterns dialog box.

2   Under Picture Format, select the Stack And Scale option button.

3   In the Units/Picture box, type **50,000**

4   Choose the OK button.

Your chart should look like the following illustration.

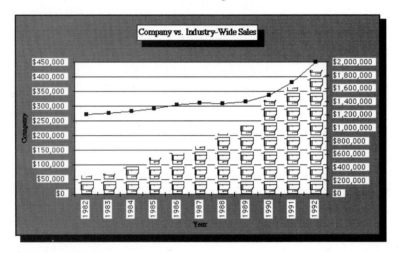

Save and close the chart

Save and close the PRINTCH chart, and close the 16PRTART worksheet. You will
use the PRESENT worksheet in the "One Step Further" exercise.

1   Click the Save File tool on the Standard toolbar.

2   From the File menu, choose Close.

3   Switch to the 16PRTART worksheet.

4   From the File menu, choose Close.

Creating a Slide Show

You can use data, charts, and graphics from Microsoft Excel or other applications as slides in Microsoft Excel slide shows.

Creating slide show presentations   You create a slide show on a special template document that is included with Microsoft Excel. To open the slide show template, you must have the Slide Show add-in macro installed. The top two rows of the template contain the buttons you use to add and edit slides and run the slide show, as shown in the following illustration.

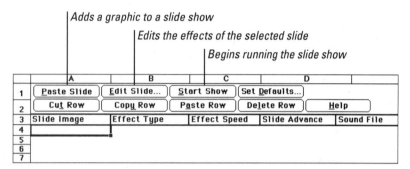

Adding slides and slide show effects   You can add any selection you have copied to the Clipboard with the Paste Slide button. When you choose the Paste Slide button, a reduced version of the image on the Clipboard is pasted into the next available row on the Slide Show template, and the Edit Slide dialog box is displayed. In this dialog box you can specify the effect used to advance to the next slide, the speed of the transition, how long each slide is displayed, and the location of any sound to be played when the slide is displayed.

In Microsoft Excel for Windows, you can play sounds only when you are running Microsoft Windows version 3.0 with Multimedia Extensions version 1.0 or later, or Microsoft Windows version 3.1 or later. In Microsoft Excel for the Macintosh, you must be running Macintosh system software version 6.07 or later.

Open a new slide show

You will create a slide show with the worksheet that you just formatted. You will display the data and the chart embedded in the PRESENT worksheet as a slide show.

1   From the File menu, choose New.

2   In Microsoft Excel for Windows, select Slides.

In Microsoft Excel for the Macintosh, select Slide Show.

Note   If the slide show template does not appear in the New dialog box, rerun the Setup program to install the Slide Show. For more information about adding or removing add-in macros, see "Managing Add-in Commands and Functions" in Chapter 4 in Book 2 of the *Microsoft Excel User's Guide*.

---

3   Choose the OK button.

The template for creating slide shows opens.

Create a slide from a range of cells

You will create a slide from the data in the PRESENT worksheet and have the slide automatically advance after 5 seconds.

1   Switch to the PRESENT worksheet.

2   Select cells B13:E24.

 3   Click the Copy tool on the Standard toolbar.

4   In Microsoft Excel for Windows, switch to SLIDES1, the slide show template.

In Microsoft Excel for the Macintosh, switch to SLIDE SHOW1, the slide show template.

5   Choose the Paste Slide button.

A picture of the slide is pasted into the slide template. The Edit Slide dialog box is displayed.

6   In the Effect box, select Vertical Blinds.

You can choose the Test button to view a sample of the effect.

7   Under Advance, choose the Timed (Sec) option button.

8   In the Timed (Sec) box, type **5**

9   Choose the OK button.

Create a slide from an embedded chart

You will create a slide from the Fiscal Year 1982 chart embedded in the PRESENT worksheet and have the slide automatically advance after 5 seconds.

1 Switch to the PRESENT worksheet.

2 Select the embedded chart for Fiscal Year 1982 .

3 Click the Copy tool on the Standard toolbar.

4 In Microsoft Excel for Windows, switch to SLIDES1, the slide show template.

In Microsoft Excel for the Macintosh, switch to SLIDE SHOW1, the slide show template.

5 Choose the Paste Slide button.

A picture of the slide is pasted into the slide template. The Edit Slide dialog box is displayed.

6 In the Effect box, select Vertical Blinds.

7 Under Advance, choose the Timed (Sec) option button.

8 In the Timed (Sec) box, type **5**

9 Choose the OK button.

Run the slide show

Once you copy data or graphics to the slide show template, you can run the slide show on any size monitor or on a screen projection device for presentations.

1 Choose the Start Show button.

2 Choose the OK button.

Your slide show presentation begins on your screen and automatically advances to the next slide after 5 seconds. After you run a slide show, the slide show template reappears.

Save the slide show

You will use the slide show presentation and the PRESENT worksheet in the "One Step Further" exercise.

▶ Save the slide show presentation as SLIDPRES.

Using Microsoft Excel Graphics with Other Applications

You can export worksheet data or objects into another application. You can copy these items or pictures of these items into a graphical word processing or presentation application, such as Microsoft® Word or Microsoft® PowerPoint®. To import data into Microsoft Word and link it to Microsoft Excel, select the chart, graphic, or worksheet cells you want to copy, choose the Copy command from the Edit menu, switch to Microsoft Word, choose the Paste Special command from the Edit menu, and choose the Paste Link button. If you make changes to the original Microsoft Excel data, you can update the pasted data in Microsoft Word with the Links command on the Edit menu and choose the Update Now button.

To import a picture into Microsoft PowerPoint, select the chart, graphic, or worksheet cells you want to copy, hold down SHIFT, and choose the Copy Picture command from the Edit menu. If you are copying a chart, Microsoft Excel will ask you whether you want to copy the chart as it appears on the screen or as printed. If your computer is set up with a color printer, select the As Shown When Printed option button. Otherwise, select the As Shown On Screen option button. Switch to Microsoft PowerPoint and choose the Paste command from the Edit menu.

One Step Further

In this lesson, you created a worksheet with embedded charts, arrows, and text boxes. In this exercise, you will use the Rectangle tool to add bars at the top and bottom of the worksheet. Finally, you will create a slide of the second chart and run the slide show.

1 On the PRESENT worksheet, change the row height of row 3 to 20 points.

2 Change the row height of row 34 to 6 points.

3 Double-click the Rectangle tool on the Drawing toolbar.

Double-clicking the tool enables you to draw multiple objects.

To cancel a drawing tool selection, click the same tool again.

4 Hold down ALT in Microsoft Excel for Windows or COMMAND in Microsoft Excel for the Macintosh, and drag from cell A3 to cell I3.

5 Hold down ALT in Microsoft Excel for Windows or COMMAND in Microsoft Excel for the Macintosh, and drag from cell A34 to cell I34.

6 Select both rectangles. Select the first rectangle, and then press CTRL in Microsoft Excel for Windows or SHIFT in Microsoft Excel for the Macintosh while you select the second one.

7 From the Format menu, choose Patterns.

8 Under Borders, select the None option button.

9 Under Fill, select dark cyan in the Foreground list (the third from last color).

10 Choose the OK button.

11 Select cells A1:I4.

12 Click the Center Across Columns tool on the Standard toolbar.

13 Select cells B13:E24.

14 From the Format menu, choose AutoFormat.

15 Select the Colorful 1 format.

16 Choose the OK button.

Your worksheet should look like the following illustration.

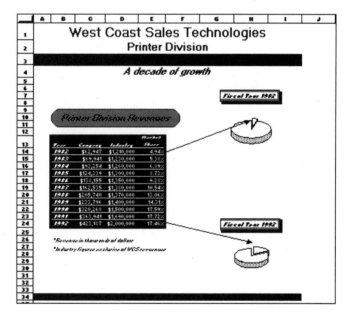

17 Select the Fiscal Year 1992 chart.

18 Click the Copy tool.

19 Switch to the SLIDPRES slide show.

20 Paste the slide.

21 Format the slide to have a vertical blinds transition effect and to automatically advance after 5 seconds.

22 Run the slide show.

Your worksheet and slide show are complete. Save and close the worksheet and the slide show.

Lesson Summary

To	Do this
Add graphic objects to a worksheet	Use the drawing tools on the Drawing toolbar.
Format graphic objects	Choose the Patterns command from the Format menu.
Add text boxes to a worksheet	Create text boxes with the Text Box tool; then type and format text in the boxes.
Create a picture chart	Copy a picture from another document and use it to replace a data marker. Format the picture data marker as stacked or stretched.
Create a slide show	Open the slide show template and paste the data and graphics you want into the template.

For more information about	See in the *Microsoft Excel User's Guide*
Using graphic objects in worksheets and creating slide shows	Chapter 15, "Working with Graphic Objects," in Book 1

Preview of the Next Lesson

In the next lesson, you will use the macro recorder to record macros that update and print your worksheet. You'll edit these macros and assign them to buttons on the worksheet so that you can click the buttons to run the macros.

7 Working with Macros

Recording Macros

In this lesson, you'll create a small application in Microsoft Excel. The application will make it easy for you to update a worksheet, print the worksheet data, and plot the data in a chart by clicking buttons on the worksheet.

You will use the Microsoft Excel macro recorder to automate work that you do regularly. You'll find out how macro sheets differ from worksheets. You'll learn techniques for documenting macros so that they're easier to read and understand. You'll run a macro, and you'll learn how to test it by running it one step at a time. You'll also create worksheet buttons, assign macros to the buttons, and run the macros by clicking the buttons.

You will learn how to:

- Record a macro.
- Understand a macro sheet.
- Edit and document a macro.
- Run a macro.
- Interrupt a macro.
- Step through a macro.
- Assign macros to worksheet buttons.

Estimated lesson time: 45 minutes

Start the lesson

1   Open the 17LESSN worksheet.
2   Save the worksheet as WCSSALES.
3   Close any other open windows.
4   From the Window menu, choose Arrange.
5   Choose the OK button.

Define the area as a database

By taking advantage of Microsoft Excel database features, you can write shorter macros to update and print data and plot it in a chart. Use the Set Database command on the Data menu to define the range where you'll enter data as a database. Microsoft Excel names the selected cells "Database."

1   Select cells C9:F20.
2   From the Data menu, choose Set Database.

Now you're ready to display the Macro toolbar and record a macro.

Using the Macro Toolbar

The Macro toolbar contains tools for creating macro sheets; for pasting functions and names into formulas; for recording, running, and stepping through macros; and for resuming interrupted macros.

Display the Macro toolbar

▶ From the toolbar shortcut menu, choose Macro.

The Macro toolbar is shown in the following illustration.

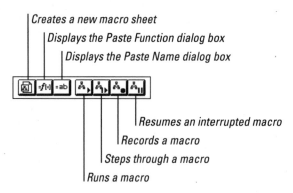

Creates a new macro sheet
Displays the Paste Function dialog box
Displays the Paste Name dialog box

Resumes an interrupted macro
Records a macro
Steps through a macro
Runs a macro

Now you're ready to start creating a macro.

Recording a Macro as You Work

With the Microsoft Excel macro recorder, you can easily create a macro that automates your tasks. Just start the macro recorder, go through your tasks, and then stop the macro recorder. Microsoft Excel records your actions as a macro on a macro sheet. You can run the macro whenever you want to repeat the tasks.

The Record command is like /Worksheet Learn in Lotus 1-2-3 Release 2.2.

The Record Macro tool With the Record Macro tool, you can start recording a macro without any preparation at all. The Record Macro tool opens a new macro sheet and prompts you to enter a macro name and an optional shortcut key. You don't need to look at the macro sheet until you finish recording your tasks. Clicking the Record Macro tool is equivalent to choosing the Record command from the Macro menu.

Start recording a macro

Use the Record Macro tool to start recording a macro that updates the WCSSALES worksheet data. You'll name the macro "Update" and give it the shortcut key U.

If you make a mistake while recording a macro, keep going. You can edit the macro later to remove unnecessary steps.

1   Click the Record Macro tool.

2   In the Name box, type **Update**

3   In Microsoft Excel for Windows, move to the Key: Ctrl+ box and type **u**

In Microsoft Excel for the Macintosh, move to the Option+⌘ Key box and type **u**

4   Select the Macro Sheet option button.

5   Choose the OK button.

Display the data form

You won't change any data right now. Just choose the Form command from the Data menu; then close the data form without making any changes.

1   From the Data menu, choose Form.

2   Choose the Close button.

The macro recorder recorded your actions so that the data form will be displayed when you run the Update macro.

Stop the macro recorder

You have finished recording the Update macro. Stop the macro recorder by clicking the Record Macro tool again.

▶   Click the Record Macro tool.

The Stop Recording tool   Microsoft Excel also provides a Stop Recording tool, which is displayed when you use the macro recorder to assign a macro to an object. You can also display it by using the Toolbars command on the Options menu. Clicking the Stop Recording tool has the same effect as clicking the Record Macro tool a second time or choosing the Stop Recorder command from the Macro menu.

Understanding Macro Sheets

Microsoft Excel macros are stored on a macro sheet, not on a worksheet.

Microsoft Excel macros are stored in documents called macro sheets. Now you'll see how macro sheets differ from worksheets.

Save the new macro sheet

1   Switch to Macro1.

2   Save the macro sheet as SALES.

Your macro sheet should look like the following illustration.

	A	B
1	Update (u)	
2	=DATAFORM()	
3	=RETURN()	
4		

The macro recorder recorded formulas for the steps you followed. If you didn't follow the steps exactly, your macro sheet may look slightly different from the illustration. You can edit the macro sheet to make it match the illustration.

Microsoft Excel macros are based on formulas, whereas 1-2-3 macros are based on strings representing keystrokes.

Displaying formulas in a worksheet or macro sheet is like using /Range Format Text and /Worksheet Global Format Text in 1-2-3.

Macros display formulas instead of values   Macro sheets usually display formulas, whereas worksheets usually display values. Macros are made up of formulas you write and Microsoft Excel functions, so it's more important to see formulas in a macro sheet than in a worksheet.

The Display command   With the Display command, you can control whether a worksheet or macro sheet displays values or formulas.

Macro functions and worksheet functions   Microsoft Excel has two types of functions: worksheet functions and macro functions. You can use worksheet functions on a worksheet or a macro sheet, but you can use macro functions only on a macro sheet. DATA.FORM and RETURN are examples of macro functions.

Change the display from formulas to values

Displaying the values returned by your macro functions is useful when you're testing a macro. You can also use a keyboard shortcut to alternate between displaying formulas and displaying values.

1   From the Options menu, choose Display.

2   Under Cells, clear the Formulas check box.

3   Choose the OK button.

You can also press CTRL+` (left single quotation mark) in Microsoft Excel for Windows or COMMAND+` (left single quotation mark) in Microsoft Excel for the Macintosh to switch between displaying formulas and displaying values.

Your macro sheet should look like the following illustration. Each macro function returns the value FALSE, because the functions haven't been calculated yet.

	A	B	C
1	Update (u)		
2	FALSE		
3	FALSE		
4			

How macros are calculated   Another difference between macro sheets and worksheets is that the formulas and functions in a macro sheet are calculated only when you run the macro. The macro is calculated one cell at a time, starting at the top of the macro, following the flow of logic, and ending at the RETURN function.

Change the display from values to formulas

Change the display back to formulas so that you can see the macro functions again. This time, use the keyboard shortcut.

▶   In Microsoft Excel for Windows, press CTRL+` (left single quotation mark).

In Microsoft Excel for the Macintosh, press COMMAND+` (left single quotation mark).

Defining a macro name   When a macro sheet is active and you choose the Define Name command from the Formula menu, the Define Name dialog box contains an extra box for defining macro names. When you write a macro on the macro sheet instead of using the recorder, you choose Define Name from the Formula menu to name the macro and to specify whether it is a command macro or a custom function. If it is a command macro, you can also assign a shortcut key. You used a custom function to convert Fahrenheit to Celsius in Lesson 6, "Putting Formulas to Work."

Display the names in the macro sheet

Choose the Define Name command from the Formula menu to see the names that the macro recorder defined in your macro sheet.

1   From the Formula menu, choose Define Name.

2   In the Names In Sheet box, select Update.

The Define Name dialog box is shown in the following illustration.

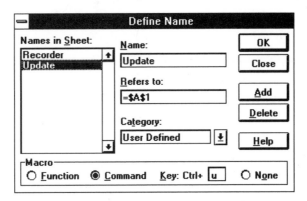

3   Choose the Close button.

Recording a Macro on an Open Macro Sheet

New macro sheets and the global macro sheet   When you click the Record Macro tool without a macro sheet open, Microsoft Excel displays a dialog box in which you specify the name of the macro, the shortcut key, and whether to store the macro in a new sheet or in the global macro sheet. If you select the Macro Sheet option button in the Record Macro dialog box, Microsoft Excel opens a new macro sheet and records your macro in column A. If you record a second or third macro on the same sheet, those macros are recorded in columns B, C, and so on.

If you select the Global Macro Sheet option button in the Record Macro dialog box, the macro is recorded in the next available column in the global macro sheet. The global macro sheet is always open and hidden when you start Microsoft Excel, so any macros stored there are available to all documents.

Once you have an open macro sheet, you may prefer to record a macro in a specific location.

The Set Recorder and Start Recorder commands   With the Set Recorder command, you can specify where you want the macro recorded in your macro sheet. If you select a single cell, all of the cells below that cell in the same column become the recorder range. Once you've specified where you want to record the macro, you can choose the Start Recorder command from the Macro menu or click the Record Macro tool to start recording your macro. Unlike the Record Macro tool and the Record command, the Start Recorder command does not display the Record Macro dialog box before recording the macro.

Action-equivalent functions   Whenever you use the macro recorder, you create a macro made up of action-equivalent functions. All of the functions in the recorded macro represent actions that you can also perform manually in Microsoft Excel.

Record a short macro to switch to the worksheet

You want the WCSSALES worksheet to be active whenever you run the Update macro. You can use the macro recorder to record the action of switching to the worksheet. Set the macro recorder to start recording in cell A5.

1   On the SALES macro sheet, select cell A5.

2   From the Macro menu, choose Set Recorder.

3   From the Macro menu, choose Start Recorder.

4   From the Window menu, choose WCSSALES.

Notice that the Record Macro tool appears pressed on the screen, indicating that the recorder is running.

5   Click the Record Macro tool to stop recording.

6   Switch back to the SALES macro sheet.

7   Double-click the column A heading boundary to display all the text in column A.

Your macro sheet should look like the following illustration. In Microsoft Excel for the Macintosh, the filename does not have the .XLS extension.

	A
1	Update (u)
2	=DATA.FORM()
3	=RETURN()
4	
5	=ACTIVATE("WCSSALES.XLS")
6	=RETURN()
7	

Editing and Documenting Macros

You edit a macro sheet the same way you edit a worksheet. You can edit cell contents in the formula bar, clear cells, move cells, insert cells, and delete cells. However, if you have macros in many different areas of a macro sheet, you may often need to insert or delete ranges of cells, not entire rows and columns as you usually do in worksheets.

Documenting a macro sheet is just as important as documenting a worksheet. Your macro sheet should be presented in an organized way so that it's easy to understand.

Insert the ACTIVATE function in the Update macro

Move your recorded ACTIVATE function to the beginning of the Update macro so that the Update macro will always switch to the WCSSALES worksheet first. Move cell A5 and insert it between cells A1 and A2.

1 Select cell A5.

2 Hold down SHIFT and drag the cell border to the top of cell A2. Don't release SHIFT until after you release the mouse button.

Clear the extra RETURN function

The RETURN function ends a macro, just as a blank cell ends a 1-2-3 macro.

The RETURN function ends a macro.

1 Select cell A6.

2 From the Edit menu, choose Clear.

3 Choose the OK button.

Your macro sheet should look like the following illustration.

	A	B	C
1	Update (u)		
2	=ACTIVATE("WCSSALES.XLS")		
3	=DATA.FORM()		
4	=RETURN()		
5			
6			

Add comments to the macro functions

Now add comments to each of the macro functions so that you can remember what the Update macro does.

▶ In column B, type the comments shown in the following illustration.

	A	B
1	Update (u)	
2	=ACTIVATE("WCSSALES.XLS")	Make sure the worksheet is active
3	=DATA.FORM()	Display data form
4	=RETURN()	End macro
5		

Format and document the macro sheet

It's okay to have blank cells in Microsoft Excel macros.

You'll eventually have other macros on this macro sheet. You'll use column A for cell names, column B for macro statements, and column C for comments. You can widen columns B and C to see more of the cell contents. Remember that you can move a block of data by dragging it with the mouse.

▶ Format your macro sheet to look like the following illustration.

	A	B	C
1		COMMAND MACROS	
2			
3	Cell Names	Macro name or statement	Shortcut key/Comments
4		Update	(u)
5		=ACTIVATE("WCSSALES.XLS")	Make sure the worksheet is active
6		=DATA.FORM()	Display data form
7		=RETURN()	End macro
8			

Running a Macro

When you run a macro, Microsoft Excel calculates the formulas in the macro sheet one cell at a time.

You can run any macro created in Lotus 1-2-3 Release 2.01 in Microsoft Excel.

Running a macro   With the Run command on the Macro menu, you can run any command macro that is on an open macro sheet. You can select the name of the macro to run, or you can specify the cell in the macro sheet at which to start calculating. You can also run a command macro by pressing the keyboard shortcut you assigned to the macro or by selecting the first cell in the macro and then clicking the Run Macro tool.

Run the Update macro

Run the Update macro to see how it switches to the WCSSALES worksheet and displays the data form.

1   Select cell B4 on the SALES macro sheet.

2   Click the Run Macro tool.

Pressing CTRL+ (or COMMAND+SHIFT+) the shortcut key in Microsoft Excel is like pressing ALT+ the shortcut key in 1-2-3.

You can also press CTRL+U in Microsoft Excel for Windows or COMMAND+OPTION+U in Microsoft Excel for the Macintosh instead of doing steps 1 and 2.

3   Choose the Close button to close the data form.

4   Switch back to the SALES macro sheet.

Interrupting a Running Macro

Pressing ESC to interrupt a macro is like pressing CTRL+BREAK in 1-2-3.

Interrupting a macro   You can interrupt a running macro by pressing ESC. In Microsoft Excel for the Macintosh, you can also press COMMAND+PERIOD. When you interrupt a macro, a dialog box appears. You can choose the Step button to run the macro a single statement at a time, the Halt button to stop the macro, the Continue button to resume running the macro, the Goto button to select the cell at which the macro was interrupted, or the Help button to get help.

In Microsoft Excel for Windows, the dialog box looks like the following illustration.

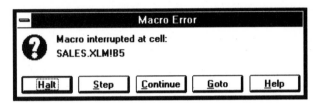

In Microsoft Excel for the Macintosh, the dialog box looks like the following illustration.

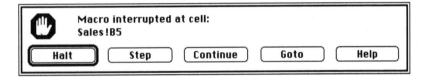

Stepping Through a Macro

The Single Step dialog box is like STEP mode (ALT+F2) in 1-2-3.

The Step Macro tool   Calculating a macro one formula at a time can be useful when you're testing the macro. If you run your macro by clicking the Step Macro tool instead of the Run Macro tool, you can run the macro with the Single Step dialog box displayed.

Step through the macro

Use the Step Macro tool to step through a macro one formula at a time.

1   Select cell B5 on the SALES macro sheet.

   2   Click the Step Macro tool.

The Single Step dialog box appears, showing the next formula that will be calculated in your macro.

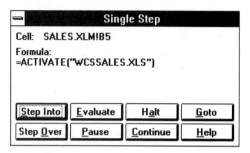

3 Choose the Step Into button to calculate the next formula.

4 Choose the Halt button to stop running the Update macro.

5 Switch back to the SALES macro sheet.

The STEP function You can include a STEP function in your macro to start stepping through the macro at a specific cell. This is useful if you want to run most of the macro normally but need to step through certain cells to debug them.

Add a STEP function to the Update macro

You'll insert cells at the beginning of your Update macro and add the STEP function. Instead of typing the STEP function, try pasting it into the macro with the Paste Function tool. You can always use the Paste Function tool if you forget the exact name or syntax of a function.

1 Select cells B5:C7.

2 Drag the selection to B6:C8.

3 Select cell B5.

4 Click the Paste Function tool on the Macro toolbar.

5 In the Function Category box, select Macro Control.

6 In the Paste Function box, select STEP.

In Microsoft Excel for Windows, you can also press S to move quickly to the first function that begins with "S," and then use the DOWN ARROW key to select STEP.

7 Choose the OK button.

8 Click the enter box or press ENTER.

9 Add left and right borders to cells B5:C5.

10 Type a comment for your STEP function, as shown in the following illustration.

	A	B	C
1		COMMAND MACROS	
2			
3	Cell Names	Macro name or statement	Shortcut key/Comments
4		Update	(u)
5		=STEP()	Calculate one function at a time
6		=ACTIVATE("WCSSALES.XLS")	Make sure the worksheet is active
7		=DATA.FORM()	Display data form
8		=RETURN()	End macro
9			

Step through the Update macro

When you run your Update macro, it will start by displaying the Single Step dialog box.

1 From the Macro menu, choose Run.

2 Select SALES.XLM!Update in Microsoft Excel for Windows or SALES!Update in Microsoft Excel for the Macintosh.

3 Choose the OK button.

The Single Step dialog box appears, showing the next formula that will be calculated in your macro.

4 Choose the Step Into button to calculate the next formula.

5 Choose the Halt button to stop running the Update macro.

6 Switch back to the SALES macro sheet.

Stepping into vs. stepping over a macro formula When you're using the Single Step dialog box, you can choose the Step Into or Step Over button to calculate the next formula. These two buttons perform the same action unless the macro formula contains a *subroutine*. A subroutine is a macro that is run by another macro. Choosing the Step Into button steps through each formula in the subroutine. Choosing the Step Over button runs the subroutine without stepping through each of its formulas.

Watching Microsoft Excel evaluate a single macro formula When you're using the Single Step dialog box, you can choose the Evaluate button repeatedly to see how Microsoft Excel evaluates a single macro formula. This is useful for testing long macro statements with many nested functions.

Disable the STEP function in the Update macro

If you delete the equal sign from STEP, Microsoft Excel can't calculate it as a function. Later, if you want to use the STEP function again, you can retype the equal sign.

1 Select cell B5.

2 In the formula bar, delete the equal sign to change =STEP( ) to STEP( ).

3 Click the enter box or press ENTER.

Recording and Naming Another Macro

Now you're ready to create your second macro. The Print macro will display the WCSSALES worksheet in print preview.

Start recording your Print macro

You'll use the Set Recorder and Start Recorder commands on the Macro menu to record the macro starting in cell B11.

1   Select cell B11.

2   From the Macro menu, choose Set Recorder.

3   From the Macro menu, choose Start Recorder.

Record a macro to preview the worksheet data

You'll set the Database range on the SALES worksheet as the print area. That way, no matter how many rows of data you enter, the macro will preview all of your data.

1   Switch to WCSSALES.

2   From the Formula menu, choose Goto.

3   In the Goto box, select Database.

4   Choose the OK button.

5   From the Options menu, choose Set Print Area.

6   From the File menu, choose Print Preview.

7   Choose the Close button.

Stop the macro recorder and switch to the macro sheet

1   Click the Record Macro tool.

2   Switch to the SALES macro sheet.

Name the macro "Print"

Use the Define Name command on the Formula menu to name your macro "Print", define it as a command macro, and assign the shortcut key P. You'll also type the macro name in the macro sheet so that it's easy to remember.

1   Select cell B10.

2   Type **Print**

3   Click the enter box or press ENTER.

4   From the Formula menu, choose Define Name.

5   Under Macro, select the Command option button.

6   In Microsoft Excel for Windows, move to the Key: Ctrl+ box and type **p**

In Microsoft Excel for the Macintosh, move to the Option+⌘ Key box and type **p**

7   Choose the OK button.

Document the Print macro

▶   Format and add comments to your Print macro so that it looks like the following illustration.

	A	B	C	D
1		COMMAND MACROS		
2				
3	Cell Names	Macro name or statement	Shortcut key/Comments	
4		Update	(u)	
5		=STEP()	Calculate one function at a time	
6		=ACTIVATE("WCSSALES.XLS")	Make sure the worksheet is active	
7		=DATA.FORM()	Display data form	
8		=RETURN()	End macro	
9				
10		Print	(p)	
11		=ACTIVATE("WCSSALES.XLS")	Make sure the worksheet is active	
12		=FORMULA.GOTO("Database")	Select area named "Database"	
13		=SET.PRINT.AREA()	Set selection as print area	
14		=PRINT.PREVIEW()	Print preview	
15		=RETURN()	End macro	
16				
17				
18				

Running Macros with Buttons

You can make your macros easier to use by assigning them to buttons or other worksheet objects.

Creating Worksheet Buttons

You create buttons on your worksheet the same way you create text boxes and other graphic objects. Click the Button tool on the Utility toolbar, and then drag to create a button on the worksheet. When you release the mouse button, the button appears with the name "Button." Microsoft Excel displays the Assign To Object dialog box so that you can select the macro you want to assign to the button. You can format the text in the button by choosing the Font command from the Format menu. If you want to edit or format the name of a button after the button is active, hold down CTRL in Microsoft Excel for Windows or COMMAND in Microsoft Excel for the Macintosh while clicking the button, and edit or format the button name as you would any text.

Splitting the worksheet window and freezing the panes   You can use the Freeze Panes command on the Window menu to create an area for buttons that will not scroll up or down with the worksheet.

Create an area for buttons

You will create an area for buttons at the top of the WCSSALES worksheet.

1   Switch to the WCSSALES worksheet.

2   Select rows 1 through 3.

3   From the Edit menu, choose Insert.

4   Point to the horizontal split box on the scroll bar, and drag the split box to row 3.

The split box in Microsoft Excel for Windows

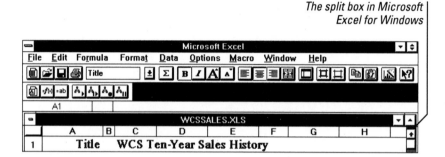

The split box in Microsoft Excel for the Macintosh

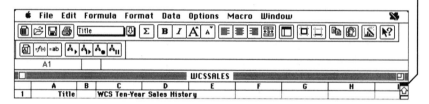

5   From the Window menu, choose Freeze Panes.

6   Select row 2.

7   From the Format menu, choose Row Height.

8   In the Row Height box, type **18**

9   Choose the OK button.

Your worksheet should look like the following illustration.

	A	B	C	D	E	F	G
1							
2							
3							
4	**Title**		**WCS Ten-Year Sales History**				
5	**Created by**		Sam Bryan				
6	**Date Modified**		17-Jun-93				
7							
8	**Purpose**		This worksheet summarizes West Coast Sales' gross revenue				
9			for the previous 10 years.				
10							
11	**Sales History**					**Market**	
12			Year	Company	Industry	**Share**	
13			1982	$62,947	$1,210,000	4.94%	
14			1983	$69,941	$1,230,000	5.38%	
15			1984	$93,254	$1,260,000	6.89%	
16			1985	$124,339	$1,300,000	8.73%	
17			1986	$138,155	$1,350,000	9.28%	
18			1987	$162,535	$1,380,000	10.54%	
19			1988	$205,740	$1,370,000	13.06%	
20			1989	$233,796	$1,400,000	14.31%	
21			1990	$320,268	$1,500,000	17.59%	

Display the Utility toolbar

▶   From the toolbar shortcut menu, choose Utility.

Create an Update button

Add a button at the top of the worksheet to run the Update macro.

1   Click the Button tool on the Utility toolbar.

2   Hold down ALT in Microsoft Excel for Windows or COMMAND in Microsoft Excel for the Macintosh while dragging the pointer across cell C2.

This aligns the button with cell C2.

3   In the Assign Macro box, select SALES.XLM!Update in Microsoft Excel for Windows or SALES!Update in Microsoft Excel for the Macintosh.

4   Choose the OK button.

Format the button text

1   With the button still selected, type **Update**

2   Select the button by clicking the border or by holding down CTRL in Microsoft Excel for Windows or COMMAND in Microsoft Excel for the Macintosh while clicking the button.

3   From the Format menu, choose Font.

4   In the Font box, select MS Serif in Microsoft Excel for Windows or Times in Microsoft Excel for the Macintosh.

5   In Microsoft Excel for Windows, select Bold Italic in the Font Style box.

In Microsoft Excel for the Macintosh, select the Bold and Italic check boxes under Style.

6   Choose the OK button.

Create a Print button

Add a button at the top of the worksheet to run the Print macro.

1   Click the Button tool on the Utility toolbar.

2   Hold down ALT in Microsoft Excel for Windows or COMMAND in Microsoft Excel for the Macintosh while dragging the pointer across cell E2.

This aligns the button with cell E2.

3   In the Assign Macro box, select SALES.XLM!Print in Microsoft Excel for Windows or SALES!Print in Microsoft Excel for the Macintosh.

4   Choose the OK button.

Format the Print button

1   With the button still selected, type **Print**

2   Select the button by clicking the border or by holding down CTRL in Microsoft Excel for Windows or COMMAND in Microsoft Excel for the Macintosh while clicking the button.

3   From the Format menu, choose Font.

4   In the Font box, select MS Serif in Microsoft Excel for Windows or Times in Microsoft Excel for the Macintosh.

5   In Microsoft Excel for Windows, select Bold Italic in the Font Style box.

In Microsoft Excel for the Macintosh, select the Bold and Italic check boxes under Style.

6   Choose the OK button.

Your worksheet should look like the following illustration.

	A	B	C	D	E	F	G
1							
2			*Update*		*Print*		
3							
4	**Title**		WCS Ten-Year Sales History				
5	**Created by**		Sam Bryan				
6	**Date Modified**		17-Jun-92				
8	**Purpose**		This worksheet summarizes West Coast Sales' gross				
9			revenue for the previous 10 years.				
11	**Sales History**						
12			Year	Company	Industry	Market Share	
13			1982	$62,947	$1,210,000	4.94%	
14			1983	$69,941	$1,230,000	5.38%	
15			1984	$93,254	$1,260,000	6.89%	
16			1985	$124,339	$1,300,000	8.73%	

Test the buttons

You've set up buttons to run the macros. Run each macro by clicking its button.

1   Click the Update button.

2   Choose the Close button in the data form.

3   Click the Print button.

4   Choose the Close button in the print preview window.

Save your work

You will continue to use the worksheet and the macro sheet in the "One Step Further" exercise.

1   Click the Save File tool.

2   Switch to the SALES macro sheet.

3   Click the Save File tool.

One Step Further

You've just created macros to update a worksheet and view it in print preview. Now you'll create a macro that plots the database in the WCSSALES worksheet in a chart. Then you'll create a button to run the macro.

Once you've created the chart macro and assigned it to a worksheet button, you'll add 1993 company and industry revenues to the WCSSALES worksheet, plot the data in a chart, and preview the printed page by clicking the Print button.

1   In the SALES macro sheet, select cell B18 and set the macro recorder.

2   Start the macro recorder.

3   Switch to the WCSSALES worksheet.

4   Use the Goto command on the Formula menu to select the database.

5   Open the 17SALECH template.

6   Enlarge the chart window to fill the screen.

7   Stop the macro recorder.

8   Switch to the SALES macro sheet.

In the following illustration, the macro has comments and formatting added. Your macro may be slightly different, depending on the location of the 17SALECH template in your directory or folder.

9   Use the following illustration to add comments and formatting to your macro.

	A	B	C
1		COMMAND MACROS	
2			
3	Cell Names	Macro name or statement	Shortcut key/Comments
4		Update	(u)
5		STEP()	Calculate one function at a time
6		=ACTIVATE("WCSSALES.XLS")	Make sure the worksheet is active
7		=DATA.FORM()	Display data form
8		=RETURN()	End macro
9			
10		Print	(p)
11		=ACTIVATE("WCSSALES.XLS")	Make sure the worksheet is active
12		=FORMULA.GOTO("Database")	Select area named "Database"
13		=SET.PRINT.AREA()	Set selection as print area
14		=PRINT.PREVIEW()	Print preview
15		=RETURN()	End macro
16			
17		Chart	(c)
18		=ACTIVATE("WCSSALES.XLS")	Make sure the worksheet is active
19		=FORMULA.GOTO("Database")	Select area named "Database"
20		=DIRECTORY("C:\EXCEL\PRACTICE")	Change the directory
21		=OPEN("17SALECH.XLT")	Open the 17SALECH template
22		=WINDOW.MAXIMIZE()	Enlarge the chart window
23		=RETURN()	End macro
24			

10   Use the Define Name command on the Formula menu to name the macro "Chart" and specify "c" as the shortcut key.

11   Add a button to the WCSSALES worksheet, and assign the Chart macro to the button. Format the button to look like the others.

12 Click the Update button, and enter the information in the following table as a new record in the data form.

In this field	Type
Year	**7/1/1993**
Company	**552000**
Industry	**2200000**

13 Click the Chart button to plot the data in a chart.

Your chart should look like the following illustration.

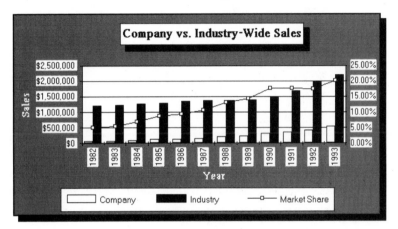

You've completed the WCSSALES worksheet. You can decide whether you want to save the chart. If you want to use the WCSSALES worksheet together with the SALES macro sheet, save the documents together as a workbook file. To see a solution to this exercise, open the 17STEP workbook file. Close all of the documents when you are finished.

Lesson Summary

To	Do this
Record a macro	Choose the Record command from the Macro menu, or click the Record Macro tool. You can also record your macro in a specific location by choosing the Set Recorder command and then the Start Recorder command from the Macro menu.
Edit and document a macro	Select the cells in the macro sheet and edit them in the formula bar, just as you would edit cells on a worksheet.

To	Do this
Interrupt a macro	Press ESC. In Microsoft Excel for the Macintosh, you can also press COMMAND+PERIOD.
Step through a macro	Click the Step Macro tool, or choose Run from the Macro menu and then choose the Step button. You can also include a STEP function in your macro to start stepping at a specific location.

For more information about	See in the *Microsoft Excel User's Guide*
Creating and using macros	Chapter 6, "Automating Tasks with Command Macros," in Book 2

For an online lesson about	Start the tutorial Learning Microsoft Excel and complete this lesson
Macros in general	"What Is a Macro?"
Recording macros and writing custom functions	"Using a Macro"

For information about starting an online tutorial lesson, see "Using the Online Tutorials" in "Getting Ready" earlier in this book.

Preview of the Next Section

Congratulations! You have completed all of the lessons in this book. You now have the skills you need to use Microsoft Excel efficiently and productively. If you need to brush up on specific tasks, you can repeat any of the lessons at any time.

In the appendixes that follow, you can learn how to set up a printer. You'll also find a list of the new features in Microsoft Excel version 4.0 that are covered in this book, including the lessons in which they are used. The last appendix contains a list of books that you might find useful as you continue to learn Microsoft Excel.

Appendixes

Installing and Setting Up Your Printer

Your selected printer is used for other applications, not just Microsoft Excel.

This appendix provides information about selecting a printer for use with either Microsoft Excel for Windows or Microsoft Excel for the Macintosh. You should also go through this appendix if you are unfamiliar with installing and configuring a printer for Microsoft Excel for Windows.

For more information about installing your printer for use with Microsoft Excel, see Chapter 16, "Printing," in Book 1 of the *Microsoft Excel User's Guide.* For more information about printing in your operating environment, see the documentation for your operating environment.

You will learn how to:

- Install a new printer for use in Microsoft Excel for Windows.
- Configure a printer for use in Microsoft Excel for Windows.
- Set up a printer for use in Microsoft Excel for Windows.
- Select a printer for use in Microsoft Excel for the Macintosh.

Setting Up a Printer for Use in Microsoft Excel for Windows

Installing a New Printer

There are two ways you can install a new printer after you've installed Microsoft Excel.

Control Panel   The easiest way to install a new printer is to use Control Panel, a utility application that you can run while using Microsoft Excel for Windows.

Setup program   The Setup program you use to install Microsoft Windows includes printer and plotter setup. You can rerun the Setup program and specify new printers.

Using Control Panel is the most convenient way to install a new printer, because you can make the changes without leaving Microsoft Excel. This appendix explains how to use Control Panel. For more information on installing printers, see your Microsoft Windows documentation.

Start Control Panel

1   From the Control menu in Microsoft Excel, choose Run.

2   Select the Control Panel option button.

3   Choose the OK button.

The Windows Control Panel window looks like the following illustration. The exact positions of the icons may vary.

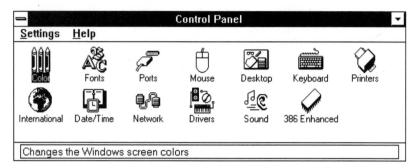

You can do more than install a printer with Control Panel. For example, you can select the Mouse option and change the double-click speed. You can also change other operating environment settings such as date and time, background colors, and network configuration.

Install a new printer

1 Double-click the Printers option.

The Printers dialog box is shown in the following illustration.

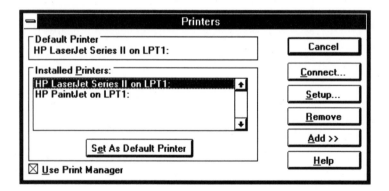

2 To install a new printer, choose the Add button.

The Printers dialog box expands.

3 In the List of Printers box, select the type of printer you want to install.

4   Choose the Install button.

You will see a message asking you to insert the disk that contains the printer driver software for the printer.

5   Insert the disk and choose the OK button.

You can select a printer port by using Control Panel.

Configure a printer

1   With the Control Panel dialog box displayed, double-click the Printers option.

2   In the Installed Printers box, select the printer you want to configure.

3   Choose the Connect button.

The Connect dialog box is shown in the following illustration.

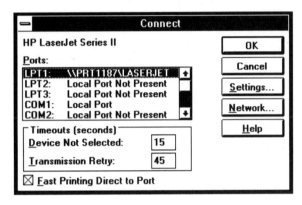

4   Select the port to which you want to connect the printer.

5   Choose the OK button.

6   Choose the Close button to close the Printers dialog box.

Quit Control Panel

▶   In the upper-left corner of the Control Panel window, double-click the Control-menu box.

Changing Printer Settings

You can change printer settings for all applications with the Page Setup command.

You can also use Control Panel to change printer settings, or you can change them from within Microsoft Excel. You can change the default settings for paper orientation (portrait or landscape), paper size, paper source (such as a specific tray or manual feed), and print resolution (measured in dots per inch).

Control Panel   To change printer settings from Control Panel, select the Printers option and choose the Setup button. Select the options you want and choose the OK button.

*The Printer Setup
button is like
/Worksheet Global
Default Printer
in 1-2-3.*

Printer Setup   You can display the same dialog box and make the same changes by choosing the Page Setup command from the File menu and then choosing the Printer Setup button. In the Printer Setup dialog box, you can select a printer from among the printers you've installed and then choose the Setup button to change paper orientation, paper size, and other settings.

Note If you choose the Printer Setup button in the Page Setup dialog box, you will change the printer settings for all of your applications. If you want to change the settings for the active document only, change the settings in the Page Setup dialog box as described in Lesson 11, "Setting Up the Page and Printing."

Set up your printer

1   From the File menu, choose Page Setup.

2   Choose the Printer Setup button.

3   In the Printer box, select the printer whose settings you want to change.

4   Choose the Setup button.

   The printer dialog box is displayed.

5   Select the options you want to change.

   For information on the dialog box options, choose the Help button.

6   Choose the OK button.

7   Choose the OK button in the Printer Setup dialog box.

8   Choose the OK button in the Page Setup dialog box.

Selecting a Printer for Use in Microsoft Excel for the Macintosh

On the Macintosh, you use the Chooser desk accessory on the Apple menu () to select printers for all your applications. Using the Chooser desk accessory is a convenient way to change printers, because you can make the changes without leaving Microsoft Excel.

Open the Chooser from the Apple menu

▶   From the Apple menu () in the upper-left corner of the Microsoft Excel window, choose Chooser.

The Chooser dialog box is shown in the following illustration.

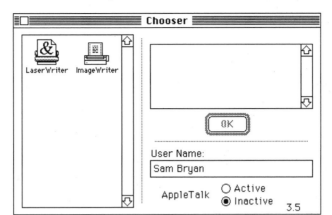

Select a new printer

1 Click the LaserWriter, ImageWriter, or other printer icon.

2 If you are printing on an ImageWriter printer, click the icon for the port (printer or modem) to which the printer is attached.

If you are on an AppleTalk network, select the AppleTalk zone and then the name of the printer.

Close the Chooser

▶ Click the close box to close the Chooser.

Summary

To	Do this
Install a new printer for use in Microsoft Excel for Windows	Use Control Panel and choose the Add button.
Change your printer configuration	Use Control Panel and choose the Connect button.
Change your printer settings	Use the Page Setup command on the File menu, and choose the Printer Setup button; then choose the Setup button.
Select a printer for use in Microsoft Excel for the Macintosh	Use the Chooser desk accessory to select a printer.

New Features in Microsoft Excel Version 4.0

The following tables list the features that are new in Microsoft Excel version 4.0, along with the lesson in this book in which you can learn about each feature. For comprehensive descriptions of new features, see Chapter 3, "What's New in Version 4.0," in Book 1 of the *Microsoft Excel User's Guide*.

New Ease-of-Use Features

To learn how to	See
Create a series of incremental or re-peating dates, numbers, or other values	Lesson 2, "Entering Numbers and Formulas"
Get quick access to the most frequently used commands and actions by using the Standard toolbar	Lesson 5, "Copying and Moving Cell Data and Formats"
Display several new toolbars that group related tools and that are easily customized	Lesson 3, "Formatting a Worksheet"
Use shortcut menus to display essential commands directly under your mouse pointer	Lesson 3, "Formatting a Worksheet"
Select number formats from format categories in the Number Format dialog box	Lesson 3, "Formatting a Worksheet"
Freeze panes to keep row or column titles displayed as you scroll through a worksheet	Lesson 5, "Copying and Moving Cell Data and Formats"
Move and copy data with the mouse	Lesson 5, "Copying and Moving Cell Data and Formats"
Group related or dependent Microsoft Excel documents into workbooks	Lesson 7, "Linking Worksheets"

New Formatting and Presentation Features

To learn how to	See
Quickly format a range of data, such as a table, with professionally designed font, color, and format combinations	Lesson 5, "Copying and Moving Cell Data and Formats"
Create custom reports consisting of named views and scenarios	Lesson 11, "Setting Up the Page and Printing"
Create onscreen slide shows of Microsoft Excel documents	Lesson 16, "Creating a Presentation Using Charts and Graphics"

New Analysis Features

To learn how to	See
Define named views of worksheet areas and print the views you want	Lesson 4, "Working with Formatting and Display Features"
Create scenarios to apply to "what-if" models	Lesson 10, "Analyzing Data"

New Printing Features

To learn how to	See
Create headers and footers for your printed Microsoft Excel documents	Lesson 16, "Creating a Presentation Using Charts and Graphics"

New Chart Features

To learn how to	See
Get step-by-step assistance when creating charts	Lesson 14, "Creating and Formatting a Chart"
Use the Chart toolbar for quick access to chart types and formatting	Lesson 14, "Creating and Formatting a Chart"

New Database Features

To learn how to	See
Create crosstab tables to summarize and compare your database information	Lesson 13, "Database Reporting"

New Customizing and Automating Features

To learn how to	See
Use the Macro toolbar to record and run macros	Lesson 17, "Recording Macros"
Use a global macro sheet on which you can store the macros you want to use with all of your worksheets	Lesson 17, "Recording Macros"

For More Information

Following is a partial list of books that you may find useful as you continue learning about Microsoft Excel. Many of the titles listed below are appropriate for either classroom or individual training and reference.

For introductory learning material, see:

- Soucie, Ralph. *Getting Started With Microsoft Excel 4 for Windows,* 2nd Edition. Redmond, WA: Microsoft Press, 1992.

  This book is written for new Microsoft Excel users.

For general-purpose tutorial and reference material, see:

- The Cobb Group. *Running Microsoft Excel*, 3rd Edition. Redmond, WA: Microsoft Press, 1992.

- Person, Ron. *Using Excel 4 for Windows,* Special Edition. Carmel, IN: Que Corporation, 1992.

Both of these books offer comprehensive tutorial and reference information. They are written for Microsoft Excel for Windows only.

- The Cobb Group. *Microsoft Excel 4 Companion*. Redmond, WA: Microsoft Press, 1992.

  This comprehensive reference book is written for Microsoft Excel for the Macintosh only.

For information on writing macros and designing spreadsheets, see:

- Kinata, Chris and Kyd, Charles. *The Complete Guide to Microsoft Excel Macros,* 2nd Edition. Redmond, WA: Microsoft Press, 1992.

  This book will appeal to anyone who wants to use the powerful Microsoft Excel macro programming language to automate tasks or develop custom applications.

- Wexler, Steve and Julianne Sharer for WexTech Systems, Inc. *Microsoft Excel Macros Step by Step*. Redmond, WA: Microsoft Press, 1992.

  This book provides self-paced hands-on tutorials for the Microsoft Excel user who is interested in macro programming.

Both of these books are written for both Microsoft Excel for Windows and Microsoft Excel for the Macintosh.

- Nevison, John M. *Microsoft Excel Spreadsheet Design*. New York, NY: Brady Books, 1990.

  This book provides a compendium of practical advice regarding spreadsheet design. It is especially valuable for anyone who designs worksheet models for others. This book is written for both Microsoft Excel for Windows and Microsoft Excel for the Macintosh.

Glossary

Argument   Information you supply to a Microsoft Excel function for calculation.

Array   Used to build formulas that produce multiple results or that operate on a group of arguments arranged in rows and columns. There are two types of arrays in Microsoft Excel: array ranges and array constants. An array range is a rectangular area of cells sharing one common formula; an array constant is a specially arranged group of constants used as an argument in a formula.

Automatic linking   A form of data exchange in which changes in data are reflected immediately in all documents linked to the data. This form of linking allows you to see any changes to data immediately, but it gives you less control over when shared data changes are incorporated into your document.

Axes   Lines bordering the plot area that provide a frame of reference for measurement or comparison on a chart. A two-dimensional (2-D) chart has two axes. A three-dimensional (3-D) chart has two or three axes, depending on the data view selected.

Balloon Help   In Microsoft Excel for the Macintosh, a form of Help that is available only to users of Macintosh system software version 7.0. When Balloon Help is active, just point and a brief explanation of whatever the mouse is pointing to appears.

Bound   When a document is bound to a workbook, it can only appear in that workbook. A bound document is saved in the workbook file.

Chart   A graphic presentation of data from a worksheet. You can create a chart in a separate document or embedded on a worksheet. An embedded chart can be linked to data on other worksheets.

Chart data series   A group of related data points to be plotted on a chart. Each data point consists of a category and a value. You can plot one or more data series on a chart.

Clipboard   The holding place for information you cut or copy with the Cut, Copy, or Copy Picture command. If you cut or copy worksheet cells, the Clipboard does not display the actual cells. Instead, it displays the action you are taking and the location of the cells you are cutting or copying; for example, "Copy 2R x 3C" or "Cut 2R x 3C."

Command macro   A sequence of commands you record on a macro sheet. Later, you can run the recorded macro to automate your work. A command macro can be assigned to a shortcut key, a button, an object, or a tool, for easy use.

Comparison operators   There are six standard comparison (logical) operators you can use in Microsoft Excel formulas, as shown in the following table.

Operator	Meaning
=	Equal to
>	Greater than
<	Less than
>=	Greater than or equal to
<=	Less than or equal to
<>	Not equal to

Consolidation by category   Consolidates worksheet cells based on their category name. The worksheet cells you want to consolidate must have identical category labels, but the position of the categories within each worksheet may vary.

Consolidation by position   Consolidates worksheet cells based on their position. The worksheets that contain the cells you want to consolidate must have identical layouts so that similar categories of data occupy exactly the same location in each source area.

Constant   A number value, text value, logical value, or error value that does not start with an equal sign (=).

Criteria   Information you enter in a worksheet range that determines which records will be affected when you choose the Find, Extract, or Delete command from the Data menu.

Crosstab table   A summary of fields in a database. You create a crosstab table with the Crosstab ReportWizard.

Data sheet   A worksheet in which you save input values that you want to substitute in your worksheet cells.

Data table   A range of cells summarizing the results of substituting different values in one or more formulas on your worksheet. In Microsoft Excel, there are one-input tables and two-input tables.

Database   A range of cells on a worksheet. The first row of the database contains the field names. Each additional row of the database is one record; each column in the record is one field.

Dependent worksheet   A worksheet that contains an external reference formula or a remote reference formula. When you link two Microsoft Excel worksheets, the dependent worksheet relies on another worksheet for the value in the external reference formula. When you link a Microsoft Excel worksheet to a document in a different application, the worksheet is dependent on that document for the value in the remote reference formula.

Dynamic linking   A form of data exchange in which changes in data are reflected when the document is saved. This form of linking provides more control over when shared data changes are incorporated into your document.

Embedding   The process by which an object is copied into another document. Embedding can take place between documents within the same application or between documents in different applications, as long as both applications support the embedding process. Because an embedded object maintains "ties" with its original application, you can open that application and edit the object by just double-clicking the embedded object.

External absolute reference   An external absolute reference consists of the name of the source worksheet, followed by an exclamation point (!) and the absolute reference to the cell range. Example: "SALES!$A$1:$H$1".

External reference   A reference to another Microsoft Excel worksheet. An external reference can designate a single cell, a cell range, or a named cell or range.

External reference formula   A formula in a worksheet that contains a reference to a single cell, a cell range, or a named cell or range in another worksheet. An external reference formula creates the actual link between Microsoft Excel worksheets.

Extract range   A separate area on a worksheet set aside for data retrieved and copied from the database.

Field   A column or cell in a database. Each column in a database contains a different category of data, and each cell in a database shares a common characteristic with other cells in the same column.

Field name row   The first row of a database. Each cell in the row contains a name describing the contents of the cells beneath it.

File format   The way information in a document is stored in a file. Different programs use different file formats. You can save documents in a variety of file formats using the Save As command on the File menu.

Floating toolbar   A toolbar that is in a window with a title bar, stays on top of the other windows, and is not docked.

Formula   A sequence of values, cell references, names, functions, or operators that is contained in a cell and produces a new value from existing values. A formula always begins with an equal sign (=).

Formula bar   A bar at the top of your Microsoft Excel window that is used to enter or edit values and formulas in cells or charts. It displays the constant value or formula contained in the active cell.

Function   A built-in formula that takes a series of values, uses them to perform an operation, and returns the result of the operation. Functions can be entered in the formula bar as part of formulas.

Global macro sheet   A hidden macro sheet that is automatically managed by Microsoft Excel. Macros recorded in the global macro sheet are available every time you start the program.

Graphic object   A line or shape (button, text box, oval, rectangle, arc, picture) you draw using the tools on the toolbar, or a picture you paste into Microsoft Excel.

Group   A temporary grouping of worksheets and macro sheets. Any changes you make in data or formatting on the active sheet are reflected in all sheets in the group.

Handles   Small black squares located in the lower-right corner of selected cells or around selected graphic objects, chart items, or text. By dragging the handles, you can perform actions such as moving, copying, filling, sizing, or formatting on the selected cells, objects, chart items, or text.

Input cell   The cell into which values from a data table are substituted.

Legend   A key that identifies the series markers in a chart. Includes each pattern or symbol used as a marker, followed by the corresponding data series or category name.

Linked documents   Separate documents that are dynamically connected so that a formula in one document refers to a value in another document. Because the link enables Microsoft Excel to update the value when it changes, the changes made in one document are immediately reflected in the other. Any time you build a formula or define a name in one worksheet by entering a reference to a cell, cell range, or name in another worksheet, Microsoft Excel links the two worksheets.

Logical value   The result of a formula that contains a logical function or equation, such as 1=1, that is either true or false. Microsoft Excel recognizes both TRUE and FALSE and 1 and 0 as logical values.

Macro sheet   A document that is similar to a worksheet and that contains sets of instructions (macros) for accomplishing specific tasks.

Menu key   The menu key activates the menu bar. In Microsoft Excel for Windows, the ALT key and F10 both function as menu keys. In Microsoft Excel for the Macintosh, the SLASH key (/) activates the menu bar. In addition, you can specify an alternate menu key in the Workspace dialog box.

Moving border   A moving dotted line that surrounds a cell or range of cells. A moving border appears around a cell or range that has been cut or copied, or around a cell or range you are inserting in a formula.

Name   An identifier you create to refer to a cell, a group of cells, a constant value, an array of values, or a formula. When you use names in a formula, the formula is easier to read and remember than a formula containing cell references.

Nonadjacent selections   A selection of noncontiguous cells and/or objects.

Normal style   The style automatically applied to cells until you apply your own style.

One-input data table   A table you produce using the Table command on the Data menu. Using a formula containing one variable and a series of values to be substituted for that variable, you can generate a one-row or one-column series of results based on the series of values you entered.

Paste area   The destination for data you cut with the Cut command or copy with the Copy command.

Plot area   The area of a chart in which Microsoft Excel plots data. On a 2-D chart, the plot area is bounded by the axes and includes all markers that represent data points. On a 3-D chart, it is defined by the walls and floor of the chart. The walls and floor can be formatted independently.

Range   On a worksheet, a rectangular section containing two or more cells.

Record   One row in a database. The first row of the database contains the field name. Each additional row of the database is one record. Each record contains the same categories of data as every other record in the database.

Reference   The location of a cell or group of cells on a worksheet, indicated by column letter and row number. Examples: "C5", "A1:D3", "R1C1", and "R[1]C[3]".

Reference style   A method of identifying cells in a worksheet. In the A1 reference style, columns are labeled with letters and rows are labeled with numbers. In the R1C1 reference style, R indicates row and C indicates column; both columns and rows are labeled with numbers.

Reference type   A relative reference (A1) in a formula indicates the location of another cell in relationship to the cell containing the formula. An absolute reference ($A$1) always refers to the exact location of a specific cell. A mixed reference ($A2; A$2) is half relative and half absolute.

Remote reference   A reference to a document in a different application. A remote reference can designate a single cell, a cell range, a value, or a field of data in the other document.

Remote reference formula   A formula in a Microsoft Excel worksheet that contains a reference to a cell, cell range, value, or field of data in a document from a different application. A remote reference formula creates the actual link between a Microsoft Excel worksheet and the other document.

Scenario   A set of input values you can apply to a worksheet model. You create scenarios with Scenario Manager.

Scroll bars   Bars along the right and bottom sides of your worksheet or macro sheet that allow you to scroll through the document vertically and horizontally, using a mouse. Clicking an arrow moves one column or row at a time. Clicking a shaded area moves one window at a time. The length of the scroll bar represents the entire document. Dragging the scroll box to a different position on the scroll bar and releasing the mouse button displays the part of the document that is in that relative location.

Series formula   A formula that contains the data used to plot a data series on a chart. When you create a new chart, Microsoft Excel automatically builds a series formula for each data series. The formula consists of the SERIES function followed by four arguments, each of which defines one aspect of the data series.

Shortcut menu   With the mouse pointer pointing to a selection on a chart, worksheet, or macro sheet, click the right mouse button in Microsoft Excel for Windows or press COMMAND+OPTION while you click the mouse button in Microsoft Excel for the Macintosh to display a menu of useful commands. You can display shortcut menus from cells, columns, rows, text boxes, objects, buttons, charts, chart items, toolbars, tools, or workbooks.

Source document   A Microsoft Excel worksheet referred to by an external reference formula or a remote reference formula. The source document is the source of the value contained in the external reference formula or the remote reference formula; it provides "source data" to the dependent worksheet.

Startup directory or folder   In Microsoft Excel for Windows, the startup directory is an optional directory named XLSTART, which is located in the same directory as EXCEL.EXE. In Microsoft Excel for the Macintosh, the startup folder is named EXCEL STARTUP FOLDER (4), and it is located in the System folder of your Macintosh. Any documents you place in the startup directory or folder are automatically opened when you start Microsoft Excel. Templates placed in the startup directory or folder are not automatically opened, but they are listed as options in the New dialog box.

Status bar   The bar at the bottom of the screen that displays information about the currently selected command, the active dialog box, the standard keys on the keyboard, and the current state of the program and the keyboard.

Templates   Templates are worksheets, charts, or macro sheets created as patterns for subsequent documents. Because templates keep all of the formatting, styles, and formulas—including row and column titles—of the original documents, they offer a quick way to create similar documents with variable data in them, such as quarterly reports or annual budgets.

Tick mark   A small line that intersects an axis like a division on a ruler. Tick marks are considered parts of an axis. Double-clicking an axis displays the Patterns dialog box, in which you can specify what kind of tick marks you want.

Toolbar dock   The region above the formula bar and below the menu bar, or the regions on the left, right, and bottom sides of the application window, where toolbars can reside.

Two-input data table　A table you produce using the Table command on the Data menu. Using a formula containing two variables and two series of values to be substituted for those variables, you can generate a two-dimensional matrix of results based on the series of values you entered.

Unattached text　Text that is not linked to a chart item and can be moved anywhere on the chart.

Unbound　An unbound document can be a part of several workbooks and is saved as a separate file.

Wildcard　A character (? or *) that stands for one or more characters. A wildcard character is used for finding data in a worksheet or as part of database criteria. Use the asterisk (*) to represent any number of characters. Use the question mark (?) to represent any single character in the same position as the question mark.

Workbook　A Microsoft Excel document in which you can store other documents. A workbook can include worksheets, macro sheets, and charts.

Worksheet　Also called a spreadsheet. The worksheet is the primary document you use to store and manipulate data in Microsoft Excel. A worksheet consists of cells organized in columns and rows.

XY (scatter) chart　A 2-D chart that has numeric values plotted along both axes rather than having values along the vertical axis and categories along the horizontal axis. This kind of chart type is typically used to analyze scientific data to see whether one set of values is dependent on or affects another set of values.

Index

Symbols

 See Apple menu
! See Exclamation point
+ See Plus sign
, See Comma
. See PERIOD key
... See Ellipsis
/ See SLASH key
    See also Lotus 1-2-3 commands
? See Question mark
@functions 21
@HLOOKUP 84
@VLOOKUP 84
▶ See Triangular bullet

Numbers

1-2-3 See Lotus 1-2-3
2-D chart See Chart
3-D chart 195
3-D chart format 35
3-D formula 121
3-D Lotus 1-2-3 worksheet xxii, 93

A

A1 reference style 281
Absolute reference 58, 279, 281
Action-equivalent functions 250
ACTIVATE function 251
Activating documents
    See Switching

Activating formula bar 11
Activating menu bar xxx
Active cell 7, 8, 10, 11, 17
Active window 71
Add Legend command 195
Adding
    arrow 205, 228–229
    chart gridlines 196
    chart legend 195, 209
    chart title 195
    data series 213–214
    footnote 232
    formula 128
    slide show 237
    summing 23
    text 206
    text box 230
Adjacent cells 56, 75
Alignment 38, 41, 43–45
Alignment tools 37
ALT key xiii
Alternate Navigation Keys 8, 38
Analyzing data 125–141, 188, 274
Annotation 85, 87
    See also Commenting, Footnote,
    Text box
Apple Macintosh See Macintosh
Apple menu ( ) 270
Apply Names command 103
Applying
    chart border 200
    names 112
    range format 35
    style 43–44, 49, 53
Area
    chart 197, 200
    plot 197, 201
    print 150

Argument 22, 82, 277
ARGUMENT function 82
Arrange command 72
Arranging window 72, 76
Array constant 277
Array formula 80–81, 87
Array function 80, 81
Array range 81, 131, 277
Arrow 205–206, 209, 228–230
ARROW keys xxx, 7, 8
    See also DOWN ARROW,
        LEFT ARROW, RIGHT ARROW,
        UP ARROW
Ascending order 164
Asterisk (*) 174
Attach Text command 195
Attribute 43, 66, 76
AutoFormat command 35
Automatic linking 277
Automation
    creating buttons 257
    macros 245
    new features 274
AutoSum tool 23
Axis
    attaching text 203, 218
    chart 198, 277
    tick mark 282

B

Balloon Help 12, 277
Best Fit column width 30, 41
Black and white monitor options 46
Blank
    cell 252
    worksheet 70
Blanking See Clearing
Bold text 45, 46

Great Resources from Microsoft Press

Running Microsoft® Excel 4, 3rd ed.
The Cobb Group
This updated edition of the all-time bestselling Microsoft Excel for Windows book is a complete reference to Microsoft Excel version 4.0. Features clear instructions, scores of examples, and detailed reference information. A great combination of tutorials and reference information for all users.
896 pages $29.95 ($39.95 Canada)   ISBN 1-55615-488-7

Complete Guide to Microsoft® Excel Macros, 2nd ed.
Covers version 4 for Windows™ and the Apple® Macintosh®
Chris Kinata and Charles W. Kyd
Here is all the information, advice, and examples you need to realize the full potential of Microsoft Excel's timesaving macros. Included are dozens of shortcuts, tips, and case studies that take you from the basics of creating your first spreadsheet to advanced techniques that include developing interactive macros.
512 pages, softcover $29.95 ($39.95 Canada)   ISBN 1-55615-526-3

Running Microsoft Access®
John L. Viescas
Here is a practical, hands-on guide to Microsoft's relational database, packed with inside tips and strategies—many not covered in the documentation. Covers all the features of Microsoft Access, and includes general information on managing data and on how a relational database works.
544 pages, softcover $29.95 ($39.95 Canada)   ISBN 1-55615-507-7

Information...Straight from the Source

Running Windows™ 3.1
Craig Stinson

Build your confidence and enhance your productivity with Microsoft Windows quickly and easily, using this hands-on introduction to version 3.1. You'll find a successful combination of step-by-step tutorials, helpful screen illustrations, expert tips, and real-world examples. Learn how to install and start using Windows 3.1, how to use applications with Windows, and how to maximize Windows performance.

560 pages, softcover $27.95 ($37.95 Canada)   ISBN 1-55615-373-2

Windows™ 3.1 Companion
The Cobb Group

"Covers the basics thoroughly.... An excellent reference featuring dozens of live examples.... Beautifully produced."   **PC Magazine**

This thorough, comprehensive resource— for beginning to advanced users—covers Windows 3.1 and its built-in applications and desktop accessories. First-time users will appreciate the tutorial-style introduction to Windows 3.1. More experienced users will find this reference invaluable. Packed with a wealth of examples, helpful tips, and techniques.

544 pages, softcover $27.95 ($37.95 Canada)   ISBN 1-55615-372-4

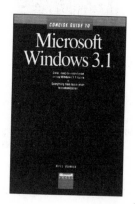

Concise Guide to Microsoft® Windows™ 3.1
Kris Jamsa

The handiest and most readable reference to Windows 3.1, offering information on everything from installation to customization. It's the ideal computerside reference! For beginning and intermediate users.

208 pages $12.95 ($17.95 Canada)   ISBN 1-55615-470-4

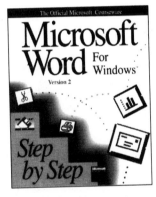